Flood, Fell, And Forest

FLOOD, FELL, AND FOREST

FLOOD, FELL, AND FOREST

FLOOD, FELL & FOREST.

LADIES BYWAIT-FEN LO INE

FLOOD, FELL, AND FOREST

BY

SIR HENRY POTTINGER, Bart.

AUTHOR OF 'BLUE AND GREY', ETC.

IN TWO VOLUMES

VOL. I

LONDON

EDWARD ARNOLD

41 & 43 MADDOX STREET, BOND STREET, W.

1905

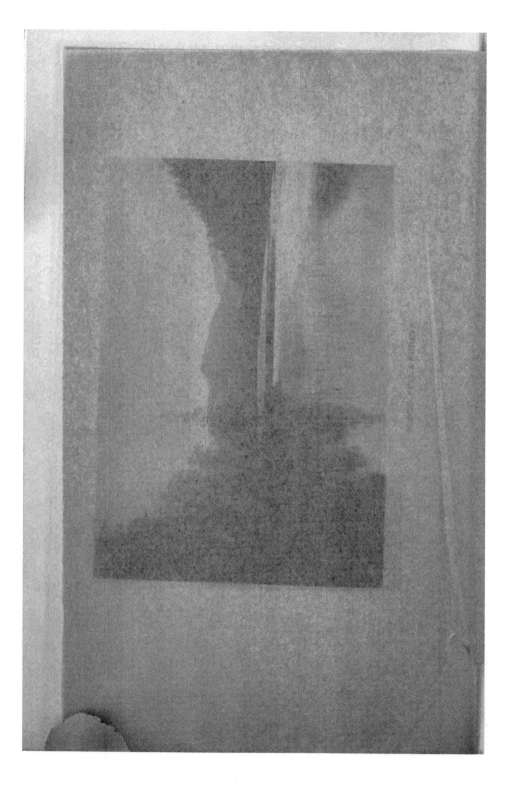

FLOOD, FELL, AND FOREST

BY

SIR HENRY POTTINGER, Bart.

AUTHOR OF 'BLUE AND GREEN,' ETC.

IN TWO VOLUMES

VOL. I

LONDON

EDWARD ARNOLD

41 & 43 MADDOX STREET, BOND STREET, W.

1905

F 5242.84

TO

MY DEAR DAUGHTER

IN REMEMBRANCE OF

HAPPY SCANDINAVIAN DAYS

PREFACE

THIS book is, as readers will discover, more a series of essays on sport and adventure than anything else. Although its chapters are here and there connected by reference, in six only of the twenty—namely, in those dealing with an expedition to the river Tana, in Finmark—is there any attempt at consecutive narrative. And this, describing, as it does, the travels of two young men nearly fifty years ago, will probably appeal to the sympathy only of those readers who are specially interested in Norway, and may have some curiosity to learn what the remote regions of the country were like at that date. The matter of these chapters first appeared in the form of letters to the *Field;* but, while retaining a few of the original passages, I have thought it best to rewrite nearly the whole narrative, at the same time endeavouring by the aid of my own and my companion's contemporary journals to retain its eminently youthful tone.

Chapters X., XI., XIII., XIV., XV., XVII., XVIII., have appeared as articles in the *Fortnightly Review,* but have undergone to some extent the processes of excision, alteration, and addition. At the end of No. XI., especially, is included an episode of elk-hunting taken from my contribution to the Badminton volume on 'Big Game'; and again in Chapters XII.

and XIII. are blended with original matter extracts from articles entitled 'The Rifle in Norway' and 'The Shotgun in Norway,' published in the *Badminton Magazine*. Chapters XVI. and XIX. respectively contain sketches contributed to the Norwegian Club 'Year-Book,' and an extinct magazine called *The Squire*. To the proprietors and editors of each and all of the above-named books and periodicals I beg to tender my thanks for their kind permission to reprint.

In Chapter XV., on trout-fishing, a little solitary, forlorn bit about England, which I had not the heart to eliminate, still keeps its place like a stranger in a foreign land; otherwise the book treats of Scandinavia only. Did I think that it was incumbent on me to allege any kind of excuse or pretext for its appearance, I would select a very venerable one, and plead the request or suggestion of kind friends, expressed in my case much in this fashion: 'Why not republish some of those old things?' And, indeed, the last five monosyllables would serve, to my mind, as a by no means inappropriate inscription for the title-page.

H. P.

RICHMOND, 1905.

CONTENTS OF VOL. I.

CHAPTER I
PAGE
NORDENFJELDS - - - - - - 1

CHAPTER II
ELSKEDE LAND - - - - - - 16

CHAPTER III
ON THE DOVRE ROAD - - - - - - 42

CHAPTER IV
TO THE COUNTRY OF THE KING OF THE NORTH - - 62

CHAPTER V
THE REALM OF THE GRAY TERROR - - - - 87

CHAPTER VI
TO THE HAVEN OF REST - - - - - 106

CHAPTER VII
TO THE TANA - - - - - - 126

CHAPTER VIII
DOWN THE TANA - - - - - - 158

CHAPTER IX

PAGE

FAREWELL TO TANA   -   -   -   -   -   - 184

CHAPTER X

AN APPRENTICE TO ELK-HUNTING   -   -   -   - 218

CHAPTER XI

A HANDFUL OF LEAD -   -   -   -   -   - 248

LIST OF ILLUSTRATIONS

FLOOD, FELL, AND FOREST - - - *Frontispiece*

SIR HYDE PARKER (FROM THE PORTRAIT AT
    MELFORD HALL) - - - - *To face page* 10

'SOFT AND SMILING AS ARCADIA' - -   ,, 30

'UNEQUALLED ON THIS SIDE OF THE ATLANTIC'   ,, 34

A CARRIOLE INCIDENT - - - -   ,, 46

BOSEKOP IN 1857 - - - -   ,, 82

THE ARCTIC FJELD - - - -   ,, 110

THE REALM OF THE GRAY TERROR - -   ,, 114

GOOD FAIRIES TO THE RESCUE - - -   ,, 116

A SKETCH AT KARASJOK - - -   ,, 138

THE CAMP AT VUOVDE GUOIKA - - -   ,, 178

THIS LORDLY MANSION IS OURS - -   ,, 186

SHOWING HIM THE BUTT - - -   ,, 198

DESCENT OF THE STORFOS - - -   ,, 210

A HUT IN THE ELK-FOREST - - -   ,, 250

THE DEATH OF THE BEAR - - -   ,, 258

THE END OF THE SEASON - - -   ,, 286

FLOOD, FELL, AND FOREST

CHAPTER I

NORDENFJELDS

To the long narrow half of Norway which, extending north of the Dovre Fjeld and Trondhjem into the wild regions of Tromsö and Finmark, lies chiefly within the Arctic Circle, and rejoices during the summer months in the strange radiance of the midnight sun, the term 'Nordenfjelds' is applied.

The word is a Norsk adverb, and its kindred adjective is 'Nordenfjeldsk,' which nowadays all northward-bound tourists well know as connected with the line of steamers running from Trondhjem to Vadsö, the ultimate station beyond the North Cape.

Familiarity does not always breed contempt; on the contrary, it often begets love and admiration. There are many things which men never appreciate to the full until they have become thoroughly intimate with them, and learnt the secret of their attractiveness. But it certainly has, in some cases, a tendency to sow the seeds of merely practical esteem, and thereby annihilate mystery and romance. At the present time the attraction of Norway is probably greater than it ever was, but expressions such as I have used above, 'north of the Dovre Fjeld,' 'the Arctic Circle,' 'the midnight sun,' 'beyond the North Cape,' have all but lost the weird fascination that they possessed even fifty years ago. At that time a man who had journeyed through Norway from south to north gained the right to be considered a genuine traveller. His rank, if below that of the Asiatic or African explorer, was far above that of the ordinary continental tourist. Even the Mediterranean and a glimpse of the East, with all its colour and romance, failed to give precedence over him who had wandered by the light of the nocturnal sun or the Aurora Borealis, had ventured to the frozen confines of Folgefond or Svartisen, and overlooked from the most northern headland in Europe the gloomy expanse of the Arctic Ocean.

It is true that a large majority of the Englishmen —and they were altogether but few in number— who at that time crossed the North Sea were influenced simply by one of the great primary factors in man's nature, the instinct of the chase, the search for sport ; but in the hearts of some of them, young, enthusiastic, and to some degree imaginative, the idea of Norway, and especially of Northern Norway, excited an undefinable thrill, akin to the sensation which is awakened by the proximity of a dark impending cliff or a gloomy mountain tarn, a suspicion of the mysterious which might expand into the terrible. This, if traced to its source, would probably have been found referable to some faint but not extinct recollection of very early days, a ballad, a legend, a picture, or even a school geography-book, with its prosaic romance and suggestive outline.

Was there some indistinct association with the stern mythology which found its last stronghold in the wilds of the Far North? Could we think of Norway without a transient idea of Odin, Thor, and Freya, of Vikings, Valkyries, and Valhalla? Did visions of trolds and gnomes flit before our eyes, of warlock Finns and Lapland witches? of krakens and sea-serpents, as depicted in the pages of old Pontoppidan and Olaus Magnus? Was it, as Charles Kingsley suggests, some stirring within us of the old viking blood which ran in the veins of our remote ancestors? or was it, in fact, merely that our venatorial and piscatorial instincts were excited by the thoughts of a land where there were grouse * as big as turkeys and salmon that rivalled the sturgeon, where the bears were possessed of the strength of ten men and the cunning of twenty, and whence came the wild-fowl and the woodcocks?

It cannot be denied that to many of the old hands —and there were old hands in Norway even half a century ago—the idea of there being any romance connected with the country or people was absurd; old tales there might be, a pack of lies and humbug, but nothing more. These were men who regarded a mountain as useful in shading a salmon-pool, and a waterfall as a detestable obstruction in the course of a river; who valued a native solely according to his skill in handling a boat and gaffing a fish, or his knowledge of the haunts and habits of wild animals. And what undaunted, indefatigable pioneers of sport were some of these old hands in their youth! What discomfort and even hardship did they undergo in its pursuit! It is a pity that their earliest experi-

* The capercailzie (*Tetrao urogallus*).

ences are not on record. Out of several hundred
volumes all dealing with Scandinavian travel, adventure, and sport, which I have during many years
collected, I can find none which describe the doings
of the men who, in the absence of steamers, were
content to cross the North Sea in slow and uncertain
colliers, timber, or merchant ships, to rough it, in
default of the comfortable stations of the present
day, in any quarters they could find, and to get
back how they could.

I have heard lamentable tales relating to these
heroes. One, for example, was once upon a time
approaching the coast of Norway in a small sailing
ship, the little town and haven whence he could
reach his quarters of the previous year being actually
in sight after a good and comparatively speedy
voyage. He had left England early, and the fishing would be at its best. Nothing intervened
between him and his goal except the usual barrier
of dangerous skerries, through which the vessel had
to find a channel. Then suddenly the wind shifted ;
it began to blow hard, and the experienced eye of
the skipper detected the signs of a coming tempest,
of real bad weather. The passage of the narrow
channel could not be attempted ; the heavily-laden
ship went about and stood out to sea again. Not
until full three weeks later did that unfortunate
angler find himself once more approaching with a
fair breeze the dangerous skerries, and during the
whole of that time he had been obliged to put up
with not only the wretched accommodation on board,
but also the ordinary seaman's fare, for the few
supplies he had provided for himself were consumed
on the original passage. I do not doubt that he

bore his misfortunes like a man, but he was heard to declare that he had far sooner have taken his chance of shipwreck and drowning.

I could tell more, but one such harrowing tale is sufficient. Think of it, ye who now go to Norway, perchance with your wives and families, in fine swift steamers, with at least ample wholesome food and comfortable cabins, who find on landing excellent hotels for your accommodation, and move on to well-appointed, often luxurious, fishing-stations, to enjoy your cut-and-dried sport under the most favourable conditions, think of what ye owe to those who showed you the way! No, books we have in plenty and to spare, but I feel that, as Owen Meredith puts it, 'greater souls have passed unheard,' and at the same time have my suspicions that their reticence did not arise from any reluctance to 'break faith with angels by a word,' but from a selfish desire to conceal from their fellow-men what sport they had, and to keep it to themselves. If I wrong them may their shades forgive me!

In the last chapter of his interesting book, 'A River of Norway,' 1903, Mr. Thomas Standford devotes a few pages to the subject of the early English anglers in that country; but, having myself made many notes on the same topic, I shall risk the charge of plagiarism in referring to it here on the same lines. After consulting as many books as I have been able to lay hands on, I regard it as certain that the piscatorial raid of Englishmen on Norwegian rivers did not begin before 1830. They have never lost their grip of them from that day to this, and it would be deeply interesting to know beyond

all doubt who was the very first man to cast a line
on those waters. In the absence of evidence to the
contrary, I believe it to have been Sir Hyde Parker.
We should know little or nothing of his doings were
it not for the brief extracts from his letters given by
L. Lloyd, the well-known Scandinavian sportsman,
who seems to have been in frequent correspondence
with most of the early fishermen. He states in his
'Scandinavian Adventures' that Sir—then Mr.—
Hyde Parker was trying the fishing in Sweden, without much success, as far back as 1828. He succeeded
to the baronetcy in 1830. Subsequently, according
to the same authority, he tested the principal Norwegian rivers from south to north, and some few
particulars of his success are given ; but on the
Alten, which he was the first to visit, in 1836, for
the express purpose of salmon-fishing, we hear
simply that he had 'great sport.' He died in
1856, aged seventy-one. A few years before his
death he wrote to Lloyd as follows (Mr. Thomas
Standford quotes the same words) :

'At the present day it is not altogether easy to
command a first-class stream. . . . I consider the
game nearly up, at least, for an old one like
myself, and not worth going the distance.'

The above is somewhat strange reading for those
who now find themselves classed among the early
invaders of Norway, because in the fifties they were
exploring its coast in the hope of finding streams
which had been overlooked. But the game which
Sir Hyde Parker meant was that of the first comer,
who had the supreme delight of discovery, and the
satisfaction of having the fun all to himself, without
paying anything for it, the distribution of the fish

among the natives being sufficient recompense for permission to use the rod.

In his delightful and now very scarce book, 'Two Summers in Norway'—also referred to by Mr. Thomas Standford—Belton, the author of that equally fascinating work, 'The Angler in Ireland,' describes the grand sport he had on the Namsen in 1837 and 1839, and his volumes give besides an admirable picture of the country and its people as they were in his day, with many valuable notes on geology and other interesting subjects. If he did not actually join in Sir Hyde Parker's lament, he was also among the prophets. 'A few adventurous brothers of the rod,' he writes, 'have already explored the Scandinavian wilds. That country will probably in its turn soon become overstocked, and then nothing will remain for the more daring enthusiasts of this fascinating sport but to follow the tide of civilization into the New West, and there pursue their mimic war against the gigantic tenants of the vast lakes and rivers of that continent.'

This prophecy has been fulfilled to the letter, but the overstocking of Norway by the British angler has simply resulted in permanent occupation. To many people the question I raised above as to who threw the first line on Norwegian waters may seem a trivial one, but it is really quite the reverse. From the casting of that line dates the great and still increasing prosperity which Norway enjoys under the friendly invasion whereby the Anglo-Saxon requites the raids of the old Norse rovers. The success of the fisherman attracted others, some of whom spread the tale of the glorious scenery amid which they had their sport, which attracted the lovers of sublime Nature and the writers of books, which attracted the eyes of the world, which resulted in the multitude of tourists of all nations. Q.E.D.

This is no fallacy, but logical truth. Perhaps only the few who, like myself, have watched for close on fifty years the aforesaid increase of prosperity, and always traced it to the same source, can realize how undeniable is that truth. Later on I may give proofs of it. The Norwegians might with reason erect a statue to Sir Hyde Parker, dressed in the costume which, by the courtesy of the present Baronet, I have been informed he bears in his full-length portrait at Melford Hall; brown clothes, wading-boots, and a tall white felt hat, into which he is putting a fly. The few travellers who explored Norway before the advent of the fishermen wrote interesting accounts of their adventures, but they attracted no visitors to her shores.

If the enthusiastic novice whom I left some way back meditating a descent on Norway, about half a century ago, had indeed cherished any romantic notions regarding its inhabitants, they must have received a somewhat rude shock before he had been long on shore; for to this very day, of all people who inhabit the earth, there are probably none who have less outward romance about them than the Norwegians, unless indeed a tendency, chiefly feminine, in certain districts towards picturesquely pastoral costume, manifested in bright bodices and extensive linen head-dresses, may be held as verging on romance. 'And these are,' he might have said, calmly overlooking, as opinionative young men will, the lapse of ages and the many

vicissitudes that Scandinavia has undergone since
the days of the old Kings and great Earls—'these
are the modern representatives of those fierce rovers
who lived by ravaging the lands of their neighbours
with fire and sword, and revelled in the idea of a
violent death ; these painfully commonplace citizens,
close-cropped and smooth-shaven, rejoicing in cheap
waterproofs and wholesale Wellington boots, intent
on their petty traffic in second-rate goods and dis-
gusting dried fish ; these ungainly ursine mariners,
clothed even in warm weather in sticky oilskins,
woollen wrappers, and monstrous fingerless gloves,
who stare at us and expectorate ; these stolid lounging peasants who have not even energy enough to
properly repair their rotten harness or caulk their
leaky boats, much less to help us with our baggage !
And the smallness, the insignificance of everything !
How about your traditional beakers and tankards ?
the biggest tumbler I can get will not hold a full
quarter of a pint.   There is plenty of wood in the
country ; why on earth, when they set about
making a bedstead, couldn't they make it more
than five feet long, or a chair with a seat more than
a foot square ?   Look at the blades of their oars,
about two inches wide; they don't feather, and
always shuffle, never put their backs into it or
pull the oar through.   What is the use of a basin
the size of a soup-plate, or a towel no bigger
than a pocket - handkerchief ?   Even in the pot-
houses they call hotels I can't get a really square
meal ; they give me a lot of doll's plates with
scraps, and poor eating at that.   Their horses are
all ponies, and their cattle the size of calves.
Then, look at their dwelling-places !   Can anything

be more terribly dull, more hopelessly prosaic, than these kidney-paved streets, cutting each other at right angles between rows of wooden cottages, mere rabbit-hutches, and paltry shops ? It is a little better in the bigger towns, perhaps, but all purely modern and pettily commercial. Show me a sign of a really old building, or even a decent ruin, any traces, I say, of a noble, even respectable, antiquity. Well, there may be a few here and there, perhaps an old church or two, but I haven't seen them yet. Then the women. Where is your golden-haired beauty, or any remnant of it, which might inspire us with divine fury, as it did the old Berserks ? There are plenty of Ragnilds, Ingebords, Minnas, Gunhildas, and the like, fine-sounding names enough, I grant you, but is any one of them as good-looking as—well, say the chambermaid at Hull ?'

And, warming to his theme, this young traveller might have continued : ' You fellows know something of the South ? I do a little. Look at the difference. There a great people may have sunk so low as to be despicable and utterly demoralized. I allow it, but the life, warmth, and colour still survive ; the sun never dies out of the blood of either man or woman. A Greek or Roman may be an Alcibiades or Themistocles, a Giulo or a Mario, and both be a very satire on the names they bear ; but it is likely enough that either is a picturesque ruffian, with sufficient extremes in his nature to vivify a whole tribe of these Northerners. There are thousands of peasant-girls in Italy and Spain who might glow on canvas as the Queen of Heaven, if only a Raphael or Murillo could be found to paint them, and you may be sure that under many a

SIR HYDE PARKER.
From the portrait at Melford Hall.

languid Spanish eyelid lurks the fire of the maid of
Saragossa. But when the sea-king relinquished his
vocation he relapsed into an obtuse fisherman, and
the Valkyries themselves, their occupation gone,
into amiable dowdies. It is the old story. Directly
the main characteristics of a Northern people cease
to be active, they become, as it were, frozen out ;
all the dash and sparkle of the current of humanity
disappears, and there is left just the sluggish, pon-
derous element, saved from complete stagnation only
by the necessity to keep flowing, the struggle for
existence. The nearer the frozen pole you get, the
more does mute endurance become the prominent
virtue, and stolid selfishness the most conspicuous
vice. No, I don't want to argue. I'm not arguing:
I'm philosophizing. Yes, by all means let us have
a couple of bottles of Bayersk, about the best
thing in the country, if there was a decent glass to
drink it out of.'

Now, in some of this querulous tirade, the result
of first impressions, there might be a few grains of
truth, but the rest is all fallacy and sophism ; and
when the novice had been longer in the country,
learnt something of the language, and become
better acquainted with the people, he would have
come to understand how much of sterling worth
underlies the habitual undemonstrativeness of the
average Norseman. Average, because it goes without saying that the many Norwegians who have
during, say, the last century become prominent
figures in every branch of art, literature, science,
and in political history, are beyond the scope of
such criticism, as also are the many gentlemen
deeply engaged in mercantile pursuits, who have

been and are occupied in developing the internal
resources of the country, and in promoting her
wealth and dignity.   Besides, it is with the average
lower and middle class Norseman that the tourist
and sportsman have mainly to do.   He is, as my
novice would soon discover, slow, sometimes painfully so, but he is sure; a dilatory starter, but a
far goer; not given to protestation, but honest
and trustworthy; not as a rule, jocular, but often
gifted with much dry humour.

One of his finest qualities, a not uncommon
source of irritation to the ordinary tourist, is his
perfect serenity, or, as the tourist might call it,
stolidity, under annoying circumstances.   This often
displays itself in small matters connected with travel,
over which the traveller grumbles and becomes impatient.   Not so the Norseman.   He accepts the
situation in his ponderously philosophical fashion,
as one who might say: 'Of course, things go wrong,
they generally do in this world, but what is the
use of exciting one's self over it?' and sets to work,
very deliberately, and perhaps awkwardly, to put
things right again.   In the end he succeeds.   It is
this quality, which is clearly hereditary and en-
gendered by a perpetual struggle, generation after
generation, against the antagonistic forces of Nature
and the proverbial viciousness of inanimate things,
and which ought especially to enlist the sympathy
of Englishmen, who have themselves a knack,
despite initial outspoken annoyance, of pulling
through under difficulties, that, combined with his
physical hardiness and endurance, renders the
Norseman one of the finest emigrants in the world,
while at the same time it inspires that desire for

emigration and for possible betterment which checks increase in the population of Norway. Hard work and serious obstacles have no terrors for him as long as he can with patience attain in other lands to some decided amelioration in his condition of life.

To the richer farmers, who have some capital, probably a banking account, and large comfortable homesteads, with leisure and opportunity enough during the winter to join in social gatherings and to occasionally indulge in field sports, this last remark about the condition of home life is not applicable; but to their poorer brethren, and to the 'husmænd,' who are not landholders, it is most strongly. Ask the hard-working, charitable priests, who are best acquainted with the subject, what is the state of these poor folk during the long, dark, bitter winter months, especially in districts where they cannot obtain work as lumbermen. Have I not myself, when saying farewell to my men in the late autumn, and receiving their thanks for the moderate wages that they had so well earned, heard the remark : ' And now we have to think how to get through the winter ' ?

It is not, therefore, surprising that among this class one finds so little of that pride in, and patriotic appreciation of, the wild beauties of their native country which is popularly supposed to be always characteristic of the dwellers in a mountain land. To the Englishman's loudly-expressed—or, when elk-hunting, whispered—admiration of some glorious expanse of fjeld or forest, of some dark glen or cliff-girt tarn, they will yield a quiet assent, not seldom neutralized by the after-remark, ' But

it is so dreary and desolate'; and in their turn
they will, not unjustly, eulogize the beauty of a
green patch of clearing, where the piles of gathered
stones and boulders show with what toil it has
been reclaimed from the wild.

I know that there are some who will, perhaps
indignantly, repudiate on behalf of any class in
Norway this idea of chronic dejectedness produced
by their surroundings. I can but indicate the impression gained during my own long experience of
the North, and will allow that there must be many
exceptions to such a doctrine. Moreover, I must
point out that my remarks refer chiefly to the
inhabitants of Nordenfjelds, and entirely to what,
out of respect to a patch or two of potatoes and rye,
and a little hay laboriously won from the wilderness,
I will call the agricultural population. The case of
the fishermen, who ply their calling as well during
the winter and early spring as in the summer months,
is different. Great toil and terrible peril they certainly undergo, but the harvest of the sea seldom
fails, and the market is always certain.

And I know also that others may be disposed to
deny the truth of my assertion regarding the Norseman's habitual equanimity under adverse circumstances, and be ready to affirm that they have known
him give way in trying moments, especially connected with the chase, to much undue excitement,
accompanied by language showing the most intimate
acquaintance with artistic malediction. I am bound
to declare that this is contrary to my experience,
but it may be so. Human nature is weak, and since
the spread of the game of golf in England it is
recorded on the best authority that instances of a

similar want of equanimity and of fervid utterance
have occurred in the most unexpected quarters.

After all, whatever I may have said, I feel sure
that my novice of the fifties must have soon discovered that there was more sterling merit in one
of these simple sons of the North than in a dozen
flashy Southerners, however picturesque ; and may
also have realized—I will go so far—that somewhere
in his nature there lurked, like the spark in flint,
that germ of fire which might under rude knocks
flash into a flame not unworthy of Saga days,
mingled with the tender sentiment and chivalrous
reverence exhibited by the old-world champions
towards things feminine, weak, and dependent, as
witness the womanly position of woman, and the
respect paid to her throughout Scandinavia, and the
invariable care and kindness bestowed on ordinary
domestic animals.

And now, having brought my novice to his senses,
and induced him to abandon an erroneous line of
thought, grounded on misleading first impressions,
I am minded to identify myself with him, or at
least to transport myself back to the date of his
novitiate, and become his companion, trying to
recall memories of what we saw and felt together,
not only as new-comers bound for the far-off region
of Nordenfjelds, but when later we had developed
into comparatively old hands. It is time to do
so, for those visions of bygone days are growing
faint and blurred, and the day is not far distant
when they will die out altogether, past hope of
resuscitation.

CHAPTER II

THE dear old long-suffering land, through or along
the seaboard of which we used to pass in our journeys
due north, has been described in scores of volumes,
until the reading public may well be weary of the
theme. Moreover, it has been regarded and treated
of from every possible point of view by different
authors, so that the attempt to say anything new
about it may well be considered a hopeless task.

Omitting all mention of the older writers, to
Laing it presented itself as a desirable place of
residence for the study of moral and political
economy; to Forester, Biddulph, and others as a
land still fitted for adventurous exploration; to
Price, Pritchett, and Walton as a glorious field for
artistic rambles. Du Chaillu marked it as a delightful change from gorilla-land, and a mine of interesting research, antiquarian and otherwise; Dasent
as a splendid basis for romantic historical fiction;
Metcalfe as the same for learned philological inquiry;
and by the latter it was also represented, as by
Belton, Jones, and Sandeman, as the angler's
paradise. Wyndham extolled the joys of wild life
on its fjelds, Hubert Smith of camp life with gipsies
in its dales, Williams its attractions for a pedestrian

16

with a knapsack, Lees, Bromley-Davenport, and Chapman the exciting pursuit of its reindeer and elk. Forbes has expatiated on the magnificence of its glaciers, Campbell on its wonderful revelations to a geologist, Willson on the history of its Church and State, Slingsby and Oppenheim on its perilous fascinations for the Alpine climber. Other specialists have dealt with its flora and fauna, its fisheries, commerce, people, and general statistics, and from the time of the ' unprotected females ' and Lady Di Beauclerc, a whole host of writers of both sexes have gushed, or raved, or drivelled over its charms as a summer playground or a winter resort, nor left undescribed one scrap of scenery, one incident of travel, from the Naze to the North Cape.

It is, therefore, just as well that my humble pen does not aspire to saying anything new about the country ; on the contrary, I propose to indulge, for a while at least, in the same gushing, perhaps drivelling, which I have imputed to others, over ill-defined themes, without the least pretence to novelty or dignity. And when later I attempt to assume a distinctive rôle as a writer, it will be chiefly, if not entirely, that of the mere sportsman. Now, frequently as I use them, and utterly impossible as I find it to discover any terms to take their place, I have to confess that ' sportsmen ' and ' sport ' are words I dislike, in fact, I regard them as more or less blots on the English language. Why this should be I cannot tell : I have forgotten its origin. It may be in consequence of the frequent vulgar misapplication of the words ; it may be on my part just one of those unaccountable and obstinate eccentricities known as ' fads ' ; but apart from my

sentiments, which I need not discuss, I firmly
believe that the shorter word of the two has a good
deal to answer for. Its light-heartedness and
frivolity contrast disagreeably with the sterner
monosyllables with which it is so constantly associ-
ated. The familiar questions, ' Did you have good
sport ?' ' What did you kill ?' ' Were you in at the
death ?' have no harsh and unpleasant sound to
ears accustomed to their conventionality, but they
frequently jar on minds disposed to, possibly
prejudiced, reflection and analysis. Shakespeare
forcibly illustrates this disagreeable verbal anti-
thesis when—in ' King Lear '—he puts into the mouth
of Gloster the words :

> ' As flies to wanton boys are we to the gods :
> They kill us for their sport.'

Now, I know that to many worthy persons given to
serious thought on matters which the majority of
men regard more lightly there appears to be but
little difference between the practice of the wanton
boys in the above quotation and that of the person
called the sportsman. To these good folk killing,
death, and sport appear to be practically synonymous
terms. But there I feel compelled to join issue;
although the main object of every chase is undoubtedly to kill, sport—for having recorded my
dislike to the word, I have no choice but to continue
using it—lies chiefly in the pursuit, which may be
arduous or dangerous, or in the skill required to
attain success, the death of the object of the chase
being the climax of that success; but regarded as a
mere act of blood-shedding, it affords the true sportsman no satisfaction whatever, and his invariable

desire is to terminate physical suffering as instantaneously or as quickly as possible. There are some phases of the chase, to be noticed later, in which he cannot carry out this desire, but the prolongation of the death struggle does not afford him pleasure as such, but because it is the unavoidable and essential feature of an exciting sport.

And now it is my intention to enter upon a rather long digression, for which I shall not apologize. Seeing what an important factor sport has nowadays become in human existence, in the lives even of those who are habitually hard workers, and have but a limited time to devote to relaxation and recreation, I maintain that it is the right of every experienced follower of sport, nay, more, that it is his duty, to express as clearly as possible his views regarding it, even though his individual opinion, as in my case, may have little weight or value.

It is but natural that the young should accept the situation to which they are born and treat sport as a trivial matter, to be indulged in according to fancy, without troubling their brains about the pros and cons in favour of or against it, but it seems incredible, although I fear it is frequently the case, that those who have attained the age of sober reflection should not have analyzed the question with some care. If they have done so they are bound, having the opportunity, to express their opinions on it one way or another. There is nothing extravagant in the doctrine that all sport, except for a supply of food or the killing, where necessary, of dangerous and destructive animals, is at the first glance absolutely unjustifiable ; that is, it requires strong and conscientiously thought-out arguments to justify it.

Without going into extreme cases such as have appeared more than once in the sporting papers, as, for instance, where a so-called sportsman records, apparently without the slightest remorse, that having got, with considerable daring, I allow, into the middle of a herd of elephants, he fired heavy bullets into a dozen of them without bagging a single one, let me take at random an extract from recent reports of the last hunting season :

'Hounds hunted beautifully, if slowly, to a patch of gorse, where the fox jumped up in their midst, and had a marvellous escape; then, skirting D——, he went back to M——, where he was marked to ground after a hunt of two hours and a half, with but two or three insignificant checks. The sewer he availed himself of had a second outlet, out of which the fox bolted, and had nearly escaped unnoticed when a bystander saw him come out, and gave the alarm. Then followed another fifteen minutes all round the hill, when a very beaten fox took shelter under a small rock, but was pulled out and eaten, after affording a fine run of two hours and forty-five minutes.'

All hunting men know that the immediate justification for the death of this gallant fox who was 'pulled out' and eaten alive was blood for the hounds ; moreover, a fox is a marauder and deserves to die, and if he be neither trapped nor shot, but allowed to live on the fat of the land—which has to be paid for—he must expect, and probably prefers, to run for his life. On the merciless 'bystander's' head be his blood! But surely the sport which affords such incidents as the above requires on the face of it some special justification.

It must be remembered that a minority, I allow that it is but a small one, has decided against sport, and its decision, even if one does not agree with it, must be treated with due respect. A friend of mine, unhappily now no more, whose opinion on all subjects was of the greatest value, after being a preserver of game and using the gun freely, gave up sport because, after due consideration, it appeared to him unjustifiable. He was no stay-at-home dreamer, but a practical, high-spirited man who had visited most parts of the world, an athlete, a great pedestrian and climber, and a devoted lover of Nature. For many years before his lamented death in Norway he suppressed his individual sporting instincts, and I have heard him say how much satisfaction it gave him to watch the stag, the reindeer, the ibex, and other wild creatures in their native haunts without any desire to molest them. He was at the same time no bigot in his views, but invariably tolerant to those who obeyed their primary instinct of the chase. The memory of such a man must always be held in reverential affection.

The morality, then, of field-sports, as I have suggested above, does not depend on any question of cruelty, which may at once be dismissed, but on whether man has a right to kill an animal simply for his amusement. I remember that some years ago, when I was playing golf, the man who usually carried my clubs, and who frequented some free library where he could read the periodicals, made the following remark : ' I have read your article, sir, in the *Fortnightly*—" An Island Deer Forest " [one of the chapters of this book], with the account of that, I hope you'll excuse my saying so, that murder,

as I call it, of the big stag.' To which I naturally
replied : ' Why murder ? I killed it fairly, after a
deal of hard work.' Whereat he rejoined : ' That
is true enough, sir; but why do you say in the
article, " poor beast " ? When you say that yourself, there surely must be something wrong.'

Now, the reasoning of my ' caddie ' appears to
me to condense the opinion of a good many other
people, which may be stated briefly as follows :
' If you kill an animal for your amusement, you
are a hypocrite if you pretend to be sorry for it ; if
you are really sorry, you have no right to kill it.'
That is the dilemma on whose horns the sportsman
is in danger of impalement, for it is a fact that, in
the case of big game especially, when the appeal to
the senses is strongest, he is even during the
excitement of the chase frequently sorry for the
animal whose wounds have not proved immediately
fatal, and his glow of triumph when standing over
the slain is not seldom succeeded by some reaction
of pity ; but that very transitory emotion will not
deter him from deliberately repeating the attempt
to kill whenever he gets the chance.

And in this the man is obeying the call of one of
the great primary and dominant instincts of his
earthly nature, that of the chase, the other two
being those of love and war. To make love, to fight,
and to hunt, have been from time immemorial,
from the earliest records of man's history, still
are, and, until all mankind has attained the higher
life, in all probability will be, the mainsprings of
existences to be reckoned by millions, by whole
nations. It might, if necessary, be proved without
difficulty that to these all other human impulses,

even those of money-making and self-preservation,
have repeatedly been made subservient.

Now, as regards man's right to indulge this instinct
of the chase, to pursue animals to the death for his
recreation, passing by the purpose of providing
food, I think it will be conceded by all who have
given any attention to the subject—I have myself
taken much trouble to investigate it—that he has
been left almost absolutely .to the guidance of his
own instincts, reason, and conscience in framing any
rules of conduct as to his treatment of wild creatures.

The terms of the so-called Noachian Charter are
familiar to all ; whether nowadays all regard with
due reverence its origin I will not pause to ask, but
one thing is certain, that never had the terms of
that charter greater meaning and force than they
have at the present day. Verily the fear of man
and the dread of man is upon every beast and
fowl and fish, upon all that moves on the earth ;
verily into his hand are they delivered.

It is not to be expected in this age of free-
thought, philosophic inquiry, and disbelief, or
very modified belief, in inspiration or revelation,
that a code especially framed for the instruction of an ancient and peculiar people should be
unanimously respected, or carry with it unques-
tioned authority; but all, of whatever creed, will
at least confess that historical writings bearing
strongly on the early education of the world
are eminently worthy of consultation. If, then,
anyone, whether orthodox believer or philosophic
freethinker, will search the Mosaic books of the
Bible for passages which may throw some light on
the question, he will find them absolutely blank of

precept or example bearing upon it, whilst at the
same time it will be clear that the shedding of brute
blood was held to be an utterly trivial occurrence.
The command to spare the hen bird when robbing
the nest (and this has the character of expediency)
is the *only direct monition* in the Pentateuch, or,
indeed, in the whole Bible, that touches on men's
dealings with *wild* animals. Here and there are
scattered sundry brief and peremptory directions
referring to domestic animals, such as the pro-
hibition to muzzle the ox when treading out the
corn, or to seethe the kid in its mother's milk ; but
these and other similar precepts are purely senti-
mental, for it is evident that the forbidden seething
could affect neither the kid nor its mother, and
that the ox, if allowed a good feed, say, of the
corn itself, would not need a share while treading
it out. Whether regarded, according to belief, as
emanating from human wisdom or from Divine
inspiration, they are indubitably protests, for man's
special benefit, against his tendency to callousness
of feeling ; they indicate that temperate and
humane tone which he should endeavour to preserve
in his dealings with the lower creation, and which
the sportsman will do well to remember in the
midst of his sport, but they do not render any
distinct and practical service to the animals themselves.

Now, that the first law-giver, whilst otherwise
ordaining many minute regulations relating to the
offices of humanity, and particularly directed against
brutality and violence, should preserve on this
special head all but absolute silence, is noticeable,
seeing that we may well believe the chase to have

been in those early days a not unimportant calling
or occupation; and when we find this silence corro-
borated, so to speak, in all subsequent codes of
morality or historically authoritative documents to
which men might reasonably turn for instruction,
the fact becomes very remarkable. It must be
either the result of accident or design. If the
former, it may be argued that only in comparatively
recent times has the question been considered other
than trivial and unworthy of notice, but this has
the unmistakable ring of a false conclusion; if the
latter, it may be fairly held to prove that man
has been designedly left to work out the problem
by the light that is within him.

Is it possible to doubt that the same legislative and
monitorial wisdom which took from the beginning,
and continued to take, note of all passions and
propensities in man, the appointed earthly lord of
creation, whether for good or evil, did not overlook
the fact of his habitually deriving pleasure and
benefit from the chase, with its attendant bloodshed,
but regarded him as both empowered by his position
and qualified by his nature to make his own laws
with regard to it, to undertake the probationary
task of striking a balance between his instincts,
without the interference, as in other cases, of
absolutely didactic authority ?

It is at least certain that, with the usual exceptions, the mass of society over the whole civilized
world has taken this view of the case, and that the
love and practice of field-sports has been encouraged
to spread coincidently with the extension of humane
and enlightened ideas regarding the claims of the
animal world. This decision is not less valuable

than that of a deliberative assembly specially
constituted to inquire into the right and wrong of
any given question.   But to take the very lowest
ground, to put the matter in its harshest light, it
may be said that society has agreed to condone the
inhumanity which some people maintain is inherent
in sport in consideration of the enormous benefit
which, irrespective of mere enjoyment, the body
and mind of man can, especially in this age of high
pressure, derive from the pursuit of it; in fact, it
pleads so gigantic, so overwhelming a set-off that
the charge of inhumanity dwindles into absolute
insignificance.   In every quarter of the globe, in
the remotest and wildest lands, the preservation of
big game is now being enforced by legislative enact-
ments, not, be it observed, purely in the interest
of the animals themselves, although they temporarily
benefit by it, but in order that they may survive
in sufficient numbers for man's recreation, chiefly
as a sportsman, with some sub-recognition of his
enjoyment as a naturalist.

There is, however, implanted in man another
instinct of a far higher nature than those already
mentioned, that of mercy or compassion.   Its
spark is too often dormant; it has at times been
enfeebled to the faintest glimmer by racial and
social influences, has been smothered almost to
extinction even in the heart of Christian com-
munities, is too often invisible amid the appalling
darkness of heathendom; but, for all that, has never
been extinguished, and is ever ready to burst with
due encouragement into a clear flame.   This instinct,
Divine and inextinguishable, is one of man's most
precious possessions, for by its aid he is able to frame

a code of mercy independent of his terrestrial surroundings. From Nature, in the midst of whose
operations he is set, he can gain no instruction on
this head; except where the sexual and parental
instincts come into play, she is absolutely merciless,
as merciless in her own realm and towards her own
subjects as she can be, on occasion, towards man
himself, and with him she is in constant antagonism.
Seated on the throne of the universe, the autocrat
finds himself encompassed by rebellion; only by
unceasing vigilance and untiring energy in con-
trolling, as far as he is able, her conspiracy of secret
agencies can he hope to hold his own. As regards
the mercilessness of Nature, what says that close
observer, Tennyson?

' Nature is one with rapine, a harm no preacher can heal:
  The May-fly is torn by the swallow, the sparrow speared by the
      shrike,
. And the whole little wood where I sit is a world of plunder and
      prey.'

But man is in this respect independent of Nature,
and if I were to define him as a hunting animal
inclined to mercy, the definition would be fairly
exhaustive, for the instinct of compassion is
peculiar to him, while that of the chase he has in
common with all more or less predatory animals on
earth. It may be noticed that friendship, affection,
gentleness, which animals that have been for many
generations under the influence of man, like the dog
and the horse, often exhibit towards each other
in a strong degree, are wholly distinct from mercy
considered as an original instinct.

It is this higher instinct that the sportsman

should encourage to the utmost. If his standard of pity and compassion be not buried in the hardness of his heart, as the standards of weight and measure are immured within the wall at Westminster, to be glanced at once in twenty years, he must be conscious that his path is ever perilously on the borderland between humanity and inhumanity, and that in his ardour for the chase he may at any time overstep it. Granting that the large majority of civilized mankind has decided in his favour, that the death of a wild animal is allowed to be of no more consequence than that of a tame 'one, that he is conscious of being humane and unwilling to cause suffering, he has to confess to himself that in some degree he must cause it. He knows that, in spite of all his good intentions and his skill, he cannot be sure of inflicting instantaneous death; nay, more, that in certain most popular forms of the chase, such as fox-hunting and salmon-fishing, he does not desire to do so, for in them to prolong the pursuit, to protract the death struggle, is to enhance the sport.

This irrepressible cry of the instinct of compassion against its co-instinct is not likely, as long as human nature remains such as it is, to put an end to the practice of the chase, nor is it, indeed, desirable that it should; but its voice cannot and must not be disregarded, for it will save a man from the danger of bloodthirstiness, and perhaps from what is far worse, callousness to suffering. Under the excitement of sport acts of what I may call thoughtless inhumanity are not seldom committed and afterwards regretted; but a man who can calmly and in cold blood watch the

agonized struggles of beast, bird, or fish without
caring or trying to put it out of its agony is a monster
beside him who, vicious with disappointment, fires
unduly long shots at game, or in the mad emulation
of a hard run half kills his horse in trying to be
the first to see a fox torn in pieces.

Magna est veritas, et prævalebit. There is no escape
from my own recorded exclamation, 'poor beast!'
Nevertheless, whilst I hope that no true sportsman
will ever be free from the wholesome thorn in his
side, the instinct of compassion, I believe firmly
that if he pay due attention to its monition he may
indulge his love of sport and practice of the chase
without blame. When he is out for a day in the
fields, the woods, the wilderness, in the saddle or
on foot, with rifle, gun, or rod, let him buckle to his
work as an Englishman should, without squeamish-
ness or false sentiment, but let him avoid the chronic
desire for wanton or capricious bloodshed, for
persecuting everything that comes within his reach,
simply because it is wild. And I will, in that case,
boldly uphold the proposition, that whereas it is
certain that the abuse of his instincts and passions
entails upon a man much evil and misery in this
world, it seems equally certain that he has an absolute right to derive whatever enjoyment and benefit
he can from a reasonable use of them, and especially
from those which appear to have been implanted
in him for the express purpose of conducing to his
personal happiness and welfare, among which the
passion for the chase stands out conspicuously, if
not uniquely.

Let anyone who desires to learn all that can be
justly said in favour of it, to imbue his mind with

the spirit of the true sportsman, with its almost
heroic vigour, its almost boyish enthusiasm, its
almost feminine tenderness, its majestic breadth
of view, its acquaintance with detail, its appreciation
of all that is good, beautiful, attractive, evil, ugly,
repellent in Nature, turn to the works of no mean
poet—whether he write prose or verse, a poet always
—the late Charles Kingsley, and study them right
through, from his novels down to his hunting songs
and his glorious ode to the north-east wind ; and
let me here quote the words which, in ' Hypatia,' he
puts into the mouth of Synesius, the squire-bishop :

' " And so I speak of these, my darling field-
sports, on which I have not been ashamed, as you
know, to write a book."

' " And a very charming one ; yet you were still
a pagan, recollect, when you wrote it."

' " I was, and then I followed the chase by mere
nature and inclination; but now I know I have a
right to follow it, because it gives me endurance,
promptness, courage, self-control, as well as health
and cheerfulness." '

As I have said, I shall not apologize for this long
digression, because that which originally attracted
me to what in the first words of this chapter I call
' the dear old land ' was the hope of sport. With something of the same hope I propose to revisit it this
very year,* and the pages of this book will, for the
most part, be occupied with sketches of it, chiefly
in Scandinavia ; therefore I seized the opportunity
which presented itself of recording my present views
on the subject. Moreover, having for the time none

* 1904. With the result that my friend and I took 163
salmon and grilse in two months.

"Soft and smiling as Arcadia."

of the serious responsibilities of an author, not being
bound to develop either plot or character, nor even
to evolve a consecutive narrative, I claim the right
to be erratic and discursive, to go as I please.

To return, then, to the dear old land. Can I
deny myself, before I relapse into the mere veteran
sportsman, the wielder of gun and rod, a brief but
general retrospect of its many fascinations, besides
those connected with the instruments of death ?

> ' Country beloved ! of the cloud-kissing ranges,
>   Bountiful vales, and munificent sea,
> Eager we plight thee the troth that ne'er changes ;
>   Ask it, our blood shall be lavished for thee.'

In this lame fashion I try to render the stirring
words of the Norsk poet, Bjerregaard, who sums up
in these four lines the salient physical attractions
of the land, as well as the strong affection she inspires in her children ; and may I not add in aliens
who come to know and love her well ?   We others
cannot reasonably give our blood for Norway, but we
can acknowledge with deep gratitude the enormous
debt we owe her for a lavish display of glorious scenes,
for a constant renewal of health, nerve, and spirits,
and for an unfailing supply of delectable recreation.

Elskede Land !   A land so beloved of the old
North Sea that he has suffered himself to be
led by a labyrinth of channels into her very
heart, and there, like the amorous giant that he is,
lies hundreds of fathoms deep in the embrace of
the mountain shoulders, now in sportive mood and
not wholly forgetful of his might and majesty, lashing
with white-crested billows the base of the inland
precipice ; now content to placidly mirror the pine

and birch, and nurse the wild-duck's brood, like the
veriest upland tarn.   And again, does he not, when
the terrible breath of the ice-giant strikes from the
frozen pole upon her northern shores, guide to them
a genial current from the balmy south, to mitigate
the terror of that deadly blast ?

Elskede Land!   A land so beloved of the heavens
that for long their great monarch never with-
draws from her his light, but grants her con-
tinuous day, while they lavish on her all the wealth
of their celestial palette, the most delicate tints, the
most gorgeous colours, the most richly sombre
shades; and when at last they have clothed her
in a mantle of virgin white, shoot across the sky a
bow of lambient radiance to illumine her unearthly
loveliness.

A land rich in pastoral vales, soft and smiling as
Arcadia; in pathless glens, about which 'a horror
lies'; in vast ranges of cliff and mountain, unsurpassed
in the massive grandeur of their primeval rocks:
in hoary wildernesses of fjeld and solemn depths
of forest; in countless lakes and rivers; in waterfalls
unequalled on this side of the Atlantic; in snowy
summits and stupendous glaciers.   A land of huge
lights and shadows, of wondrous effect and un-
imaginable outline.   A land which suggests its
history and prompts its traditions, whose mythology
is written in the grand characters of mountain and
precipice, and its legends heard in the moan of
waters and the sobbing whisper of the pine.   Were
there not extant a single ballad to commemorate
the deeds of its ancient race, a single wild tale of
the Spirits of Flood and Fell to whom has ever been
conceded an equal possession, the poetic faculty

would graft such on the stern physical aspect of the
mainland, on the outer bulwark of storm-lashed
islets and the sheltered havens of the fjord, on the
silence of the gray waste and the melancholy waters
of the inland sea.

A paltry half-century, which can develop such
astonishing transformations in a newly - settled
country, converting desolate prairies into fertile
champaigns abounding in flocks and herds and
flourishing homesteads, barren uplands into areas
of rich cultivation, and forest tracks, once the haunt
of savage tribes and wild beasts, into the site of
noble cities, can effect but little conspicuous change
in the features of a land like Norway, ' the aged of
nations,' always sparsely peopled, and never increasing in population, incapable, indeed, of supporting
more than a limited number of human beings. Here
and there a railroad may have been laboriously
forced through the rugged glens, or even through
the heart of the hills, to connect one chief town with
another, and the latter may have greatly increased
in size, importance, and prosperity ; here and there
a road, possibly a triumph of engineering, may
have opened out for a mass of tourists some wild
region previously accessible only by the adventurous
pedestrian, and, as a consequence, here and there
great wooden hotels may have usurped the place
of the insignificant station-houses of old days; but
there it all ends. Half a mile in any direction from
the railway, road, and hotel the wilderness reasserts
itself; the bear and the elk leave their trail where
they have passed over the lines of man's progress.

The vast forests may have been thinned for the
requirements of the timber trade, but where this

has been judiciously done, as it usually is, with an
eye to future growth, there is no outward sign of the
axe's work ; the serried battalions of the woodland
maintain their primeval stations far over hill and
dale, and only he who penetrates their sombre
ranks can detect where their comrades have fallen.
And amid the eternal desolateness of the high
fjeld, in the region of the glacier and the snowfield,
of the ' tind ' and ' skar,' what tokens of man exist ?
The ashes of a fire, the skeleton of a hut, where
the hunter has made his bivouac, the mountaineer
or the nomad Lapp his camp; a small cairn, forlorn
witness of valiant deeds, a Bauta-stone of athletic
victory, marking where the nerve and muscle of a
Slingsby or a Heftye once triumphed over the
terrors of the highest peaks.

But if the superficial features of the old Norway
have remained practically unaltered through the
ages down to the present day, a peculiar change
has of late years come over her social aspect and
condition, a change justly hailed with immense
satisfaction by her inhabitants, and by thousands
upon thousands of annual visitors. She has made
great efforts to adapt herself to modern requirements, has doffed her simple peasant garb and
assumed more fashionable attire, has become, as
people say, more civilized, for which, if I may coin
a word, I would substitute continentalized. And
this change, slowly developed, I firmly believe, as
I have said before, to date from the appearance of
the first Englishman who cast a salmon-fly in the
country.

One cannot deny that Norway, always slow in
starting, rose gradually to the situation ; she had

"UNEQUALLED ON THIS SIDE OF THE ATLANTIC."

ample encouragement to do so. Valleys which
I remember in my youth as almost poverty-
stricken have bloomed into prosperity under the
continued tenancy of Englishmen who have rented
the sporting rights; small roadside stations have
developed into large hotels. The encouragement
increases yearly. In the Bergen district alone the
expenditure of tourists amounts in a good season
to two millions of kroner; it has been quite recently
calculated that a single Anglo-Norwegian fishing
association leaves behind it about one million seven
hundred thousand. These are enormous sums for
Norway, and they are for the most part evenly
distributed among the local population.

It is only the old hand, grizzled and grumpy, who
is inclined to growl over this new condition of things,
and in his heart even he is ashamed of doing so,
just as he was afterwards ashamed of his querulous
irony as a novice. Shall not the beloved land which
has been his scene of recreation for so many years,
and afforded him such immense enjoyment, become
the favourite playground of a multitude, and
thereby reap a rich summer harvest, without his
regarding it, when in one of his tempers, as a personal
injury? Out upon him for a selfish veteran,
incapable of entertaining up-to-date ideas! If he
consider, as did Sir Hyde Parker sixty years ago,
that the game is nearly up for an old one like himself, let him stay away, and the country is well rid
of him—that will be the verdict of all right-minded
persons in his case. But at least none will resent
his cherishing possibly absurd visions of the old
days in his armchair at home, and some may even
bear with him if he tries to put those visions into

3—2

words, and listen to his foolish explanation of how
great a charm, not to be felt elsewhere, lay (for him)
in the very littleness and simplicity over which he
was at first inclined to be satirical, in the liliputian
scale of travel and daily life, as contrasted with
the magnificent immensity of Nature.

Where could so strange and withal so pleasant a
voyage be found as the long run in old days in one
of the steamers, scarcely bigger than an ordinary
Gravesend boat of the same date, which threaded
the mazes of the entire coast from Christiania to
Hammerfest ? The whole time in salt water, but
seldom in sight of the sea, doubtful if the breeze
had in it more of the ocean or the upland, if day
was only a brighter night or night only a softer day,
we glided from fjord to fjord, from mountain to
mountain, to break at intervals on the repose of
some pigmy settlement, raising a whirlpool in the
tiny harbour and a storm of excitement in the small
community of the ' children of the creek.' For in
those days the call of the weekly or fortnightly boat
was an event.

It is true that the same inland sea voyage is continued to the present day, and has become familiar
to countless thousands of tourists; but the peculiar
littleness, the intense simplicity and, as it were,
domesticity which characterized it in old times have
disappeared. There is certainly nowadays a great
increase of comfort and convenience; the steamers
are far larger and better appointed, the passengers
of a superior class, and, I suppose I ought to add,
take them in the mass, of superior manners; the
rules of etiquette which obtain in ordinary social
circles are at least better observed, if that is an

advantage. No Norseman of the present day approaches an Englishman and, after eyeing some article of dress, ornament, or baggage which he covets, abruptly opens conversation by the terse and in no way offensively meant inquiry, 'Will you sell ?' or 'What did that cost ?' And yet in old days this was no uncommon occurrence. I allow that the Briton would at first set up his back at this strange forwardness, and even assume an air of haughty surprise; but when he began to understand the ways of the people this initial annoyance passed, his insular reserve gave way, and he only smiled when the inquisitive or acquisitive native suggested that the value of the said article was about the tenth of its cost price. In the end he might even become inoculated by the local spirit of barter and exchange. I remember once buying a coat lined with splendid wolf-skins off the back of a man on board, and on another occasion a silver-mounted gourd-flask, which a chatty passenger of respectable appearance produced out of his handbag. In any case those small traffickers were far more tolerable than the German bagmen with whom the seaboard of Norway now teems—as a rule, most obnoxious specimens of their class, trying to impose on the natives by vulgar swagger and airs which would not be tolerated in their own country, without the politeness of a French or the quiet self-assertion of an English commercial traveller.

Nowadays people seem to be in a greater hurry than they used to be. At the chief stopping-places there is a rush which recalls a railway-station in England; individuality is merged and lost in the mass of moving humanity, and amid the crowd on

board there is greater isolation for the stranger and
visitor—it is quite possible, I allow, that he prefers
it.   In the old days, after two or three voyages,
how surely did we hail, as a matter of course, the
reappearance of the same types, and not seldom of
the same individuals; for during the summer months,
when day and night are confounded, when it is of no
consequence at what hour you go to bed or get up,
arrive or start, the whole mercantile population
seemed to be moving up and down the seaboard,
just as one sees a tribe of ants running to and fro
on the same line of insect highway, ostensibly busy
without much apparent reason.   So it was with the
good Norsemen: intent upon some little commerce,
they dropped on and off the Prinds Gustav, the
Ægir, and the Gyler—ah, how few are now left
who can remember these names!—at every insignificant station composed of a dozen red-ochred
rabbit-hutches and a store-shed.

If we did not always recognise familiar faces and
perhaps exchange greetings, the familiar types were
always in evidence: the hearty English-speaking
merchant, who was much interested in hearing
what we had done or were going to do, though he
smiled at our enthusiasm; his fair-haired, gentle-
voiced wife, who endeavoured to impress us with
the difficulties and hardships of our proposed route
through the wilds; the blue-eyed maiden who gazed
with shy wonder at the Englishmen, blushing
charmingly under the ordeal of being sketched (at
that date the Kodak fiend was still in limbo); the
staid and somewhat reticent uniformed officer on
his annual tour of inspection.

And there were many of another class, usually

encountered in the smoking cabin: the funny man, with his stock of jokes and humorous stories, always appreciated by his compatriot audience, and which he would sometimes translate with great pains into imperfect English for our special benefit; the musical man who towards evening lifted up his voice in the old songs, and generally secured the vocal aid of some of the company; the man who made trifling bids for our field-glasses or shooting-boots; the man who invariably had bottled samples of cod-liver oil on his person, and entreated us, as a personal favour, to taste them; he who carried in his bag a store of cheap knives, and led the conversation up to cutlery; and he, but he was then a rarity, who imitated the English, and had taken 'fifty pieces of salmons'—probably sea-trout—with flies of his own manufacture.

I will not deny that it was at times possible to have too much of these good people, but they were at least, on the whole, amusing company, and were in harmony with the then mode of travel and its daily routine. One most amiable quality they possessed, a strong desire to oblige, assist, and entertain the Englishman; it was remarkable how far they would on occasion go out of their way to attain these ends, which was all the more meritorious because they could not altogether understand his ways. Ignorant themselves of vacations or any fixed period of relaxation from work or study, and with the instinct of sport but imperfectly developed, they were inclined to regard him as a wealthy mono-maniac, one of the 'Penge-folk,' whose sole object in life was to travel for the purpose of capturing beasts, birds, and fishes. The idea of payment for such an end was to them ridiculous, and the pursuit of it by the alien did not provoke in any class the bitter jealousy which is so prevalent at the present day.

It may be fairly said that, excepting the peasantry of certain wild districts and the professional hunters, all that the large majority of Norwegians know of sport they have gradually learnt from the English. I can remember when he who could kill a bird on the wing was a celebrity among his fellows, and as for taking salmon with a rod, it was an idea to be laughed at. It is, I suppose, natural that the present generation, with increasing prosperity and leisure for recreation, should in many cases envy, and I fear I must add dislike, the race from which they have by degrees absorbed instruction, and that the authorities should aim at putting obstacles in the way of aliens, synonymous with Englishmen. ' Norway for the Norseman ' is a fair cry, I freely allow it, as sound a doctrine as would be ' England for the English'; but I cannot help lamenting that the growing dislike of my compatriots should have taken the form that it did in recent years, that of ferocious exultation over the misfortunes of England. I happened to be in Norway at the time when our fortunes in South Africa were at their lowest, and my blood boils when I recollect the general tone, with a few honourable exceptions, of the Norwegian press, and the satisfaction that I have seen exhibited over the details of our disasters even in the reading-rooms of the hotels. It is, again, natural that a small, weak nationality should espouse the cause of what appears to be the weaker side and rejoice in its success, but that is a very different thing to the expressions of savage glee, which I read with my own eyes, over the loss of English life and the consequent mourning in England. And when was there an Englishman who had not a word of kindness and good feeling for Norway? Search my Scandinavian library, and see if a volume, I might almost say a chapter, can be found without one. But while I write thus I must not forget those friends who sympathized with us in our sorrow, and assured me of their sympathy.

Another long digression! And what has it to do with an 'indenskjærs' voyage up the Norwegian coast in my youth? I have again wandered from my theme, and will not revert to it, but turn over a new leaf and begin another chapter. I have already expressed my sincere gratitude to Norway for much happiness she has given me, and trust that,

'Difficilis, querulus, laudator temporis acti,
Me puero'—

I have not been led into any unduly disparaging criticisms of her under her modern and more fashionable aspect.

CHAPTER III

'There's milestones on the Dover road' was one of those inexorably practical and amazingly irrelevant statements which 'Mr. F.'s Aunt,' in Dickens' 'Little Dorrit,' used suddenly and defiantly to hurl like thunderbolts into the midst of conversation, and thereby stupefy the company in which she happened to be placed. And this immortal dictum of that afflicted lady, so useful to this day in changing a subject, I shall, with a slight transposition of two letters, adopt as my text for this chapter.

Milestones there are on the old Dovre road between Lillehammer and Trondhjem, and to revive memories of how in bygone days our carriole wheels used to flash or crawl past them is my present desire.

The use of the carriole is to some extent dying out among travellers in Norway, or it would be perhaps more correct to say that out of the mass of tourists a great number have neither the inclination nor the need to use it. Attracted by the now excellent service of large steamers up the entire length of the seaboard, or by the special facilities offered by the tourist-boats for seeing the finest fjords, glaciers, and other lions of the route, they avail themselves

42

of these means of locomotion in preference to any
other. Then, the railroads run direct from
Christiania to Trondhjem, and from Bergen to
Vosserangen; there are public conveyances on some
of the most frequented roads, and small steamboats
ply in every direction through the finest scenery.
Moreover, for journeys by land, the ' trille,' or light
phaeton, drawn by a pair, supersedes, as a rule, the
little spidery one-ponied vehicle.

But in my young days you could not think of
Norway without having carriole in the background
of your thought; the idea of it suggested itself as
naturally as that of meals or a bed. We who had
become enamoured of Norway, and resolved to repeat
our summer wooing of her whenever possible, used
to buy our carrioles outright, and on returning to
England leave them in charge of that great bene-
factor Mr. Bennett, by whom they were put into
thorough repair before the next year.

And when ready for the start, what a delightfully,
uniquely compact, self-contained means of locomotion did a well-appointed carriole represent!
It has been described by, say, a hundred writers,
which shall not deter me from being, say, the hundred
and first to do so. Of late years, and for a considerable number of them, my time in Norway has been
passed in a region where there are neither roads
nor stations, and where the carriole is consequently
unknown; it affords me, therefore, considerable
satisfaction to recall what it was like in the days
of my youth. I see it in my mind's eye as it was
turned out of Bennett's hands, spick and span,
freshly painted and varnished, the wheels neatly
picked out with colour, the shafts tested, the

springs in order; and then packed to perfection
as follows.

The portmanteau, or, better still, the wooden
trunk, which did not yield to the weight of the
' skydskarl,' or postboy, as I must call him, and
was exactly of the right size, strapped to the board
behind; the rod-box along one of the supple shafts;
the guncase underneath the body; and below it,
when a dog was taken, a pendant hammock of strong
net, in which the animal soon learnt to make himself
comfortable when tired of running. Then, firmly
secured on either side of the body, two waterproof
haversacks for books, maps, powder-flask, and shot-
belt—for breechloaders had not been invented—
provisions and sundries; close to the seat, and
under the legs of the driver, his handbag; in front
of him, on the dashboard, the receptacle for waterproofs; on the other side of it the case containing
four bottles of whatever liquor he preferred to have
with him. He sat on his folded overcoat wisely
covered by a light waterproof sheet, and under
the seat, in the body of the carriole, was a locker,
containing hammer, winch, gimlet, screws, and a
small coil of thin rope, everything, in fact, needful
for repairs. A stout leather apron, with side and
top flaps, extended from the dashboard to the seat,
and might be used as a covering in wet weather;
but in dry he who wished to be comfortable would
sit almost exactly as he would on horseback, with
his legs outside the slender body of the vehicle,
and his feet resting, as in stirrups, on the irons
provided for the purpose. And in going down a
steep pitch on one of the rough byroads at the pace
which a good Norsk pony can and will go, however

rugged the way, the sensation was not altogether unlike riding a buck-jumper; there was nothing for it but to sit well back, hold on to the apron with your knees, and let him go. For carriole-driving there was no costume like knee-boots and breeches.

In reviewing my above accurate description of a well-appointed carriole, I maintain my original contention that, toy carriage though it be, for compactness and self-containedness it is unique; never has the ingenuity of man evolved anything more admirably adapted for its purpose in life, more efficient and convenient, more flawless in arrangement. But well appointed it must be, of the best material and workmanship, with every detail carefully attended to.

There were some, not intent on sport beyond occasional trout-fishing or a stroll with a gun in the forest free to all, in no hurry to accomplish long distances in the day or to arrive at any given place, who bought pony as well as carriole, and thus attained the acme of independence. And for a man freed for a time from the cares of business, or whatever other home cares he might have, in search of the true apolaustic life, quiet enjoyment without luxury and enervation, content to take things easily, with the sublime and beautiful *à la distance*, what more fascinatingly simple mode of progress through a glorious country was there? Untroubled by the presence of a not seldom loutish, heavy, odoriferous, chattering postboy, he could in perfect serenity drive as he pleased and halt where he liked; it was as glorious as a trip through Poe's 'Domain of Arnheim,' as easy as a run by an old penny boat down the Thames. Did he sketch? was he botanist

or geologist ? did he desire to use trout-rod or gun ?
he had but to put up at the first wooden toy-house
he fancied, and betake himself to his favourite
pursuit, without let or hindrance ; no permission
to ask, no fear of trespassing, no interference by
keepers, no boundaries, no fences. And all the time
he was feasting his eyes on things of beauty, filling
his brain with glorious recollections and his lungs
with the finest air in the world.

And we who were bound from Christiania to
Nordenfjelds, when the short railroad that then
existed had deposited us at Eidsvold, and the little
Miosen steamer taken us on to Lillehammer, with
what intense satisfaction did we face the drive
before us, beside the foaming Laagen, through fair
Gudsbranddal and the steep gorge of Rusten, the
long ascent to the summit of the Dovre Fjeld and
the wild plateau round Snehetten, followed by the
downward run through glorious scenery along the
banks of the Driva and the Gula, until, on the fourth
or fifth day, we saw the splendid prospect over the
gleaming expanse of the Trondhjem Fjord, and
before evening our carrioles were rattling through
the stony streets, to stop at the door of the so-
called Hôtel d'Angleterre, the better of the two
small hostelries in the ancient capital.

How exhilarating was the sensation as the line of
carrioles swept down the long hills, no whips required
to urge the sturdy, sure-footed ponies to their speed,
while the postboys, rightly expectant of extra
gratuities, with strange labial sounds excited their
little favourites to do their best ! With what
cheery bursts of laughter, with what astonishing
linguistic efforts, often in a high key as if loud

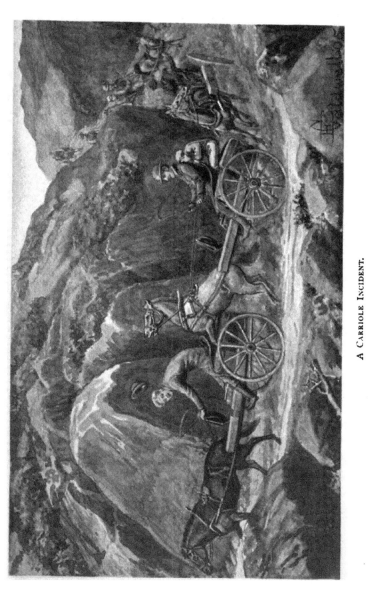

A Carriole Incident.

utterance could make up for imperfect speech, did the resonant timbers of the station-houses ring, of Oien or Laurgaard, Jerkin or Garlid! Everything was fun; there was an inexhaustible stock of jocular comment for every incident, even when it verged on annoyance or disaster; as, for example, when one of the party occasionally found himself behind a poor trotter, and, in submission to shouts ironical and expostulatory, had to draw on one side, perhaps into the ditch, and let the others flash past him; as, again, when the leader of the line, a novice at the game, neglected after a rush down a steep descent to spring his pony some little way up the opposite hill, thereby causing the rearward carrioles to run into each other like telescoping railway-carriages, and producing temporary chaos. Here a shaft doubled up and snapped, there a pulling pony rose at the portmanteau in front of him, and dropped his forelegs between it and the body of the carriole, after driving the occupant of the seat headlong, but happily unhurt, towards the dash-board. What matter? it was all a huge joke. The intelligent puller was released from his awkward position and seemed quite unconcerned, the daunt-less sitter recovered his fugitive hat and laughed, the coil of rope was routed out and the shaft spliced well enough to last for the stage, and the incident, as newspaper correspondents say, was closed.

But while I write there rises to my mind the recollection of one incident on that old Dovre road which, as far as I was personally concerned in it, went just a shade beyond a joke, although I allow that it later became a theme for many jocular utterances on the part of my merry companions.

Ought I not to suppress it altogether ?   No ; urged
by that internal goad which, as is well known to
all magazine readers, impels the long-reticent hero
of many a thrilling tale to suddenly commit to paper
certain dark passages in his life which for no other
reason is he bound to record, I yield to the irresistible impulse of the moment, and will unburden
my soul.

Once upon a time, when Crowe was Consul, and I
was *calidus juventa*, I happened to form one of a
party driving northward along the Dovre road.
We were five friends, and an excellent and versatile
' my man,' by name Paul, whom one of the party
had brought with him from England.   Now, in
those days there was a station on the road which
lay not far from the bottom of two very steep hills,
so that whenever travellers arrived at it they were
sure to be driving rapidly downhill, and whenever
they left it they were obliged to crawl slowly uphill.
Whether its inhabitants were simply soured by
their position in the hollow, whether they envied
the extra ' drikke-penge ' which drivers, exhilarated
by the pace at which they reached it from either
direction, used to bestow on their postboys, and
which they, the dwellers in the hollow, did not
receive, the said drivers generally having to dis-
mount and walk up the hills, or whether they had
conceived the idea that Englishmen were all Jehus
and drove furiously, or whether for any other reason,
the fact remains that they were a surly, ill-con-
ditioned, and discourteous lot.   Strange as it may
appear, I cannot now be certain about the name
of the place, which by the following year had
vanished from the official list of stations, and so

passed into oblivion, but I believe it to have been Sundseth; at all events, let us make it so, and I will risk the chance of an action for libel.

When we left it to proceed on our journey, we were accompanied by four postboys, a real boy and three grown men, one of whom, a hulking lout, with a particularly ugly, ill-tempered face and a harsh, disagreeable voice, perched himself on the portmanteau at the back of my carriole, which was the fourth in the line. At that time my knowledge of Norsk was but limited, but I had learnt enough to sustain a lame sort of conversation, restricted to simple sentences. As we drove slowly along the bit of level before reaching the foot of the hill we exchanged a few remarks, his being grumblings over the hard work which ponies had to do when driven by Englishmen. I at last concocted what seemed to me a very pertinent question, and said: 'If you think so much about the horses, why do you, who are so heavy, come as " skydskarl," and not send a " gut," a boy?' To which he replied: 'I come because if the Englishmen strike the horses, I can strike them.' Nobody will, I fancy, deny the malice prepense in these words. I rejoined simply, 'That you had better not do,' and then, having reached the foot of the hill, which was nearer two miles than one in length, five of us got out and walked up it, leaving the management of the carrioles to our attendants, whilst we amused ourselves in various ways, trying how far we could throw stones across the ravine, cutting sticks, searching for ferns, and so forth. With many halts to breathe the ponies, we at last all but reached the top, in fact, the leading carrioles were well on the level, when Destiny permitted the unpleasant incident to develop itself.

In the first carriole of all was the special friend with whom I had come from England—the late Captain J. H. A. Steuart—and who, being lame from a partially sprained ankle, had remained on his seat, peacefully smoking his pipe, and handed the reins to the boy, who walked beside. The latter, after waiting some minutes until the rest of the line had crawled close up, restored the reins to my friend, and mounted the portmanteau, thus clearly intimating that it was time to jog on; my friend touched his pony slightly with the whip, and it began to move. But this was the opportunity which my brute had been waiting for. I had noticed him striding up the hill to the front, but without the least notion of his intention. Directly the pony moved he rushed at its head, seized the reins, and with a volley of violent language backed the carriole until the wheels overhung the usual ditch at the side of the road, while he made a grab at the driver's whip, but this he did not succeed in getting hold of.

Now, by the Skydts law of Norway, if a horse be over-driven or ill-treated, its owner or attendant may complain to the next postmaster, who can call in two other men to decide on the compensation to be paid, and refuse horses if the traveller will not pay; but the latter may deposit the money claimed in the postmaster's hands, who must hold it until the reasonable time allowed for appeal has expired. Nothing can be fairer than this arrangement, and the postboy is strictly forbidden to take the law into his own hands, or to use any violence whatever towards the traveller. On this occasion there had not been the least provocation, we had all behaved in the most exemplary manner; my friend had waited patiently, and made no attempt to start until his own boy handed him the reins and mounted to his seat.

As my lout came swaggering down the hill again, talking loudly to his fellows, and evidently exulting in his illegal and brutal conduct, I was preparing to mount, had one foot on the step, and in my hands the reins and a whip. The latter was the ordinary hunting-whip which in those days we all used for carriole driving, being just of the right length, equal to rough usage, and useful in chastising the dogs who frequently dashed out upon us from the roadside farms; mine was luckily, as it happened, a light one, with a cane crop and a buckhorn handle.

When the man had come quite close I exclaimed, with as much indignation as I could condense into so few words of a foreign language, ' You had no right to do that,' whereupon he gave vent to what is, I believe, generally called a ' loud guffaw,' and, prompted by the evil spirit within him, lurched towards me, struck my shoulder with his, and knocked me back against the wheel. Then I dropped the rein and whip, and, facing him, spoke again; but my Norsk failing me at the moment, I have reason to believe that I expressed my feelings in my native tongue. I may have said, ' Bless you, my man, how awkward you are !' or ' Please keep on your own side, and don't jostle me,' or some remonstrance to that effect; but mere words are of little consequence, and as even our great Iron Duke

4—2

declared that he was unable to remember in what particular terms he ordered the decisive charge of the Guards at Waterloo, a humble individual like myself may be pardoned for his forgetfulness. But whatever I did say was clearly misunderstood by the poor untutored savage, for instead of being in the least degree pacified, he made a half-turn and slapped himself, rather severely, on a prominent part below the waist, a gesture which the most innocent-minded person in the world could not but interpret as one of scorn and defiance.

All experts on the subject are unanimous as to the difficulty of determining from which side in important contests came the first positive act of hostility, but I have to this day a clear, I might almost say vivid, recollection as to which belligerent struck, literally speaking, the first blow in the battle of the Dovre road.

Directly after the aforesaid gesture of defiance we were facing each other in attitudes unmistakably suggestive of a desire for personal combat, when the Norseman at once executed a dexterous manœuvre, the result, I have no doubt, of considerable practice, and took me, I confess, by surprise.

Stooping so low that for an instant I fancied he was going to butt, he brought his right hand from his knee in a swift, straight upper cut, without the least 'hook,' as the modern term is, about it. I feel sure that his fist was aimed to take me under the chin, and had it got home where intended might have well effected the 'knock-out blow' familiar to readers of glove contests; but I was then quick of sight, and although I failed in my guard, instinctively drew in my chin, so that my antagonist's fist encountered only the base of my nose, a prominent feature in my countenance, and so severely that it was later something of a surprise to find its aquiline contour unimpaired. The immediate effect of this unexpected impact was the optical delusion known as 'seeing stars,' which, however interesting it might have been under other circumstances, was for the moment distinctly unpleasant and inconvenient, accompanied as it was by a violent desire to sniff, for my nostrils became instantly conscious of superabundant moisture; first blood for the Norseman! But his repulsive face loomed through the stellar nebula which his fist had evoked, and not forgetful of the great law of counter, as explained and illustrated in the academy of that eminent instructor of youth, Professor Reed, or of the precepts governing the science of hitting as expounded in his time—hard and straight, with the knuckles well to the front—I struck at one of the glaring eyes before me as hard as I could and very savagely, for I was much annoyed by the assault on my nose. The blow got well home, of that I felt sure, but the effect of it far surpassed my expectations, and positively astonished me.

When the galaxy of stars had vanished, I became aware that my opponent was no longer confronting me, but lying on his back in the road, with his feet and knees in an attitude indicating the ambition to turn a backward somersault, and at the same time the voice of my friend Cornewall, who was in the next carriole, exclaimed: 'Well done! I never saw a neater knock-down blow. How do you like that, old fellow?'

The person to whom this thoughtful and cheery inquiry was addressed appeared to have neither time nor inclination to reply to it. For some seconds he lay where he was, probably meditating on the strangeness of his position—I dare say that it surprised him as much as it did me, its author— and then scrambled to his feet, looking uglier than ever. His eyes, or eye, as the case may be, at once fell upon the whip which I had dropped ; he snatched it up, twisted the lash round his hand, and rushed at me with the uplifted crop. We discovered afterwards that he had not with him the knife which, as a rule, every Norseman carries fastened to his waistband ; otherwise in his rage he might have been tempted to use that weapon.

My eyes were now quite clear, and the flow of blood had cooled me. As the crop descended I stepped in, throwing up my left guard above my head, and took the blow on my forearm. The cane bent, and even cracked slightly ; the horn handle just touched the back of my head, but no harm was done, and my opportunity for retaliation was splendid. The Norseman not having the faintest idea of ' guarding the counter,' I was again able to smite him with another savage ' right-hander,' this time on the mouth; and without waiting to argue, he resumed his recumbent position on the road.

But now his comrades came to his assistance, and helped him to rise, while the ready Paul picked up the whip, and thoughtfully provided me with a much-needed clean pocket-handkerchief. And so we stood, even as two old-fashioned prize-fighters might stand, face to face. with bare fists, a gallery of patrons, and seconds to administer to our necessities.

The brief remainder of the actual combat might have been described by that guide, philosopher, and friend of my youth, *Bell's Life*, somewhat in this fashion :

'*Round* 3.—This was short and decisive. The Sundseth Pet came from his corner looking savage, but decidedly weak in his understanding ; there was a large mouse under his dexter optic, which had nearly put up the shutters, and the Burgundy was distilling from his potato-trap, which was all awry. The foreigner waited in the ring, steady on his pins, and evidently meaning business ; his lower visage also showed ample traces of the ruby, tapped by the Pet's splendid visitation on his smeller in the first round. The knowing ones offered five to one on him without finding takers. The man from the North again opened with his right, but in a half-hearted way, and, as before, exposed his mug to the counter, which came in the shape of a real slocdolager on his undamaged peeper, and he once more dropped on to his mother's lap, and remained deaf to the call of time.'

But although the fighting was over, some unpleasant business had still to be done. The Norseman recovered, and when I had turned away and was standing with my back to him, the warning shouts of my friends made me turn round, to find him close behind me, with his hands clutching at my neck. Then it was half-arm work, and I was obliged to put in a quick 'one, two.' It was no time to spare, and when the gladiator is once aroused in a young man it takes some time to lay

him. He staggered back and fell heavily, the upper
part of his body disappearing into a clump of
bushes close to the roadside.

From this leafy couch he was extricated by one
of his comrades, a rather elderly man, and the father
of the boy. It turned out that he did not come
from Sundseth, but a neighbouring farm, and was a
steady, respectable man, much scandalized by the
whole proceedings; but this we did not know at the
time. The other, a sturdy, broad-shouldered young
fellow, advanced when I was still mopping my nose,
and, shaking his fist at me, revealed his intention
of avenging his comrade or perishing in the attempt.
But Paul was equal to the occasion, and in his
turn employed the hunting-crop argument; he had
a stout one of his own, with a heavy head. Grasping
this, he stepped in front of me, and simply said,
'No, ye don't,' much in the same tone as the melo-
dramatic tar of my boyhood, who in defence of
forlorn youth and beauty used to flourish his cutlass
and defy the villain or villains of the piece ; but
the sailor always spat on his hands and hitched
up his trousers, and this Paul neglected to do.
Nevertheless, his interference was sufficient ; the
aggressive skydskarl drew back, and was presently
summoned to assist the fallen champion.

What to do with the latter was now the question.
He was evidently a wreck, staggering between his
supporters and moaning dismally; he did not take
his punishment over-well. With much difficulty
he was hoisted on to his old perch on my portmanteau, where, dropping his head on the back of
the seat, he remained motionless until we reached
the next station, and bled profusely, not only

over the carriole, but, as Cornewall, who kept a
look-out behind, informed me, over the back of my
coat as well; but as the latter was but an old heather-
mixture shooting-jacket already saturated in front
with my own gore, it was not of much consequence.
But the situation was rather like that described by
the infant cherub in the charming book ' Helen's
Babies' after the combat between David and
Goliath, when everything was ' bluggy.' And so I
resumed my drive after the fashion of an Homeric
hero, with my vanquished foe at the tail of my
chariot, with the difference, that instead of dragging
him by the heels, I gave him, as it were, a friendly
lift.

When we did arrive at the next station there was
much excitement. The postboys gave their own
version of the tale, and the station-master informed
us, most respectfully, I allow, that he could not
give us horses until the Lensmand had been sent
for to inquire into the matter. He lived at a long
distance, but a messenger on horseback would start
immediately to summon him. It was not even
permissible to wash the gory carriole; it must be
kept as a witness that human blood had been shed.

There was nothing for it but to make the best
of the matter; we had plenty of time to spare
before the northern steamer left Trondhjem. Personally, I had a good wash and a complete change.
My nose, although so tender that I could not bear
to touch it, was neither swollen nor discoloured,
and I felt all the better for the blood-letting. I
was rather anxious on the subject of the Lensmand:
what kind of man would he prove to be, and what
view would he take of the case? Of course, he

could not speak English, and amongst us we could not hope to give from our point of view such a graphic account of the incident as the postboys would from theirs; they might represent their comrade as having been shamefully handled in the discharge of his duty.

We had reached the station not long after noon, and the official did not arrive until eight o'clock in the evening; but two hours before his arrival the god out of the machine appeared, for from the North there came driving up to the door the poly-glot Petersen, cheeriest of men, best of interpreters, and most intrepid of Arctic explorers. He was soon in possession of the facts, and we felt that we were sure of acquittal in the face of any charge that the native faction might bring against us.

When the Lensmand came he heard the post-boys' story, and then went to see the injured man, who had been put to bed on reaching the station, and was looking, so Petersen told us, a miserable object. The five blows which Fate had destined me to inflict on his countenance had battered it out of recognition, and both his eyes were closed. He was, as appeared later, a man who drank habitually, and in bad condition. The Lensmand—I give Petersen's account—looked grave and pondered, then he asked to be shown the other man, expecting possibly to be conducted to another bedroom. He was, on the contrary, introduced to a young man looking fresh and in high spirits, who, having just finished a hearty supper, was smoking his pipe with much satisfaction. At first he was incredulous and astonished, but after hearing and weighing all the evidence, gave his judgment to this effect:

' The skydskarl exceeded his duty in using violence and bad language, even had there been any
ground for complaint or anger, but there was none:
the Englishmen had done no wrong. As for the
fight, it was simply a fight and nothing else, and
because one man proved himself better than
the other, there is no reason for my interference.
If such a thing happened among yourselves you
would not send for me; why should you because
there was an Englishman in the case ? You will
supply horses for these gentlemen whenever they
wish to proceed, and there is an end of the matter.'
So spoke this very Daniel of a Lensmand, and as there
was no darkness, it being midsummer, we decided
to move on that night until we reached good
quarters, and did so.

By Petersen's advice, we entered in the ' day-
book ' a complaint, which he wrote for us, of the
conduct of the people from Sundseth, and an outline
of the result. There were many other complaints
in the book referring to the same place. It was
afterwards a satisfaction to me to learn that the
man whom I was obliged to thrash was a notorious
bully, frequently insolent to travellers, and that
his evil influence had done much to corrupt the
good manners of the people round him. Mr.
Bennett, the author of the road-book, who certainly
knew more about roads and stations than any other
man in Norway, was my authority. By the next
autumn the Government Commissioners had shifted
the station to another farm.

But there is yet something more to tell in connection with this unpleasant adventure. As three
of us returned over the Dovre Fjeld road in late

autumn, two being friends who had not been with me on the northward drive, we had, of course, to pass Sundseth and change horses there. We were bound to catch the English steamer on a particular day, and had only just time; accordingly, my friends entreated, and I promised, that there should be no row, and consequent delay, unless we were actually assaulted.

The news of my coming had spread, and at Sundseth we found quite a number of people assembled. My late opponent was on the steps of the house, being jostled and pushed about by the women, who were laughing at him; he had evidently been drinking. We took no notice of him, and having ordered horses beforehand, directed the change to be made as quickly as possible, whilst we went into the guest-house, a separate building, to write our names in the 'day-book.' A minute later the man entered, followed by a number of people, and fortunately by the station-master. My friend said to me, 'now, Harry, remember, no row,' to which I replied with the invariable 'all right.' But it was a near thing. Whilst I was leaning over the book writing my name I heard behind me the harsh voice, 'Hola! Herr Professor!'—I suppose he meant of pugilism, for I cannot imagine any other ground on which I could merit the title —and received a clap of his open hand on my shoulder, at which I felt—well, say annoyed, and turned quickly round, but saw the station-master close by, evidently remonstrating with him; so to him I addressed myself in my best Norsk: 'We are travellers in haste to catch a steamer; I have no time to waste over that man. You are station-master, and it behoves you to see that travellers are left in peace.' There was a murmur of assent from some of those in the room, and the supposed disturber of the peace was hustled out of it. It was the simplest way of settling the matter, but to this day I am uncertain as to his intentions, they may have been friendly in his fashion. We mounted our carrioles as soon as the horses were put to, but there were no postboys, and the station-master had to explain that no one would go with us, that carrioles had preceded us with two boys, who would bring back our horses also ; and so, for the only time in my experience of the road in Norway, we drove off unattended.

As we passed the house I again saw the ugly face of my late antagonist. He had been apparently locked into a room, and was gesticulating through an unopened window. Whether he shook his fist or waved his hand at me I cannot say, but after some demonstration of the kind he applied himself to a bottle which stood by him on the window-ledge.

CHAPTER IV

ON Tuesday morning, July 27, 1857, my friend John Young Sargent and I were lounging idly on the grass in front of the residence of Herr Meyer, Norwegian merchant, at the little steamer-station of Bosckop, in the Alten Fjord, where for the time being, according to custom, we had our quarters as paying guests. The weather was lovely, the sky cloudless, the fjord calm and blue, the hills wrapt in a tender haze—in short, Nature was at her best; but we, sad to say, were both in a shockingly bad temper.

And for this reason: Collected on the grass and in the entrance-hall of the house was a mass of baggage, comprising articles of every size and shape, from tent and saddle-bag to rod-box and camp-kettle, and for a whole day and night, both being equally serviceable for a start, the cool bright night, indeed, for choice, had we been waiting for the promised horses which were to convey that baggage across the fjeld to the goal of our summer wanderings. No fewer than twenty-four days had been expended, through no fault of ours, in reaching Alten since we left Hull on the third of the month. We were a good deal later than we expected to be,

and now every day was of consequence. Moreover, we were constrained to hang about Bosckop,
doing nothing in particular, lest if we even took a
walk to any distance the horses might arrive in our
absence. Our guide had, indeed, made his appearance at the appointed hour early on Monday, a
genuine Finn in full costume, voluminous belted
tunic and square, blue, red-bordered cap, with,
despite a humpish back and bandy legs, something
of a regal swagger, and a general resemblance to the
stage representation of Richard III. His name
was David, which must be pronounced with the
broadest possible accent—' Da-ahveed.'

Our host Meyer, annoyed because we were—for
although rather reticent, he was a friendly, well-
intentioned man—was, as we could see through the
low windows of the sitting-room, relieving his
feelings by severe exercise indoors, such being his
habit. He was the possessor of an enormous pipe,
a plain square block of meerschaum with a long,
pliant stem ; the bowl must have held three times
as much tobacco as that of an ordinary pipe, and
on that his locomotion seemed to depend. With
it in the palm of his hand, he would stride up and
down the room, puffing rapidly and violently, and
rolling out volumes of smoke when at his best pace,
but when the puffs slowed down so did he ; he went
by smoke, as an engine goes by steam. When the
pipe was exhausted he would halt by the matchbox
on the wall, refill, relight, and start again, just like
a locomotive after taking in water.

We had expended on him our choicest Norsk, but
he could not suggest any means by which the faith-
less horse-owner, who lived a long way off on the

other side of the Alten River, could be found and
made to hurry up.   There was apparently no messenger handy except Richard III., and he remained
stoically unconcerned; his business was to guide
horses, not to fetch them.   And so there was nothing
for it but to exhibit as much patience as possible
under the circumstances; ours was not a brilliant
exhibition of that virtue.   Possibly with greater
command of Norsk, and especially of vigorous,
expostulatory, minatory, or even maledictory Norsk,
we might on this and on other occasions have
worked things better, and we might, of course,
have engaged someone to do the talking for us;
but before leaving England we had, over a brew
of gin punch after a farewell dinner at that
then much-frequented tavern the old Blue Posts,
registered before witnesses a solemn vow that
not on any consideration whatever would we
be tempted to employ the services of a professional interpreter.   What little Norsk we did
know we had picked up from grammar and vocabulary, such as were found in Murray's handbook,
learning them by heart.   During the passage from
Hull, both being good sailors, and all the way up the
Norwegian coast, we used, whenever a convenient
opportunity occurred, to repeat our lessons to each
other, like very schoolboys.   I confess to some
misgivings as to what might happen when we came
to deal with a purely Finsk population, in regions
comparatively remote from Norsk influence.

I must go a long way back to account for our
presence at Bosckop; this chapter will, indeed,
be mainly a retrospect of the three weeks previous
to our arrival there.

The crown and glory of Nordenfjelds is the great river Tana, which, born of the junction of two noble streams, the Anarjok and the Karasjok, flows into an inlet of the Arctic Sea, eighty miles east of the North Cape. In the year 1857 a veil of considerable mystery still hung over the river, and it entered into the heads and hearts of six young men, forming two separate parties, to try and lift that veil. One party consisted of Messrs. Charles Hambro, Merthyr Guest, Clover and Smith, and the other of John Sargent and myself.

Since those days I have taken some trouble to discover who could claim the distinction of having first angled in those remote waters, and I believe that it belonged to two adventurous wanderers, Pretyman and Pigott, as far back as 1838; but of how those pioneers reached the Tana or of what sport they had there seems to be no record. During the next decade, according to Lloyd, in vol. i. of his 'Scandinavian Adventures,' published in 1853, it was visited by several Englishmen; but he gives no names, and for some reason conjectures that they had indifferent sport. His notice of the subject is altogether vague, and based merely on hearsay. In 1851, however, the late Campbell of Islay did certainly reach the Tana by marching over the hills from Alten; but his book, 'Frost and Fire,' which contains a brief account of the expedition, was not published until 1865. He was travelling to study the features of the land as affected by glacial action, and mentions simply that he fished, without a word as to the result. But his journal, from which the account is condensed, must be deeply interesting.

Of late years the Tana has been regularly fished by

Englishmen, who have built sufficiently comfortable houses on its banks, and made private arrangements with the Finns for the sole right of angling at certain stations. But it cannot be leased or rented to the exclusion of others; from time immemorial it has been a free river, and anyone who will pay the small price of a license to the Foged, or local magistrate, can obtain the right to fish.

In 1857, however, as I have said, but little was known about the river. I can, at all events, testify that our efforts to obtain information of any importance on the subject in England resulted in complete failure. We knew of no books that could help us; Lloyd's brief notice was of no practical value, and Murray's handbook of that date, now before me, in which, like all true Britons, we naturally put our trust, contains these passages: ' The Tana and its tributaries have yet to be explored by the angler . . . the salmon are known to be very abundant and large. With a tent, guide, and provisions, a most exciting and delightful exploring expedition down the valley of the Tana might be made from the Alten.' The date of this handbook is 1849; the third edition was published in 1858, and simply condenses Lloyd's remarks.

The other party started shortly before we did, without any precise idea of their route. We hoped to meet on the river, and indulged in visions of what a jollification we would have when we did; but Fate ruled that we should not meet, and therefore I must follow the separate fortunes of my companion and myself.

We two had already had considerable experience of each other as comrades and fellow-travellers, and

I am thankful to say that the same active experience continued for thirty years after we had disposed of Tana, while the friendship endures to this very hour. Had we not executed together a number of those minor athletic feats in which English youth delights: rambled over Irish wilds, climbed the crags and screes of the Cumberland hills, seen sunrise from Helvellyn and Skiddaw, bivouacked by the torrent and slept soundly in the heather? Only two years before had we not tramped, knapsacks on back, under a July sun, from Bayonne, through Pau, to Eaux-chaudes, and thence, enduring together the filth, vermin, and other horrors of wretched Spanish posadas, crossed on foot the Pyrenees by the well-named Sierra-di-mal-repos, descending on the ultra-Iberian town of Huesca, and thence to Saragossa; and further endured, before the time of railroads, the almost greater horrors of ten-muled Spanish diligencias, until we arrived at Madrid and our longed-for portmanteaux, which had been forwarded to meet us by another route? It is from such companionship as this that young men learn whether they are congenial spirits, able to take rough and smooth as they come without danger to friendship.

> ' No more, no more, ah! never more on me
> The freshness of the heart can fall like dew,'

wrote Byron at the age of thirty. It is to be hoped that there are not many who will sympathize with or echo the morbid lament which our great poet's peculiar temperament led him to utter at such a comparatively early age over the decay of youthful emotion and sentiment. There are, happily, a great number of people in this world who, long past middle

age, have no such dismal reflections.   Who, indeed,
does not count among his acquaintances some veritable elder who, on his temporary escape from the
serious business of life and perhaps domestic
responsibility, develops an almost boyish enjoyment of his outing and recreation, returning when
it is over to delight his friends by his renewed
energy and spirits, and to surprise them into the
extensive declaration that they never saw him
looking so well in his life ?   One cannot help regret-
ting for his own sake that Byron had not in him
a little of the sportsman.   Take the case of another
poet who was also, in his line, as hard-working
a man as ever lived, Charles Kingsley.   Note his
intensely youthful enthusiasm when he looks to
getting away for his brief holiday, as expressed,
for instance, in ' The Invitation ' to Tom Hughes :

> ' Fish the August evening
>   Till the eve is passed,
> Whoop like boys, at pounders
>   Fairly played and grassed.
>
> *   *   *   *
>
> ' Up a thousand feet, Tom,
>   Round the lion's head,
> Find soft stones to leeward,
>   And make up our bed.
>
> ' Eat our bread and bacon,
>   Smoke the pipe of peace,
> And, ere we be drowsy,
>   Give our boots a grease.'

Was there ever anything more juvenile and
refreshing ?

But, in spite of all this, it cannot be denied that

1

there are some things which a man, one, I will say, of the great majority of men, however tender and vivid may be his recollection of youth, can scarcely realize late in life, that is to say, he cannot resuscitate in himself the same psychical condition ; it has perished for ever. Men with clear brains and sound livers can reproduce such things, as they do in books and on the stage, but they are only exquisite reproductions, the result of memory, not of living sentiment or sensation. As familiar examples, take the exuberantly innocent delight with which a child hails the advent of Christmas and its festivities ; no grown man can realize how he felt that delight as he actually did feel it when a child himself. Again, and this I approach with respectful hesitation, take the sweet idiocy which overcomes a very young man, a mere boy, during his earliest experience of the tender passion, when for the first time he discovers that he has a decided and reciprocated, for that is a great point, liking for a young person of the other sex. I use no stronger term, because the chances are that in six months or less the fitful fever will be over, and the young people have regained their senses. In after-life that boy may be capable of the truest love, of passionate devotion, but he will always wonder how he could ever have been, as he would probably say himself, such a young ass. If, however, he wrote a novel or a play, he might be able to faithfully reproduce his baby spooniness for the delectation of the public.

In the same way can no man who has grown old, or even elderly, and knocked about the world to some extent, although as long as his limbs will serve him he may remain a fairly keen sportsman and an habitual rover, recover the 'freshness of the heart,' to use Byron's words, and sanguine expectation with which he entered upon his first expedition to any distant region round which still clung some romance of the unknown, and which promised to introduce him to a completely novel mode of life. To obey 'the call of the wild,' to plunge into the wilderness or among strange peoples, to become a dweller in tents, and perhaps dependent for food on his own gun or rod, to be out of the reach, except at rare intervals, of the post; how glorious was the prospect !

And then the preparation : the excitement, the suggestiveness, the positive romance of the shopping, broken by lunch at some city tavern, with careful comparison of note-books and memoranda. The erection of the tent and trying of the beds on the floor of Edgington's warehouse; the consultations over rods and tackle; the inspection of the camp-kettle, a very puzzle of compactness, and of the portable copper powder-magazine, an indispensable item in the days of muzzle-loaders ; the choice of axes, knives, compasses, and the score of other small extras which seemed necessities before starting, and might in the end be seldom or never needed. Ah ! in later life we can remember all this, but we cannot evoke the spirit in which it was transacted, the audacious optimism, the superb self-assertion of the twenties.

In looking over early journals, as I have been lately, I am struck by this triumphant tone of youth, and by the difficulty in reproducing it without literal quotations from the journals themselves ; it would at least, irrespective of the narrative, be a too severe effort of memory to do so. The Spanish journal, for instance, is full of it, sustained to the end, in spite of some disagreeable incidents and some disappointments. But in my Tana journal, although the same tone is constantly in evidence, I positively find it leavened to a serious extent by an undertone of complaint, a chronic murmur, which I allow surprises me, because unassisted memory has cherished only the gladness of those days that are no more, discarding whatever there was of evil or merging it in the good. But the evidence of a diary written at the time is unquestionable; the evil did exist, and made itself sorely felt; omnipresent, unescapable, the phantasmal terror always hovered nigh, embittering by its venomous influence the hours even of mirth and jollity, of sweet success itself.

> ' Medio de fonte leporum
> Surgit amari aliquid, quod in ipsis floribus angat.'

The above is, I fancy, an emphatically high-toned passage, not unsuitable to a weirdly sensational novel; but it does not, according to my diary, exaggerate the condition of affairs during a part of our expedition. I and John were young, I three-and-twenty, he a little the elder, but still in his happy third decade; we were both strong, I may say athletic, and in perfect health, disposed to make the best of everything, and to rough it to any extent; indeed, we rather gloried in the idea of possible difficulties; and yet it is certain that for a while we found ourselves ' sair hodden doun,' to put it mildly, as the Cumberland boy was by the ' bubblyjock,' by a creature individually as insignificant as any to be found on the face of the earth, but a veritable ogre in the vicious unanimity of its multi-myriad existence. There came, indeed, as it appears, speaking for myself, one dreadful hour, the nadir of torment and despondency, when, to my shame be it said, had I been able to turn tail, tail I would have turned and fled, glad to relinquish all ideas of sport or any other diversion in exchange for relief from the gray terror. As in the course of my narrative I shall have to say a good deal more on this painful subject, I will for the present dismiss it.

My aim, then, in rewriting and reproducing this account of unimportant travel nearly fifty years ago has been to preserve as far as possible the juvenile tone of the journal on which it was grounded when it appeared originally in the form of letters to the *Field*. And I have not, therefore, scrupled to maintain the sense of importance which as young men we attached to our expedition, while permitting myself a running comment of age on the arrogant inexperience of youth, and the judgment of my memory on details of the said journal written at the time. As noticed in the preface, the narrative can have interest only as a record of early days in what Mr. Slingsby aptly calls 'The Northern Playground.'

There was fair reason for our youthful exultation over the idea of a trip to the Tana. To travel from London to that distant river involved a journey of over two thousand miles, which was, especially in those days, a respectable distance to go for a bit of fishing. Then, as I have said, no one that we knew could tell us anything about it. A reference to the best atlas procurable—we did not get Munch's map until we reached Christiansand—showed that it ran for a long way through a region with a few strange outlandish names scattered here and there, but with little evidence of there being any population to speak of. It seemed almost certain that we should find neither decent accommodation nor food, have to live under canvas, and trust for provisions to our own resources. All this was delightful to think of. How much in doubt we were as to the best route to take appears from the fact, as recorded in my journal, that at one time we actually contemplated an overland journey from Christiania to Stockholm, and thence by steamer to Tornea, from which place we might cross Lapland to Muonioniska, and so descend into the valley of the Tana. By that route, with all our baggage, we should certainly not have reached our goal before the winter. In the end we decided to land at Christiansand, and make our way up the coast as quickly as we could to Alten, or to Hammerfest, the most northern town in Europe. There was a distinctly refreshing sound about the last half-dozen words.

And now how simple it all seems and is! From Hull there is a steamer, and from Christiania a railroad to Trondhjem, whence a 'hurtig-rute,' or express Nordenfjelsk boat, in connection with the train hurries the traveller to the Far North, and the telegraph, or even the telephone, enables him to secure quarters for the night, and boats to take him up the river. We left Hull on July 3, did not reach Trondhjem until the 16th, and the Tana not before August 4, and yet we travelled as fast as the then means of transport permitted. Between Christiansand and Alten we stopped at no fewer than sixty-four steamer stations.

During the last twenty years the telephone has extended itself throughout Scandinavia by marvellous leaps and bounds. Nowadays from my quarters on the remote Indre Folden Fjord, beyond Namsos, I can chat with the stores in Trondhjem about fresh supplies to be sent by the next steamer; but, although I live close to the sea, the said supplies, when despatched, will take between two and three days to reach me.

We left Hull, then, on July 3, in the little paddle-wheel steamer the *Courier*, of 250 tons, owned by Messrs. Wilson, and commanded by Captain Fairbairn. She was placed on the Christiania line in 1852. Before that date all anglers bound for Norway, except the early pioneers who, as I have said, crossed the North Sea as they best could, seem to have gone round by Hamburg and Gothenburg.

As it would have been next to impossible to drive from Christiania to Trondhjem with our amount of baggage, and as we were dead against the idea of parting with and sending it round by the coast, we resolved to land at Christiansand. There we were delayed for the inside of a week waiting for the northward-bound steamer, and occupied the time by a visit to Vigeland, on the Torrisdal River, where for the first time we threw a fly on a Norwegian stream. But a sawmill was in full work, and the water so cumbered by logs, which came rushing down over the Helfos, to be caught by a boom, and so thick with sawdust, that anything like serious fishing was impossible. We caught five grilse under and a few brown trout above the Fos, and made an excursion through the forest without a guide in search of a large lake said to abound with big trout. A fine sheet of water we did after a long ramble discover, and began fishing at once near the mouth of a stream which entered it. After catching two or three brown trout, I hooked and landed, to my surprise, a sea-trout, and later John actually killed on the fly an adventurous codling! The water was salt. We had rambled astray, and at least four miles too far, and struck a branch of the fjord near Lomsland. Nevertheless, we had good sport with our little rods; the best sea-trout weighed 4½ pounds.

At Bergen, Herr Sundt, on whom we had letters of credit, kindly assisted us in purchasing stores for our expedition, the chief items being a ham, several enormous and, as it turned out, very savoury sausages, a keg of ship's biscuits, ten pounds of rice, two large bottles of salad oil and six of good cognac: for the despotism of King Whisky was not then established. Our Spanish experiences had taught us the value of oil for frying anything, but especially fish. We laid in besides a stock of sardines, tins of preserved peas, fresh lemons, pickles, sauces, and other condiments. The only provisions that we had brought from England were tea, some packets of compressed vegetables, portable soup in ox-gullets, and a small keg of pickled pork of such amazing saltness that not all the waters of Karasjok, Anarjok, and Tana, rivers of Finmark, fresh or boiled, could render it sufficiently sweet to be eatable, and in the end we generously presented it to our boatmen.

At Trondhjem we had the good fortune to meet at the Hôtel d'Angleterre Mr. Thomas, the manager of the copper mines at Alten, and the one man on

the face of the earth who could best give us information about our proposed route; for he happened
to be the leader of a party which had crossed the
fjeld from Alten to Tana, in 1855, only two years
before, and which claimed to be, as he told us, the
first English expedition to that river, a claim recorded
on the logs of a hut at Karasjok, as we should see
if ever we got there ourselves. This certainly disposed, or attempted to dispose, of the pretensions of
any supposed predecessors, but it may be that
the pith of the claim lay in the word 'expedition'
as opposed to the casual wandering angler; the
latter, if he did reach the goal, is, however, without
doubt the worthier of the two. At the time we
were ourselves fairly content with the idea that we
should be the second expedition.

The ideal of a Briton, tall, stalwart, deep-voiced,
and of imposing presence, Mr. Thomas had been
resident in Norway for over twenty years, long
enough to give him the right of being elected a
member of the Storthing, and he was returning to
Alten after the conclusion of the sitting at
Christiania. He resided in a large wooden mansion
at Kaafjord, where he kept open house, and was
noted far and wide for his kindliness, courtesy,
hospitality, and sumptuous style of entertainment.
There were few imperishable luxuries that could
not be obtained at his extensive stores, including
the finest wine and cigars; for he took good care
that his outward-bound ships laden with copper
and salt-fish should bring back an ample store of
such good things among their return cargoes. He
was, indeed, until his departure from Kaafjord to
Chili, where he undertook the management of certain

mines and eventually died, universally known by
the title of ' the King of the North.' His wife was
a very charming and comely lady, a native of the
island of Hindö in the Loffodens ; she is immortalized in Lord Dufferin's ' Letters from High Latitudes ' by his enthusiastic description of ' the
chatelaine of Kaafjord.'

And this gentleman kind Fate had thrown in our
way just at the most opportune moment. We
dined together, and under the influence of a couple
of bottles of champagne his genial nature, I may
say all our genial natures, expanded. We plied him
with innumerable questions, which he was good
enough to answer without being, apparently, bored.
It is somewhat sad to relate that the immediate
result of our long conversation was discouragement.
Thomas had noticed our pile of baggage in the hall
of the hotel, and at first recommended us to take a
steamer which stopped at the mouth of the Tana
Fjord once a fortnight, to procure boats, and make
our way up the river ; but he suggested that it was
rather late in the season, that when we came to
the rapids there would be a long and difficult portage,
and that we might not get far up. The alternative
route, he said, was to cross the fjeld from Alten to
Karasjok, and there try to engage boats to descend
the river. Our baggage could, of course, be carried
by horses, several would be required, and we could
walk ourselves ; but it was a long, weary march over
rough ground, without shelter of any kind, and—
the mosquitoes were dreadful ! At these last objec-
tions to the route we smiled, at the notion of our
pedestrian powers not being equal to the task, or
of our being frightened by a lot of insects. Think

of that forty-five miles Pyrenean march the last day before entering Spanish Huesca; of the miserable posadas and their swarming vermin! Yes, we smiled.

Then, as regards the fishing. Thomas allowed that he and his party had fair sport with large salmon, but did not expatiate on that point as much as we should have liked. The fishing-stations, he said, were few and far between, a great part of the river consisting of long, still reaches, almost like lakes, without any visible current; also that the sport was always uncertain, depending as it did to a great extent on the sand and water at the mouth, the one being often too high and the other too low, whilst in some seasons there were droves of seals to waylay the passing fish. I feel sure that his friendly object all the time was not to excite in us false hopes which might result in much disappointment, and in this he was successful, for we were certainly discouraged.

The criticisms on our mass of baggage, which was a sore point, worried us considerably, and after Thomas had retired we sat for a while in gloomy consideration of the future. Then a sudden reaction set in; we vowed that cross that fjeld we would, and that nothing should deter us from accomplishing the march. The first thing to do was to reduce the weight of the baggage as much as possible, and to begin the task on the spot.

Whereupon there ensued a scene of unmitigated confusion. Stripped to our shirt-sleeves, and with needful refreshment handy, for five hours did we rummage, compress, stamp, and haul, straining every nerve to effect the required reduction. The passage became blocked, and belated guests had to pick their way over our barricades. By rejecting the frames and legs, and reserving only the mattresses, we contrived to force both beds into a single waterproof case ; a deal of the ammunition, a portmanteau full of clothes, in short, everything not absolutely necessary, we determined to leave behind. There was, of course, no darkness nor need of artificial light, and at 3 a.m., when the sun was a long way above the horizon, we turned in, and slept the sleep of men who had done their duty.

Bayard Taylor, the celebrated American author, and his devoted friend Braisted, had crossed with us in the *Courier* from Hull to Christiansand, and we met them again on the deck of the steamer in which we left Trondhjem. He and I were both, after a fashion, dabblers in water-colours, but he was a better hand at it than I was, and it was a privilege to consult with him on the subject of tints ; for in those northern latitudes Nature takes a pleasure in disconcerting the ambitious amateur by abnormal effects : now by a total absence of apparent atmosphere, so that a distant mountain appears to be within a stone's-throw, and again by a bewildering display of delicate tones which reduces its solidity to a mere phantom of itself. At Bodo, where we stopped for the night, my ill-timed zeal for spoiling paper was nearly productive of serious trouble. John and I got a boatman to land us below the town, and we enjoyed a glorious nocturnal ramble along the desolate shores of the fjord. So absorbed were we both in watching from a rocky peninsula, and I in audaciously attempting to record, the indescribable alternations of that wondrous northern hour when the delicate blush overspreading land and sea deepens to a palpitating crimson glow, which in its turn, like the change from life to death, fades slowly into a solemn universal gray, that our retreat was all but cut off by the quiet progress of the treacherous sea. We had just time to dash across the sandy bar to the mainland, and in a few minutes more the rock where we sat had become an islet a quarter of a mile from shore. A nice mess we should have been in had not some guardian spirit prompted John to look over the landward crest of the promontory to see what the tide was about.

A little beyond Tromsö all on board tendered their homage to the midnight sun, and on the following day, July 23, we entered the Alten Fjord. After dropping King Thomas at his Kaafjord palace, to which the great man gave us a hearty invitation, we found ourselves and all our baggage at length safely landed at Bosckop, on the other side of the bay. Whilst we stood on the wharf, doubtful in which direction to turn, we saw approaching us an unmistakable compatriot, accompanied by two girls, one of whom we now recognised as a passenger from the last station. He turned out to be Collingwood, who, with three other Englishmen, was then fishing the Alten River, and the young ladies were the Misses Mary and Sarah Monk, daughters of the Cornish captain of a mine not far from Bosckop, and tenant of a house called Raipas, where the anglers had their quarters.

All now went smoothly for us. By Collingwood's kind directions, our heavy baggage was deposited in a store-shed, and we were ourselves conducted

to the house of Meyer. For the second time that
morning we received a cordial invitation, which we
accepted for the next day, and then our new friend
and his fair young companions started on foot for
Raipas, about three miles distant.

Our first care was to collect all articles that
required washing, and consign them to the tender
mercies of the local laundresses, after which we
went down to the rocks and washed ourselves well
in the sea. Thankful to have escaped from our
long spell of steamer life, and quite contented with
our present lot, we wrote letters and journals,
smoked many pipes on the great white dome of rock
overlooking the blue fjord, and, after a good supper,
went early to bed.

It would be easy to write many pages about our
surprising experiences of the next two days, surprising because they were so totally unexpected.
It seemed as if Fate had determined to afford us, on
the very verge of the wilderness into which we were
about to plunge, a final taste of the delights and
amenities attendant on highly civilized social life,
either by way of sharp contrast to the then unknown
troubles before us, or to console us during those
troubles by dreams of what we might in the end
regain. And we were not prepared for this kind
of thing. Before leaving home we had steeled our
hearts, as we believed, to meet any hardship or
difficulty, but we had not anticipated the risk of
enervation by Capuan luxury; it was perhaps as
well for us that our apolaustic probation was but
brief.

These remarks are the result of finding in my
journal a rude pen-and-ink sketch representing,

as per marginal note, ' our return from dinner at
Raipas, 2 a.m.' In this sketch John, I, and
George Gillett, then one of the merry company at
Raipas, and afterwards my friendly neighbour for
some years in King's Bench Walk, Temple, are
depicted as forcibly piloting down the steep road
from the house one Nostrum, Norwegian purveyor
of horses, with whom some item of the fare provided
in that home of hospitality had clearly disagreed,
to the extent of affecting his powers of steady
locomotion, while looking over a fence in the background a row of spectators appear from their gestures to be encouraging our efforts.   And a little
later in the same diary I find these words, pur-
porting to be an excuse for some confusion of mind
whilst trying to record our visit to King Thomas
at Kaafjord : ' Perhaps the Cliquot, Hockheimer,
and Château Margot, or those big regalias, may
have something to do with it.' It is from such
slight evidence as this, afforded by contemporary
documents, that commentators on past events are
apt to draw perhaps erroneous conclusions.   But
this I can say for certain, that at Raipas we were
welcomed with the utmost cordiality; that we found
there a group of English gentlemen, good fellows
all, who did their best not only to entertain us, but
to help us in the arrangements for our proposed
expedition ; that Captain and Mrs. Monk were
model host and hostess; and that their fair polyglot
daughters, who had been educated for some years in
England, and spoke their own language, Norsk,
Lappisk, and Finsk with equal facility, provided
that sweet element of artless girlhood which leavens
and refines every household where it is found.

BOSEKOP IN 1857.

We returned to Bosckop and Raipas for a fortnight after the Tana expedition was ended, and when two of the anglers, Collingwood and Honywood, who intended to spend the winter in Norway, were still there.

Our visit to Kaafjord was equally gratifying in its way. Before dinner we strolled about the well-kept lawn, with its miniature battery and the English ensign flying, went over the works of the company and the church, walked round the bay to the Kaafjord River, where King Thomas had taken many a big salmon, and, returning to the luxuriously furnished house, inspected his immense store of fishing-tackle.

Then followed a sumptuous entertainment, with a dozen guests at table beside ourselves. I need not expatiate on the excellence of the cuisine and the choiceness of the wines. Our hostess grew every minute more charming, our host more magnificent. I can see him even now as he rose from his seat, tall and broad-shouldered, and elevating a huge beaker of champagne, drained it with a loud Skaal! to the health of his guests. The best of tobacco, coffee, and liqueurs succeeded, while we sat in the arbour overlooking the fjord, and the strains of music from the saloon floated out into the quiet Arctic night.

But parting is the one thing in this world as certain as death. Thomas and his fair wife we should in all probability never see again, as they were leaving Kaafjord shortly for Chili. A six-oared boat was thoughtfully provided to take us back to Bosckop, and reclining on the luxurious couch of reindeer skins spread in the stern, we thought how different

had been our recent experiences to those which
we expected in latitude 70° N.   But it was no dream:
the Far North was around us.   As we neared the landing-place the rays of the sleepless nocturnal sun
were beginning to gild the hilltops; the eider-ducks
swam lazily out of the course of the boat, and close
by, between us and the rocky shore, the roll of a
whale broke the glassy surface of the fjord.

About noon on Tuesday the dilatory Nostrum at
last made his appearance, with three horses and two
men, who were to accompany them.   He tried to
explain the delay by declaring that the animals,
which were loose in the woods, had wandered so far
that there was great difficulty in finding and capturing them, and then they had to be shod.   Our
bargain with him was as follows : For each horse
as far as Karasjok, reckoned at eighteen Norsk, or
126 English, miles, we were to pay twelve specie
dollars (£2 14s.), the men, paid by Nostrum, finding
their own provisions ; the journey to occupy not
more than four days, by alternate marches and halts
of about six hours ; the Finn guide to take charge
of the leading horse, and receive twelve dollars for
himself.

Regarding the weight and complex character of
our baggage, the task of arranging the loads for
the horses was not an easy one, but the men made
the worst of it.   Their pack-saddles were wretched,
and they seemed to have little idea of a sound
lashing.   Nearly two hours were consumed in weighing, shifting, and wrangling over each package
before it was announced that all was ready for a
start.   The word was given, the heavily-laden horses
moved forward, and then Providence, in the shape

of a log of wood projecting from a pile, caught the side of the leader, and in a moment precipitated the whole of his burden to the ground. I say Providence, because with three horses only we should never have reached Tana. Hence another long delay whilst a fourth was captured and shod. A lad of fifteen consented to lead him; the poor boy must have bitterly rued the hour when he did so.

About three o'clock we did get off, and for two miles followed a track through grand pine-woods to Elvebakken, where the river Alten had to be crossed, necessitating, of course, a complete unloading. John and I were ferried over in a light canoe by, as recorded in our journals, one of the prettiest girls we ever saw, and two of the horses, with great intelligence, took to the water and swam gallantly behind us; the other two followed the large boat containing the men and the baggage. Another hour along a narrow path thickly beset by trees, which sorely tested the lashings of the horses' loads, brought us to Nostrum's house, and there it was agreed that, for the fourth time, an entire repacking should take place, while John and I were regaled indoors by his pleasant little wife with a bottle of wine and biscuits, and much, under difficulties, agreeable conversation.

Then we started again in better trim, and at once began to climb. For a few miles the track was terribly steep and rugged, and very trying to the horses. Many halts were necessary, and our progress consequently slow, but at length we surmounted the crest of the last mountain ridge, and found ourselves among the snow patches, while before us lay the broad gray folds of the fjeld stretching away to the horizon, and dotted with many tarns. We trudged on until nearly ten o'clock, when the leading horse, which we had christened Black Mustang, suddenly lay down, either because he was really exhausted or because he considered it a reasonable time to halt in a spot which appeared quite suitable for a bivouac ; whatever his motive, we none of us felt disposed to question the wisdom of his action.

CHAPTER V

THE REALM OF THE GRAY TERROR

THE first bivouac on an Arctic fjeld! a delight
long looked forward to, and at length attained; a
cherished hope, a sweet dream, that has become
concreted into fact, into positive incident, inseparable
from one's life.

It is a still midnight, with all the clear luminosity
of an early summer morning, but without its indi-
cations of nascent day. The spirit of the Night,
although forced to discard his mantle of darkness,
is still regent of the hour; nevertheless, his transitory control can assert itself only in the chill that
pervades the atmosphere, in the mists that creep
among the hollows, and in the intense hush, so
unmistakably nocturnal, that overlies all Nature.
For the present he is powerless to effect more; he
bides his time—the time, not long distant, of his
terrible hibernal sway. Motionless overhead a few
fleecy clouds acknowledge with a quiet ruddy glow,
like that of dying embers, the direct influence of
the sun, who has for a brief space withdrawn the
light of his countenance beyond a low ridge due
north; to say that he has set would be to mis-
represent his absence.

The more I think of it, the more am I convinced

that before our leading horse lay down, apparently exhausted, he had carefully selected the spot for this our first bivouac, and was not altogether selfish in his choice; that his intelligent equine eye took in at a glance all its advantages; the narrow sheltered dale, so attractive amid the gray sterility of the fjeld, with its patch of greensward, through which gurgles over a rocky channel a rivulet of ice-cold water; the few wind-stunted birch-trees, happily not without dry, rugged stumps, whereon John has been using the axe, and thereby providing the best of fuel for our fire.

Having two journals, John's, which he has been good enough to lend me, and my own, to refer to, I feel that by occasionally quoting entire or abridged passages from them I shall give a truer picture of our transit of the fjeld than in any other way. And now as we lie by the fire after supper on our waterproof sheets—it does not seem worth while to unpack and erect our rather elaborate tent, and have the trouble of repacking it—John has got out his inkpot and pen, and is busily writing up his journal on the spot, by far the best plan when possible. Let me look over his shoulder, and read his sketch of our first bivouac. It is especially interesting, as it gives the first suggestion of the terrible plague that subsequently drove us nearly to the verge of despair.

' A jolly crackling fire within two yards of my nose (stopped to kill a mosquito that was biting my finger), Harry inditing as he lies resting on his haversack beside me (semicolon for one on my eye); two Norsemen and a boy lying a few yards off, and beyond them David, our trusty Finn guide (another

on the forehead), snoozing in his thick warm "pesk,"
with a heathy mossy ridge in front, complete the
groundwork of the scene.

' The only sounds are the tinkling of our horses'
bells, as they graze down the hollow, and the
bubbling of a snow-born brook behind.   The baggage
is scattered on the hillside where Black Mustang
lay down, except those few things which we require
for our personal comfort in a bivouac.   I have just
got up to replenish the fire.   It is pleasant to have a
good one, although, wrapped as I am in one of our
waterproof tent-sheets, I flatter myself I could get
well through a far worse night than this.   The
snoring of the men has now added a deep bass to
the treble of the bells and the chatter of the brook's
soliloquy (another bold mosquito on my nose) ; in
fact, sleeping seems to be the thing that they do
best, for they have not lent us a hand even in
getting fuel.   They made a short, comfortless repast
after their kind, eating cheese and raw salmon, and
then lay down at once to slumber.

' Harry and I immediately set to work to choose
our ground, light a fire, and cook supper, in which
we were successful beyond our wildest hopes.   We
brought the camp-kettle, a big sausage, some
compressed soup, a bottle of oil, and a supply of
biscuits, and there and then I ate the sweetest meal
I ever had in my life.   It was a sight to see my
comrade, who is an excellent cook, frying the
sausage in oil, and boiling the kettle of soup suspended from a stick, whilst I looked to the fire,
and then to hear the lordly tone in which he
announced that supper was ready !   We ate and
talked and praised the viands, and were thoroughly

happy, and in our pride of successful cookery arranged a dinner to which we mean to invite the other Tana party when we meet them in their encampment. Supper was followed by a pipe and some brandy punch, and a chat that was worth all. But the Finn is astir; it is half-past one in the morning, and the beasts have to be packed. I must stop writing.'

It will be evident to anyone that my modesty would alone have prevented my personally recording all the details of our repast as given in the above graphic quotation. In our youthful enthusiasm we christened the scene of our first bivouac 'The Happy Valley.' If, eager to be on the move, we left it without a sigh, we had later to confess with many a one that none other of our subsequent halting-places deserved such a euphemistic name.

As it is, however, we start about 2 a.m. in high spirits, as yet ignorant of the hours of torture that the future has in store for us. The air is cool and misty, and it seems unnecessary to lower the green veils, which, by the advice of friends, we wear round our 'wide-awakes,' or to put on our gloves. We carry our guns, being determined to harry any-thing and everything likely to be fit for food, to shoot without scruple 'for the pot.' It is still July, but there are no game-laws in Nordenfjelds to interfere with our doing as we please, and most certainly no gamekeepers in the Arctic wilderness. We have not long to wait for shooting of a kind. Scarcely have we cleared the dale and emerged again on the open fjeld, spreading into the far dis-tance in a succession of billowy undulations, like the rollers of a great gray sea, than we hear the

wailing ventriloquial pipe of golden plover, and see
a number of the birds running and flitting over the
waste.   Here indeed is a chance to replenish our
nomadic larder with delicious food.   The Arctic
fjeld is a favourite breeding-place of the plover ;
the young birds are clearly full grown and unable
to fly, and likely to be as fat as butter.   For
the next three hours we wander from the direct line
of our little caravan in pursuit of them, and bag as
many as we care to.   Their plumpness fully satisfies
our expectations.

Nothing can be drearier or more monotonous
than the features of the land, but for us there is at
present a certain fascination about its grim desolateness.   Is it possible that in the whole wide world
there can be a region more desolate ?   What strikes
us particularly is its aspect of incalculable old age.
This is due in a great measure to the abundant
growth of etiolated reindeer moss, which imparts a
universal hoariness to the landscape, and the
innumerable lichen-encrusted boulders and stones
scattered in every direction over the surface of the
waste, and all of a uniform gray.   At this early hour,
too, the tarns are sheets of dull drab, and the snow
patches of a somewhat ghastly white.

The land was ground down into lifelessness under
the inexorable dominion of the Glacial Age, which
has left its tokens in the sheep-backed ridges and the
multitude of rocky fragments deposited by the
receding ice, and the long Arctic winters have
maintained, as far as in them lies, the merciless
traditions of that remote reign of terror.   Their
gigantic notice is, as it were, inscribed on the face
of the plateau: 'Vitality is strictly forbidden here.'

But although for mile after mile the cursory glance
of the wanderer can detect no conspicuous signs of
contradiction to that stern decree, Nature has,
nevertheless, been quietly and constantly at work,
after her own fashion, to mitigate its severity.
That pale moss, for all its achromatic aridity, is
full of nourishment; there is no food on which the
reindeer thrives so well. The botanist, if he went
on his hands and knees for the purpose, would
discover among the stones many a minute Arctic
plant that dares to put forth insignificant flowerets,
to waste their sweetness—if they have any—on
the desert air. In the swampy hollows are occasional
clumps of gray-green, stunted willow, on the drier
slopes of dwarf birch,* at the best paltry, wan vegetation, yet affording shelter for the nest and brood
of wild-duck or willow-grouse; and in certain spots
at long intervals, where a man has by a brief sojourn
encouraged her efforts, Nature has succeeded in
effecting the development, not only of attractive
green turf, but even of long, sweet grass, tempting
the wanderer and his weary cattle to rest and be
thankful.

Now, had she been content with these proofs of
her creative powers under difficulties, she would have
my fervent blessing for her benign influence, I
would retract all I may ever have thought or said
about her pitilessness; but when she takes upon
herself to produce from the soil, for elsewise could
it not be produced, an innumerable host of useless,
bloodthirsty, venomous, torturing, winged and unescapable vampires, I say that she deserves the
worst that can be said of her, that she has com-

* *Betula nana.*

mitted herself to a work of malicious and iniquitous
supererogation, worthy of the most malignant deity
in the worst of heathen mythologies; and could I
use stronger language without words of positive
malediction, such as may have been wrung from
me in my agony, I would. Why condescend to
the meanest treachery? Why hold out hopes of
her own 'sweet restorer, gentle Sleep,' only to prove
it an unattainable blessing? I have often been
grateful to Nature for much direct happiness, for
much consolation under annoyance, for compensation
by her revealed loveliness for weariness of limb
and mind, poor success with gun or rod, and have
at times been half willing to allow that her pitilessness is exhibited more in her own special realm
than towards man—that is, if she does not catch
him at a disadvantage—but I cannot allow any
offset to counterbalance the atrociousness of her
conduct on the Arctic fjeld.

But all the above is an after-thought. As John
and I ramble over the fjeld in the small hours of
the first day out, we reck little of the benignity of
Nature or the reverse: we only see around us the
most desolate region imaginable, remote from the
haunts of men, and our hearts leap within us as we
realize that we are at last ' off.' That magic mono-
syllable means so much. For over three weeks have
we been travelling away from England, and have
never felt ' off' until now.

In wandering beside some of the tarns we are
inclined to long for our rods, for fishes of goodly
size, trout or char—we cannot decide which—sail
from the banks into the deeper water. There are
no snipe in the swampy ground, which appears so

suitable for them, nor, though we see ducks, do we for the present get within range of any, the few broods visible keeping well out in the water. Without a retriever they could not be recovered when shot, at all events, only by losing more time than we can afford.

About eight o'clock we discover that we are not only weary from want of sleep, but both hungry and thirsty. With rills and snow patches all round, and flask in pocket, the thirst is easily quenched, but to satisfy the hunger we must overtake the horses; and where on earth are they now? Fortunately, the faint outline of a high snow-capped mountain, promising before long some change of scenery, has been pointed out to us as the line of the march, and by pressing on in that direction we catch sight of our train, halted in a distant valley, where a patch of green indicates that there is grazing for the horses.

The sun is now well up in the sky, and has dispelled the mist. The aspect of the fjeld itself is not materially altered thereby; it has merely assumed a lighter tone of gray, and the contrast between the brown heathy ridges and the areas of pallid reindeer moss is more distinct; but the lakes and tarns are blue and smiling, and the rivulets sparkle in the light.

From that hour of apparently cheerful change in our surroundings dates the commencement of our misery. The warmth of the sun is rousing our deadly enemies into active warfare. Attacked as we are by a few score of viciously-piping skirmishers from their mighty host, we have before advancing to look to the joints in our harness, to lower our vizors, and don our gauntlets—would that they had been the real thing!—and then in descending the long slope towards the bivouac the scores of the foe are gradually multiplied to hundreds, the hundreds to thousands, the thousands to myriads, and by the time the green patch of grass is reached we are enveloped in a dense cloud of diminutive winged fiends, until, as John forcibly remarks, the air around hisses and stinks with them.

The men, having swallowed their hasty meal, are again recumbent, protected as well as may be from the attacks of the vermin by their coats thrown over their heads; but at intervals an impatient jerk, slap, or gruff exclamation shows that some insidious blood-sucker has succeeded in getting his poisoned weapon home. One advantage they have over us, their outer garments are of such stout texture that the most persistent mosquito cannot pierce it, and beneath this armour they have a casing of strong, coarse cotton, equally impenetrable, while we are clad in the ordinary light material that one chooses for a march in summer weather, and, except our flannel shirts, undergarments have we none. Now, only give him time and a fjeld mosquito will bore through flannel and tweed, especially where the web is strained, as over a bent knee or elbow, and the thickest stocking is a little holiday to him.

As for Richard III., he is all over as invulnerable as Achilles, excepting a portion of his very brown and not very clean face. His huge cap comes down over his eyebrows, his thick, coarse hair streams over his ears and temples on to his shoulders, his body and legs are encased in reindeer-skin armour of proof, and his hands in enormous gloves.

The horses are a distressing sight. From nose to tail, from hoof to withers, their unfortunate bodies are covered with what might be taken at a casual glance for gray blanket clothing, but reveals itself to inspection as a textile mass of seething insect life, so closely set that you could not anywhere put the point of your finger on the bare hide. And yet, quivering all over, stamping, shaking, lashing their tails, they continue to graze, perhaps conscious how much fuel is required to replace the life that is being incessantly drained from them. It is well that we have not a dog with us.

In defiance of the vicious swarms, we again endeavour to carry out our notion of camp life, light a fire, and meditate cooking breakfast and making tea; but flesh and blood are not equal to the task. As John leans over the camp-kettle his sight of it is obscured by the mosquitoes on his veil, I can at any moment kill the shape of my hand in them by slapping him on the back. We therefore abandon the idea of warm food and drink, and rousing one of the men, who, beyond unloading the horses, have no conception of making themselves useful, send him to bring back from a neighbouring drift a can full of snow, and concoct with mingled lemon and cognac a deliciously refreshing brew of weak iced punch.

Then we haul out our mosquito-nets, packed with some forethought uppermost in the saddle-bags, and lying down beneath them, gloomily munch dry biscuits and slices of cold sausage. Now, a mosquito-net is an excellent defence as long as it can be suspended over a bed and kept from touching the body, but when in contact with the latter it affords little or no protection, for the mosquito can with ease insert his proboscis through the fine meshes, and by perseverance reach the flesh of his victim.

That I have to dwell so much on this distasteful theme is wearisome to me, and must be so to the reader, but one might as well try to ignore the presence of vehicles and foot-passengers in the streets of London as that of mosquitoes on the Arctic fjeld. I have spoken with those who have had experience of the pests in all parts of the world as well as in that region, and for numbers, size, and venom they all give the palm to the demons of Finmark and Lapland. For such small creatures they exhibit an astonishing amount of character and diabolical intelligence. They will dash through smoke like a foxhound through a bullfinch, creep under veil or wristband like a ferret into a rabbit-hole, and when they can neither dash nor creep, will bide their time with the pertinacious cunning of Red Indians. We wore, as I have said, stout dogskin gloves, articles with which they could not have had much previous acquaintance, and yet they would follow each other by hundreds in single file up and down the seams, trying every stitch in the hope of detecting a flaw; every inch of the sewing was outlined by their unbroken ranks. Unluckily, our gloves were not gauntlets, and in carrying the gun there was half an inch of exposed flesh, which became fearfully bitten. By the time we reached Karasjok I counted over sixty separately distinguishable bites, and there may well have been many more, on that small area of cuticle on my right

wrist, despite my endeavours to shield it with strips
of wet linen; it was swollen to nearly the size of
my forearm. It may well be that only the good
condition of our blood, and constant exercise, inducing free perspiration, saved us from an attack
of fever.

The problem presents itself, Why are the vermin
so horribly bloodthirsty and so perfectly formed for
sucking blood? It is one of the great mysteries of
creation. On the uninhabited fjeld of Finmark
they must, as a rule, exist on vegetable diet, the
chance of blood so rarely occurs; there is no local
life except a few birds with impervious feathers.
In the summer-time the Lap drives his reindeer to
the sea. No native is fool enough to cross the fjeld
at that season unless he be driven thereto by the
rare call of duty, or tempted by the gold of a mad
Englishman, and there may be, at the outside,
half a dozen such madmen in half a century. In
winter, when the reindeer sleigh can skim merrily
over the universal waste of snow, disregarding the
boundaries of land and water, when the Tana itself
becomes a solid highway, when the priest and
merchant return for the church service, school, and
market held at Karasjok, travellers may not be so
uncommon; but whatever other peril or hardship
they undergo, they are at least free from the Gray
Terror.

In the valleys and by the rivers, that is,
in the permanently inhabited parts of Northern
Norway, the mosquito plague can at times be bad
enough, but in its hideous redundance it exists only
on the bare fjeld, a primeval and enduring curse,
inexplicably developed to its utmost in a region

seemingly the most unsuitable for its effective working : the less chance of blood, the more blood-suckers. That this should be so is a mercy, but my point is the mysteriousness of the whole thing. One thing alone is to me a greater mystery; naturalists affirm that it is *only the female mosquito* which bites! I can but say that I have never, in that case, met with the male insect. But what a terrible opening for a general libel on the fair sex does this affirmation afford to the cynic and satirist!

I used not to admire the character of Beelzebub, or Baal-ze-bub, ' the lord of flies,' regarding him as their patron and protector, but have taken a more lenient view of it since I discovered in the works of learned commentators that he obtained that title owing to his zeal and skill in destroying them, and can even in a measure understand why Ahab encouraged his worship. But I feel sure that his lordship, however eminent as an insecticide, would not care to visit the Arctic fjeld, which offers such a magnificent field for the exercise of his special function, simply because he would mistrust his power of dealing with the multitudinous scourge, and be in fear of suffering torments greater than any he could inflict.

It is, perhaps, needless to say that, although we got a certain amount of rest for our limbs at the second halt, which in bitterness of spirit we named ' Hell Gate '—what a change from the Happy Valley!—we failed in securing repose of mind and real sleep; the constant itching of our recent and the repeated infliction of fresh bites would not permit anything beyond brief uneasy dozes, and we were truly glad when the six hours of wakefulness

7—2

had passed. Before starting we exchanged our shooting-boots for the native 'komager,' of which we had each bought a pair at Alten. This flexible Lappish foot-gear, in shape like a boat, and made of reindeer-skin with the hair outside, is filled with dried senne-grass,* into which the foot has to be pressed until it is quite covered and surrounded by the soft stuffing, and rests on a thick cushion of it; the upper part is then bound round the ankle with gaudy blue and red bands. For dry walking this outlandish boot is light and comfortable, but as soon as the grass gets damp and matted it tends, as we found, to produce heat and footsoreness. The binding, however, outside the trousers, which at the time we were both wearing, effectually prevents the mosquitoes from biting one's ankles.

'From Hell Gate to Hawk Hollow. This stage was a dreary one; ridge after ridge of monotonous waste, where the clouds never moved through the sky, no wind blew, and the air around and ground beneath teemed with swarms of the flying vermin. It seemed as if we had passed the confines of natural existence, and gotten into an unfinished limbo, where evil only held sway, and instead of the happy life and vegetation of the known world, nothing thrived but venomous flies, and a leprous gray scurf of lichen and moss coating the spongy earth and dead stones.

'But towards the end of the stage, as we descended through broken ground, we discovered our party bivouacked in a most beautiful spot beside a stream. It had many years ago, for the fences were dilapidated and rotten, been the

* *Carex sylvatica.*

encampment of nomad Lapps, and now the circle which they had enclosed was overgrown with sweet green grass, and but for the all-pervading plague would have been a delightful resting-place.'

Thus my friend, regarding our march to and arrival at Hawk Hollow, and he exactly expresses my own sentiments. We are told that among the North American Indians it is the custom to name chiefs after any special incident or sight noticed at their birth, and on the same principle we named our places of bivouac. In descending the hill to the spot described above I shot a magnificent gyr-falcon, which with loud cries was wheeling overhead. Perhaps I ought not to have shot him, he was not fit for food; but what young Briton with a gun in his hand could resist the chance of bagging so splendid, and to him so novel, a bird ? I have no doubt that he and his mate were to a great extent responsible for the dearth of willow-grouse, birds that we especially desired to meet with; although during the latter part of the march we had passed through a considerable extent of low brushwood, forming excellent covert, not a single rype was to be seen.

At Hawk Hollow it was the same story over again. We tried to be jolly, made a huge fire, the old broken-down fences supplying plenty of fuel, plucked three golden plover, and got out the frying-pan and teapot, but in the end were driven from our anticipated feast by the harpies, and retreated with nets and waterproof sheets to a green patch some distance from the fire, its warmth in the cool of the night seeming to attract the mosquitoes. Before retiring, however, I put a cake of preserved vegetables and a couple of inches of portable soup into a big can of water, and left it to simmer on the embers until morning.

A sad incident at this place was the breakdown of the poor boy, who, after many moans, burst into a fit of hysterical sobbing. He must have suffered horribly, and, to make matters worse, had that day fallen down in crossing a river, and got soaked to the skin. But his clothes were now quite dry again, and after a while he recovered sufficiently to eat his supper and coil up among the others. Hear again the words of John :

' No sleep came to me. I lay for hours listening to the hissing of the baffled foes, and watching them crawling in troops over the net, darting their poisonous fangs through every mesh until they found a prominent part. As one had to support the net with knees and elbows, these formed good marks for the enemy, and were riddled with wounds. I may have dreamt, but I never slept. All the vermin inside I killed, and watched those outside with a painful fascination, until their hump-backed bodies and long limbs, their gray-ringed trunks and malignant faces, seemed to expand into those of afreets and monstrous demons ; and I fancied what an Inferno Dante might have imagined had he crossed from Bosckop to Karasjok before writing his poem. Take Ugolino from his bed of flame and cage him in the pit beneath a grating, with grinning fiends, in the shape of magnified mosquitoes, driving poisoned lances at him through the bars ; let him be conscious that hundreds find their way in, and that when he rises he must be pursued by them for many weary leagues across an infernal waste, with no escape, no shelter, no hope, and then he might have a notion of what we suffered—and four days would expiate his crimes.

' About two in the morning, the hostile troops being numbed with cold, if not less numerous, Harry called out to me: "I vote we get up and try to make some breakfast, for I can't sleep for these devils!" So up we got, replenished the fire, and, getting almost reckless as we warmed to the work, proceeded with our cooking in spite of them. My friend soon had the birds trussed with some neat skewers which I whittled for him, and consigned to the frying-pan, and in a short time such a breakfast was served up as a chef might be proud of. The birds, done to a turn, were pictures, and the vegetables as fresh and good as if just gathered; they had swelled out so as to be enough for half a dozen, and we were able to give a cup of soup each to the men. And then the tea, although there was no milk, never was anything so refreshing; it revived our spirits, and enabled us to face the foe again.'

I remember that when, many years ago, I was returning in a steamer down the coast of Norway there came on board an angler who had been enjoying extraordinary sport on one of the northern rivers, so extraordinary that he was himself struck by the notion that no one could possibly believe his tale of how many fish he had taken, and of what an astounding average in weight. He therefore had actually gone to the length of inducing the local bailiff, in whose house he had quarters, to attest in writing the absolute truth of his fishing register. The exhibition of this corroborative evidence was a poor compliment to himself, and not altogether

successful in its object. One humorist at least on
board gravely accepted it with much regret, as
proving what he had not previously suspected, the
corruptibility of Norwegian officials.

Now, I find myself troubled with doubts similar
to those of the aforesaid angler, namely, whether
readers will credit my account of the fjeld mosquitoes as given in this and the following chapter.
And I shall therefore also pay myself the poor
compliment of adducing, at intervals, evidence in
confirmation of it, and also begin by that of a
Norwegian official; but this, be it noticed, will be
purely independent testimony.

It happened that in the very same summer
when we voluntarily crossed the fjeld to Tana,
Herr J. B. Barth was obliged to do the same in the
discharge of his professional duties as inspector of
forests, his object being to supply the Government
with a report of the condition of the pine-woods all
over Finmark. Not that there are any woods on
the fjeld, but it was his shortest way of getting to
work, and he had as companions the boundary
commissioners for the 'moss tracts' between
Karasjok and Kautokeino. What a terrible vocation! far more dreadful than the trade of the
samphire gatherer.

In descending the Tana his boat passed one
of our encampments, but he did not accept our
invitation to land. Herr Barth was the author
of several pleasant volumes containing sketches of
sport, travel, and natural history, and known for
long as the crack shot of Norway; but, strange to
say, he never touched a rod, and in the published
account of his journey through Finmark complains

that he could get little to eat, recording his great
satisfaction over a present of cold boiled salmon,
at a time, too, when he was daily travelling on waters
teeming with fish. By trailing a fly or spinning-
bait he might have supplied himself with any
amount of food.

But I have to do with his remarks about the fjeld
mosquitoes, and will quote the following passage :

' The most remarkable, or, to speak more correctly,
the one remarkable thing in our journey across the
fjeld was the enormous mass of mosquitoes which,
as the weather was all the time clear, still, and very
warm, incessantly plagued both men and horses.
No sooner had our train occupied one of the hollows
for a bivouac than the air round about the encampment was so filled with them that they enveloped
the whole place like a thick veil, which even obscured
the brightness of the sun. I tried if the report was
true that a man could with a stick write letters
of the alphabet in the swarm of insects, and found
the truth of it so far confirmed that the letters were
actually visible when I had finished them, but the
swarm then immediately closed again over them.'

About his sufferings in pursuit both of duty and
sport Herr Barth is eloquent. There is, indeed,
such an almost ludicrous resemblance between his
published experience and ours as recorded in our
journals at the time that both narratives might have
been written by one hand. He subsequently proposed that the Government should allow the forest
inspectors of Finmark who followed in his steps
much higher pay than usual as compensation for
the tortures they had to undergo.

CHAPTER VI

TO THE HAVEN OF REST

WHEN we left Hawk Hollow the rising sun was obscured by a thick mist driven before a light breeze, and for the first two hours we travelled unmolested. As the sky cleared, our tormentors again descended on us in their myriads, but, on the whole, we accomplished the march in good spirits. Its monotony was pleasantly varied by two or three sporting incidents. Not long after starting John was able by ingenious manœuvring to kill two out of a brood of five large ducks, the tenants of a rushy tarn lying in the basin of a low hill. They fell in the water, and he had to wait nearly half an hour until the breeze drifted them to the bank, whilst I went on to keep the horses in view. Having arranged a code of whistle signals with five variations, we were able to converse even at a distance in a thick mist. The ducks turned out to be young scoters; at the moment we did not recognise the species.*

Mixed with the golden plover, which were still fairly numerous, were several well-grown families of dotterel,† a lovely little bird in whose small bosom Nature has thoughtfully implanted a desire to become as fat as possible, and fit for the table of

* *Oidemia nigra.*   † *Charadrius marinellus.*

Lucullus. I had never seen this bird but once before, on the higher slopes of Skiddaw, and on that occasion I achieved a memorable success as a youthful oologist. In those days a British example of the egg was held to be a great rarity, and to possess it was one of my boyish ambitions. The dealer in the town of Keswick had three eggs, all taken in Cumberland, which he valued at a sovereign apiece, and not a penny would he abate of this, to a boy with limited pocket-money, prohibitory price. How often was I permitted, being a fair customer according to my ability, to gloat over the coveted treasure in the little shop, until its image was graven on my brain, and I should have recognised the egg among ten thousand.

Now, it happened that one lovely day in May, 'for ever marked with white,' I ascended Skiddaw on foot with two ladies of my family on pony-back and a guide. In descending we turned off for a few hundred yards from the main track to look at a particular view, when suddenly, to the surprise and consternation of the party, I uttered a kind of shriek, and hurled myself almost under the feet of one of the patient, docile ponies, who in no way resented my unexpected collision with his fore-leg. He had, before my very eyes, set the hoof of that leg on one of two eggs which lay close together in a very slight depression of the moss; it was unluckily squashed, but its companion remained intact, and I was able to save from the threatening hind-leg the object of my great desire, a genuine dotterel's egg. Shortly afterwards we saw the birds running along the hillside. 'Dotterels, sure enough,' said the guide, and my happiness was complete. I suppose that no boy ever carried anything in the world so carefully as I did that egg from the mountain to the shop, where I exhibited it to the friendly proprietor, and received his really cordial congratulations. He blew it for me artistically, and packed it gratis in a neat box with wool. And now, ten years later, I was destined to meet the interesting little birds again on the Arctic fjeld, and to regard them chiefly as prizes whereon to exercise my culinary skill, being at least familiar with their reputation as delicacies.

From an ambush in which he got badly bitten, John, by great exercise of patience, at last succeeded in shooting three ducks out of a flock which was cruising about in a bay of one of the larger lakes, but, the breeze failing, could not spare the time to wait until they drifted ashore, and was reluctantly compelled to leave them. To strip and swim in after them, which under ordinary circumstances would have been pleasant enough, was not to be thought of in the face of the Gray Terror. As it was, he was left a long way behind me, and I was far in the rear of the caravan. But for our system of signals he might well have lost his way, for our course was now changing, and we were beginning to incline round the shoulder of the great mountain, Vuoras Duodder, of which we had never lost sight. During this stage we crossed a considerable river, the Vuorasjok, which rises amidst its snows. In default of a bathe we had a good roll in a deep snow-drift, which was decidedly refreshing, and gave us the satisfaction of annihilating our insectile overcoats. As regards the name of the mountain, I may observe that Duoddar in Lappish means ' a high, bare fjeld,' and Vuoras, with an accent on the *s*, ' a hooded or gray crow ' (*Corvus cornix*) ; without it, ' an old man ' ; and as I cannot say whether in this case there was an accent or not, readers may take their choice between Gray Crow or Old Man Mountain. In Alten there is a point of land called ' Vuoras Njarga ' ; in Norsk Kraakenæs—' Gray Crow Point.'

Close to the halting-place I at last shot a willow-grouse, the first we had ever seen. It was an old cock, the hen and brood being doubtless somewhere among the brushwood ; but to search for them without a dog was next to useless, and the young were probably still cheepers, scarcely able to fly. The scene of our bivouac was in consequence called ' Ryper Bank.'

Here, as it was a mid-day halt, we did not trouble to light a fire, and were content with cold lunch and grog, but exhibited more cunning in defending ourselves from our persecutors by forming small tents out of sundry articles of baggage and the mosquito-nets, so that the latter did not touch the body anywhere. Inside these low shelters we were fairly safe, could eat and smoke in comparative peace, and even secure a few intervals of unconsciousness. Sound refreshing sleep was still out of the question ; the maddening irritation of our bites when at rest and the incessant din close in our ears of insect life rendered it impossible.

Wearied as we were with much rough walking, combined with little or no sleep and chronic torment, the magnificently wild scenery at the commencement of the next stage made us forget for awhile our troubles. On the left of our march lay the placid waters of a vast lake, above which rose the snowy summit and rugged sides of Vuoras Duodder; on the left and in front the rolling plateau of the fjeld, studded with a profusion of waters: from one rise I counted thirty-seven of all sizes. The sun shone brightly, but a strong, delicious breeze rid us of the vampire host, which rejoices in still heat, and the soft gray shadows of the wandering clouds swept rapidly across the face of the enormous landscape. We were able to raise our veils and breathe the glorious air without fear. Ah! if this state of things would only last.

There were plenty of ducks in sight, but we could not spare time to go after them, and were satisfied with picking up a few plover and dotterel. In the distance we saw four reindeer, one of them snow-white, tame in all probability; but if so, whence they came, whither they were going, and why they were wandering about in these demon-haunted solitudes at a time when their companions had gone to the seaside, it was impossible to conjecture. Our guide, as far as we understood him, could throw no light upon the subject.

On rounding, late in the afternoon, the spurs of Vuoras Duodder we saw before and rather below us an immense tract of marshy land, intersected by streams, and spreading for miles in every direction. We felt then that our respite from torment was to be but brief, and so it proved. As we entered this region of morass the wind fell, there was not a breath of air, and a miasmatic exhalation seemed to boil up from the earth on every side; the walking became desperately bad, the soil being alternately rough and rotten, and our progress slow on account of the horses. This was at last

From Sketch
by Author.

THE ARCTIC FJELD.

the very stronghold, citadel, and head centre of the Gray Terror. Woe to those who had dared to invade it !

After shouldering our way for a couple of hours longer through the opposing legions of the foe, and traversing several more miles of broken ground and marshy tundra, a halt was effected beside a sluggish stream of considerable size. The place was well enough in its way—a tolerably dry, grassy slope, bordered by bog myrtle and the ubiquitous shrubs, dwarf birch and willow ; the river, which had cut its way down to the bed-rock, was clear, and anywhere else we should have hailed it as a rather attractive spot. But John had reason in describing it as a ' ghastly river of groans,' and in declaring that he would as soon have passed a night on the banks of Phlegethon.

In the last few pages I have endeavoured, with the assistance of my friend—for a single brain reels under the effort—to picture the dreadful condition of things since we left the Happy Valley, and if after what I have written I simply state that it was now a great deal worse, that statement ought to be sufficient for any reader with the least imagination. I begin to wish that I had never undertaken ' *infandum renovare dolorem.*'

But if suddenly despondent, we had also become savagely determined to have our own way. We lighted a fire, cooked a hot meal, drank tea—it is true that we drank it as did the knights of Branksome the red wine, ' through the helmet barred,' that is, through our veils ; the food we used to insert by mouthfuls under them—built up our dens, and, clad from head to foot in suits of water-

proof, crept inside. As I reclined with a haversack
for my pillow, I saw through the meshes of the net
the swarm of insects hovering about me like a dark
cloud, and resolved, experimentally, to lie quite
still and let the aerial Gray Terror descend upon me.
Without describing my sensations, as John has done,
I merely place on record the fact that in a quarter
of an hour the light of the sky was completely shut
out, the entire net, which was about eighteen inches
from my face, being overlaid by an unbroken film
of darkest gray.

The sound of the multitude was peculiar and
characteristic; it was neither hum, nor buzz, nor
pipe. I might liken it to the notes of a gigantic
Æolian harp mingled with a horrible, angry sibilation,
but this comparison does not convey a true idea of
its practical horror, of its plaintive yet exultant
bloodthirstiness, no words, indeed, can. If one can
conceive that the souls of monsters of cruelty, like
Tiberius and Torquemada, were after death transformed into swarms of mosquitoes and consigned
to the limbo of the fjeld, their constant wail, ' Give
us blood, give us blood!' blended with their voci-
ferous glee on finding it, and their savage murmurs
when balked of it, might together represent the
sound that I heard in my fortress that night. It
was so loud that when I addressed John, who was
lying a few feet from me, his answer in an ordinary
voice was unintelligible.

By 3 a.m. we had quitted the accursed river,
to which we gave the name of ' Acheron.' In the
words of John, ' We packed in haste and pain, so
completely dismayed that neither spoke of breakfast. Silently and grimly, with clenched teeth and

muffled heads, we got the baggage together, and departed from the valley of the substance of death.'

But throughout our expedition some guardian spirit—perhaps akin to the 'sweet little cherub that sits up aloft to look out for the life of poor Jack'—always marked the hour when our trials had been sufficiently severe to lower the overweening pride and confidence in ourselves with which we started, and brought relief that enabled us to pluck up courage again. Soon after leaving Acheron we began to ascend a hill, and on its crest met with a breeze strong and cool enough to completely rout our pursuers. The ground now becoming very rocky and dangerous for the horses by reason of deep brushwood-hidden chasms, the Finn had great difficulty in finding a practicable route, and was at last obliged to turn back and make a long détour round a lake. This gave us an opportunity of resting for half an hour. Water being handy, and our tormentors absent, we had a good wash, and then, lighting a fire, absolutely enjoyed a quiet pipe; the blaze was also agreeable, for both water and air were very cold.

The march was resumed over a succession of rocky hills, with a good deal of low covert here and there. John in his turn killed his first rype, also an old cock, and we bagged a few more plover. Several bunches of birds were now suspended from the baggage, and we felt that, happen what might, we should reach Tana with a plentiful supply of fresh food. As the sun rose the breeze freshened to a wind ; we were able to raise our veils, and by the time we reached 'Windgap,' our next halt, were in good trim for a hearty meal of biscuits and

sardines, followed by two hours of sound sleep under
a sunny, breeze-swept rock.

Grateful for our nap, which brought up the amount
of real sleep obtained during the last three days and
nights to about eight hours, we did not delay longer,
as the Finn held out hopes of our being able to
reach Karasjok that very day, and the prospect
of escaping another night on the fjeld, and finding
shelter under a roof of any kind, spurred us to fresh
exertions. After resuming our shooting-boots in
place of the sodden komager, we now left the hills
and descended to a lower expanse of prairie-like
land, where the going was tolerably firm and good,
and, the breeze holding out, we were not much
worried by mosquitos.

On we trudged doggedly, at times half asleep,
until mile after mile of the flat was left behind
us, though it was long before Vuoras Duodder
seemed to recede and the low ridge in front to grow
nearer. But at last we surmounted the latter, and
saw below us a wide valley, with a string of lakes,
bordered on the far side by actual trees; examined
through my glass, they proved to be full-grown
birches. ' Oh, joy !' exclaimed as much of the
sanguine spirit as still survived within us: 'the fjeld
and its horrors are done with ; there is the blessed
woodland !' Before we left that wood, reached
after a rather difficult descent, ' blessed ' was not
the epithet we applied to it. It was very thick, with
in some places a dense clinging undergrowth, in
others a treacherous substratum of moss-covered
stones, abounding in ankle-traps, and it was apparently pathless. The cleverness of the guide was
sorely tested in finding a passage through this

The Realm of the Grey Terror.

birchen wilderness, and the tired beasts with difficulty kept their footing under the repeated con-
cussions of their loads with the stems and branches.

Now, too, in the midst of our perplexity, the
malignant might of the Gray Terror reasserted itself;
the lowland hordes of that interminable realm rose
to attack the intruders on their primeval domain.
Under happier circumstances how one would have
admired the scenery of that forest region! In its
very depth we skirted the terminal bay of a magnificent lake, apparently about the size of Winder-
mere, stretching away for miles into its sylvan
recesses. But we had no heart to admire; our
sole thought was how to extricate ourselves from
our present surroundings. The sagacity, or knowledge, or good fortune of David did at last discover
a kind of path leading out of the wood to the banks
of a river which had to be crossed; but where we
struck it ford there was none: it was deep and
impassable.

And now occurred a lamentable catastrophe.
Whilst David, who was clearly astray, meandered
about like the river itself, searching for a ford
over it, the horse that carried our tent and beds
suddenly became entrapped in boggy ground and
fell, scattering his load right and left over the
quagmire. When the luckless beast had regained
his legs it was no easy job in such a spot to replace
the baggage. Nor was there any apparent way of
escaping from the dismal swamp; the ground
seemed to have broken up on every side; our
position was the climax of misfortune. The news
of our mishap, of course, spread among the local
demons, and they assembled in millions for their

feast of blood. The wretched horses were almost driven mad, the usually impassive Norsemen and the Finn railed at each other, and, as far as we could understand, at all creation, with violent language and gesticulations; the miserable boy, in his agony, again sobbed convulsively. We, unable to help in any way, sat down on a fallen tree and laughed the bitter laugh of despair; we could lief have wept also had we not felt so savage. The children of Israel by the waters of Babylon were cheerful compared to us.

In this terrible crisis of our fortunes our good angel again sent relief. Suddenly there appeared out of the steaming birch covert on the opposite bank of the river two weird figures, who came leaping down the rocks, and stood at gaze before us. From their appearance and the manner of it they might have been forest elves, but proved to be young Finsk girls belonging to the tribe that was encamped for fishing purposes on the neighbouring lakes; they had been attracted by the sound of our voices.

If in some degree picturesque, their garb was rough and uncouth, their head-dresses, if quaint, weather-beaten, and their locks tangled; but they were, as John remarked, as assuredly kind fairies come to the aid of virtuous mortals in distress as if they had presented themselves in tights and short muslin skirts, with spangles, wreaths, and wands complete. By their guidance David regained the right path, reached the ford, and enabled us to cross, when we soon found ourselves on the bank of another lake. Some conversation ensued, and then the good fairies jumped into a canoe and paddled off, evidently bent on a beneficent errand, the object of which we

GOOD FAIRIES TO THE RESCUE.

could not ascertain; but as the men immediately
unpacked and settled down to a meal, I suspect that
it was connected with their wants, perhaps of milk,
fish, or bread.

But John and I were desperate, and announced
our intention of going on at any cost, and as David
agreed to guide us, we slung our haversacks and
marched off, leaving the men and horses to follow
at their leisure. It now appeared that one Norsk
mile (seven English miles) of woodland still intervened between us and Karasjok, and it took us nearly
three hours to accomplish the distance. I suspect
that David overlooked the 'bitte,' or bittock, which
exists in Norway as much as in Scotland. But we
were undoubtedly very weary, and very sulky, not
knowing what evils lay before us, and meanwhile
the swarming bloodsuckers gave us no peace.

Only once did we forget them — when by the
side of the path up sprang a covey of well-grown
ryper, and settled again at no great distance. Bred
in the sheltered lowland woods, they were probably
much more forward than their brethren of the
fjeld. Here was a chance of relieving our feelings
and shooting for the pot. In five minutes we had
a couple of brace of them down and pocketed, and,
not caring to pursue the rest, continued our march.
As we descended the last slope the birch-wood
thinned out and the pines began to appear, until at
length, turning the corner of a sandy bank, along
which the path ran, we came in sight of the longed-
for village.

The scene was not unlike what we had imagined
it would be. A broad, shallow river, gliding between
sandy shoals, beautiful in its wooded banks and

glassy reflections—but these we hardly noticed at the time—a small cluster of wooden houses and out-buildings on a patch of level sward, a score of cattle grazing in a misty hollow, there was Karasjok. The Finn led the way to the largest of the houses, from which presently emerged four or five uncouth beings with tangled locks and sleepy eyes, to greet him after their fashion. They then held an animated conversation, of which we, judging by the looks of curiosity directed at us, were the chief subject, until we impatiently broke in upon it by requesting to be shown some place of shelter where we could lie down. One of the women pointed to a log-hut about eight feet square elevated on timber supports, and entered by a trap-door. It was used as a store-house for reindeer-skins, which being cleared out, our lodging was ready for us.

Miserable as it was, we crept in, glad of the chance of baffling our relentless persecutors and of resting our weary limbs. Then we asked for something to eat and drink, and an old woman brought us some huge cakes of rye-bread and two pails of milk, which we eagerly drained to the last drop. Somewhat refreshed, we stretched ourselves on the layer of birch twigs which covered the floor of the hut and closed our eyes, but not for long. Through every chink in the logs, above, below, like the rats which devoured Bishop Hatto, the mosquitoes swarmed in. Wet with per-spiration after our hard walk, we were chilled to the bone by the cold morning draughts which pene-trated through the same interstices, while burning outwardly from innumerable bites.

At this point let John continue the narrative :

' " Well, I shall have a pipe, at any rate."

' "Pshaw! what's the use of smoking? What on earth shall we do, John? We are in for it. I wish to goodness we had never heard of Tana!"'

'Now, for two whole days my friend had never sung a song, which in itself betokened an extra-ordinary state of things, and here he was refusing his tobacco! Surely the end had come! We lay on our bed of dry leaves, worried by bitter reflections as well as by mosquitoes. We were in the heart of Finmark, unable to speak a word of the language, and only about fifty of Norsk, which could be the sole medium of interpretation. Behind us the wilderness formed a barrier that we dared not pass again. To go on was to plunge into new troubles, for we now fully believed that there was not an inch of air or earth between Karasjok and the North Cape free from the poisonous pests.

'It was then, as we lay in that dismal torpor, that Harry, who was shivering with cold, first summoned moral courage [How delicately he puts it!—H. P.] to mention the words " go back." At first I was in-clined to agree to this, but the difficulties of the fjeld route, the shame of failure, and the hope of meet-ing Hambro and his party down the river, decided us against a retreat, and in the midst of our per-plexity we fell asleep.'

I trust that I repented with due shame of ever having even suggested so inglorious an ending to our expedition. In Mr. Cutcliffe Hyne's admirable book, ' Through Arctic Lapland '—he and his friend underwent, forty years later, much the same ordeal as ours—I find a passage so appropriate to the situation that I cannot help quoting it:

' We passed that night in a condition bordering

on frenzy, and let not those who merely know the mosquito in Africa, India, and the Americas, judge us too harshly when I say that at times we wished most heartily that we had never set foot in so detestable a country. Cold we could have endured, privation we were prepared for, but this horrible stew of flies ground upon the nerves till we were scarcely responsible for our actions.'

And this passage proves clearly that the horrors of the Arctic fjeld remain unabated to this day.

We were roused from our sleep by the voice of David at the trap-door announcing that the horses had arrived, and when we had crept sulkily out of our den and shaken ourselves like bears after hibernation, he astonished us by explaining that this was not the real Karasjok village, but Assebakte*—a name we had noticed on our map—that Karasjok proper, where the merchant lived in winter and the fair was held, was two Norsk miles down the river, and that, although the merchant was not in residence, his house would be at our disposal.

I conclude that our very slight knowledge of Norsk, which David spoke after his fashion, prevented our understanding all this before, for I cannot conceive him meditating an agreeable surprise or capable of a practical joke, and it is to me still a matter of wonder how we ever discovered the meaning of his words, unless it be that misfortune renders the intellect preternaturally acute.

He now invited us into the largest house, which we had called at on our arrival, and we presently found ourselves in a clean room some twenty-five feet square, with a stone chimney and fireplace in one

* It appears to mean 'the abode on the rock.'

corner, the blaze from which revealed to us the recumbent forms of thirteen people of both sexes and all ages laid side by side in beds, or rather pens, arranged on the floor along the walls, and covered with reindeer-skins. Besides these, there were astir to receive us an old grandmother and two young women, one nice-looking, with a beautiful, though rather dirty, blue-eyed child in arms, of which she appeared excessively proud. The grandmother informed us several times—she had the words quite pat—that it was ' Inglees babbi.' What land is beyond the sphere of British influence ?

Here also we found our men making coffee, and had a cup of the warm, fragrant beverage ourselves. Free from mosquitoes, and, but for the tingling of their bites, almost comfortable, we sat by the fire for two hours, conversing, as it were, with the natives, John taking much pains to give them a lesson in English, and to receive one in their language. They seemed very quick at catching and pronouncing words. Then our guide, who had left the room, returned with four of his compatriots, and it was then and there arranged that for half a specie dollar a day each—two shillings and threepence—two of them would remain with us until we reached the mouth of the Tana, David agreeing to go with us himself as far as Karasjok proper, and undertaking to find there two more boatmen.

We next settled accounts satisfactorily with the Norsemen; poor fellows ! they had to return over that horrible fjeld; pale and wretched as he looked, the boy survived the repetition of its horrors, for I saw him afterwards at Bosckop. And then we took leave of our hosts, giving them in a fit of generosity

four marks—three and fourpence—for their hospitality. It was probably three times as much as they
expected, but how grateful were we for those pails of
milk and the shelter of that room! and it cannot be
said that there was any market to spoil. John then
went to superintend the packing of the boats, whilst
I, under much persecution by mosquitoes, added our
names to the few carved on the logs outside :

'Thomas, Dodd, Campbell, Rowley, May, Skene.

The first English Expedition to the Tana, 1855.'

Oh, the luxury of gliding down the cool, misty
river, freed from protecting veils, damp handker-
chiefs, and gloves, and with pipes emitting their
blue wreaths on the still morning air! We settled
comfortably into the canoe, a man paddling at each
end, and we lying face to face propped up by the
softer baggage. The Karasjok is a broad stream,
with high wooded banks sloping to sandy beaches ;
indeed, its bed is nearly pure sand, and in places very
shallow. The current being strong, we shot round
the frequent bends and down the long reaches quietly
as the water itself, without any exertion on the part
of our boatmen. The baggage canoe waited for us
when well off, and we went side by side, the men
chattering a language that seemed to be more than
half vowels, soft and sonorous.

John and I were enjoying the reaction from our
worries too intensely to indulge in much conversation, and became very drowsy, as was natural after
our almost sleepless travel of the last four days.
How long we slept in the canoe I cannot say, but
it seemed as if we had only just dropped off when
we were roused by the grating of its keel on the

beach at the new Karasjok, or Karasjok Marked,* as it is properly called.

The merchant's steward had now to be sought, and presently appeared, an elderly Finn, beaming with smiles and gorgeous in attire. He had put on his best clothes for the occasion, blue tunic and cap, with facings of bright yellow, and led the way to a house of quite respectable size, with a brilliantly green door: vivid colour seemed to be popular in Karasjok. This he unlocked, and with significant bows and gestures placed at our disposal the winter residence of his absent master, Merchant Fandrum.

Of our discoveries in that haven of refuge I shall speak later. When we had got all the baggage stowed away inside it, and ejected with resolute courtesy the inquisitive barbarians, male and female, who swarmed in after us, we managed by David's intelligent aid to make arrangements for fresh boats, and secure the, at first reluctant, services of two more boatmen, who in the end consented to accompany us to the sea, one of them a schoolmaster who spoke Norsk, and proved himself a most valuable ally.

And then we paid and dismissed our trusty guide, who declared that he was in a great hurry to get back with the horses to Alten. As John remarks, ' he seemed sorry to leave us, companions in hardship, and shook hands again and again with his "kjœre venner."† Two hours afterwards he returned. This time he was quite overcome by his emotions ; indeed, he could hardly walk straight. The thoughts of parting and the proceeds of his

* Norsk for market or fair.
† Dear friends.

" drink-money " had thoroughly melted that genial heart. He wept as he shook hands once more.'

By his departure was severed the last link that connected us with the world on the other side of the fjeld. Left to ourselves, we had first of all to perform a stern duty which was also a sweet revenge, and resumed our komager as the most suitable foot-gear during its performance, the British boot being too clumsy for the foot of the swift and active avenger. We meant business. A host of mosquitoes had somehow found their way into the house, accompanied by a strong contingent of their almost equally vicious lowland allies, the sand-flies. The majority, conscious, let us hope, of impending doom, were now trying madly to escape through the glass of the windows, but a large number were still sailing and piping about the apartment. Closing the doors, and as an extra precaution hanging the mosquito-nets over them, that none might escape, we armed ourselves with damp towels, and fell upon the myriads, even as the Goths in ' Hypatia ' fell upon the trapped ' wild beasts of Alexandria,' and there ensued ' a murder grim and great.'

In an hour there was not the faintest hum audible, nor the glint of a wing visible in any corner of the house. It was hard work, but the itching of our many bites under the exertion stimulated us into the utmost efforts of vengeance, until, wearied by, but not satiated with, slaughter, we laid down our blood-stained weapons. In that house, for a time at least, the Gray Terror had ceased to be.

Then, while John unpacked and arranged on the two beds our blankets and pillows, I prepared, in a kitchen well provided with all necessary apparatus a savoury meal, which we washed down with a bottle of excellent claret. We might have had champagne, port, or sherry, had we preferred them! The sweetest of all pipes followed; but, always of a practical turn, we resolved to utilize the hour of repose by plucking some of our birds, an empty keg in the kitchen serving well as a receptacle for the feathers.

In the midst of our industry the irresistible hand of the sleep-god was suddenly laid upon us. John was the first to succumb entirely to the beneficent touch, and, sitting in his chair, fell into so deep a slumber with a half-plucked plover in his hand that it was a difficult matter to rouse and persuade him to move as far as a bed. The komagers were easily got rid of, but that was all; clothed as he was, he threw himself down, and in ten seconds was as unwakeable as if dead.

I finished plucking my rype as Hood's poor sempstress sewed on her buttons, ' in a dream,' and, reeling with somnolence, retained just sufficient reason to tear off my garments before plunging in among the blankets. It was 1 o'clock p.m. on Saturday when I lost consciousness; I regained it at 3 a.m. on Sunday, having slept uninterruptedly for fourteen hours by Fandrum's clock, and John did not wake until two hours later.

CHAPTER VII

At this point I feel obliged to make a few remarks on a rather bewildering subject. I have spoken of our guide, David, of the girls who came to our rescue in the dismal swamp and their tribe, and of the inhabitants of Karasjok as Finns. Now, the river Tana, to which we were bound, divides Norwegian Finmark from Russian Finland, and the population of the latter country are the Finns proper. But the Norwegians almost invariably call the aboriginal inhabitants of Finmark and of the North of Norway generally Finns also, which naturally causes a good deal of confusion. Professor J. A. Friis, of Christiania University, of whom I shall make further mention, has published a series of ethnographical maps of all the ' Præste-gjæld,' or parishes in Finmark, including a chart of the river Tana, and shows clearly that, although there is in that huge, sparsely-inhabited province a considerable admixture of the Russian Finnish element, the large majority of its population is of the Lappish race. We are accustomed to regard the Lapps as a purely nomad people, whose occupation is tending the herds of reindeer by which they support existence ; but there are a great number of them settled

126

on the fjords, lakes, and rivers of Northern Norway
who have no ostensible connection with the deer,
although they may in many cases have a possibly
vested interest in them, for it is probable that some
members of every tribe are genuine fjeld-Lapps and
herdsmen.

The characteristics of the pure fjeld-Lapp are unmistakable. Of very short stature, with, as a rule,
very dark hair, eyes, and complexion, and a Mon-
golian cast of countenance, he is the most complete
contrast to the tall, stalwart, often blue-eyed and
fair-haired Finn ; and yet we are told by ethnolo-
gists that both peoples belong to the great Ural-
Altaic family, which is said to comprise forty millions,
and to ' stretch through Central and Northern Asia
into Europe, overlapping the European border in
Turkey, and reaching across it in Russia and Scandinavia to the very shore of the Atlantic.' We are
also told that Finns, Esthonians, and Lapps may
probably ' be bracketed together as Ugrians or
Uralians.' I feel sure that in these last few lines I
have piled up the agony to such an extent that
the reader will metaphorically put his fingers in
his ears, and implore me to stop, which is exactly
what I wish to do, but am impelled to go on a
little longer. I will, however, try to avoid being
learned.

Certain districts in Northern Norway, such as the
valleys of the Alten River and of the Lax River in
Porsanger Fjord, are occupied by tribes of pure
Finns, and these the Norwegians distinguish by the
name of Kvæns, or, as we say, Quains, thus separat-
ing them from the so-called Finns of Finmark.
There are, perhaps, in Norway about, in round

numbers, 20,000 Lapps and 9,000 Quains. The latter, of course, came out of Finland, and have kept up the purity of their race by marrying amongst their own people. In appearance they are frequently just what we can imagine the old vikings to have been. But a number of their brethren have mingled and intermarried with the river, lake, and sea Lapps, thus in course of time producing half-breeds, in whom either of the two types may be dominant, or both indistinguishably blended into the commonplace.

Then as regards the language. When we began, as will be seen later, to pick up words from our boatmen, one of whom was a schoolmaster at Karasjok, and to form the same into a vocabulary, we were, in our ignorance, under the impression that we were learning Finsk or Finnic, whereas it proved afterwards to be pure Lappish. As we wrote down the words phonetically, many of them were not easy, some impossible, to find in Professor Friis's lexicon of the Lapp language, but we were later able to identify enough of them to prove to which tongue they belonged, such as 'luossa' (salmon), 'gumpe' (wolf), 'muorra' (wood), 'dolla' (fire), 'chaccé' (water), 'butes' (clean), 'olmai' (man), and many more. According to the Professor, the languages are cognate, but entirely different. In his maps he takes immense pains to distinguish by symbols those families of Lapps and Finns over the whole of Finmark who cannot speak a word of each other's language, those in which at least one member can speak Finnic or Lappish, as the case may be, and those who can speak Norsk as well. The labour of compilation must have been enormous, and he specifies also with the minutest care the mixed tribal elements in each village or settlement.

I have now, I think, ventured sufficiently far into this ethnological labyrinth, and shall be glad to retreat before I find myself inextricably involved in its mazes. I shall continue to call the people with whom we came in contact and our following on the Tana Finns, after the Norwegian fashion, without scrutinizing their nationality. They would probably have described themselves as Lapps; I believe them to have been all more or less hybrids. At this distance of time my memory cannot recall any unmistakable specimens of the pure Lappish type at Karasjok, and as far as I remember only one of our boatmen, who will be introduced to the reader as 'Little Savage,' bore strong traces of that type. Of one thing only am I pretty certain, that they spoke Lappish.

And so I sneak out of my difficulty, which is no inconsiderable one. That a river should divide two regions, both having names beginning with 'Fin,' whereof the inhabitants, although of different nationalities, are in common parlance indiscriminately called 'Finns,' is in itself bad enough; and to make confusion worse, they are all Laplanders, for Lapland so called runs right across the extreme North of Europe, including a part of Finland, there being Russian, Swedish, and Norwegian Lapps, with several aliases and four distinct Lappish dialects. How many Finnic there may be I cannot conjecture. Finland itself was Swedish for nearly six hundred years, and, as is well known, has belonged to Russia only since 1809, when it was ceded to that empire by the treaty of Frederikshamm.

The Finns, who are said, whether truly or not I cannot offer an opinion, to have originally driven the Lapps out of Finland, which, one would say, must have been an easy job for them, were in remote ages a powerful independent people, but were conquered by the Swedes in the twelfth century. They have magnificent mythological traditions, collected by the labours of Dr. Elias Lönnot into a celebrated epic, the ' Kalevala,' which Professor Max Müller declares to be the equal of Homer's ' Iliad ' in length, completeness, and beauty, and one of the five great epics of the world. For the benefit of the curious, who may not have met with Mr. F. Vincent's book of 1881, ' Norsk, Lapp, and Finn,' I give a specimen of the original poem, taken from that work. I hope it will not make readers gasp. It will be noticed that the run of the metre is that of the American poet Longfellow's ' Hiawatha,' which is, indeed, a splendid imitation of the ' Kalevala ':

> ' Vaka vanha Wainaimoinen ;
> Sen Varsin valehtelitki,
> Ei sinna silloin nahty,
> Kan on merta kynnetihin,
> Meren kolkot kuokittihin,
> Kala-harat kaivettihin,
> Kuuhutta kuletetaissa
> Aurinkoa autellaissa,
> Otavoa ojennettaissa
> Taivod tahitettaissa,
> Mjekkojasi, mieliasi,
> Tauriasi, tuumiasi,
> Waan kuitenki, kaikitenki,
> Lahe en miekan mittelohon
> Sinum kanssasi katala,
> Kerallasi kehno rankka.'

Fandrum's winter residence at Karasjok was not an abode of luxury. It could not, according to English ideas, be considered even comfortable. There were no carpets; what furniture it contained— and the supply was but scanty—was of the most strictly simple and utilitarian description. It was not clean: the dust lay thick about it; for he of gorgeous attire who placed it at our disposal had evidently not thought himself bound to perform any menial services beyond winding up the clock. It is possible, I allow, that the vivid green of the door may have been his handiwork, for the paint was fresh and shining; his real line may have been decorative art.

The ground-floor accommodation was limited to a small parlour, a double-bedded room, and a kitchen; overhead were two attics. But no fabled hero of Arabian romance, when placed by the good offices of friendly Genie in sudden possession of a magnificent jewelled palace, ever felt half the satisfaction and surprise that we did when that small plain dwelling was handed over to us. As John remarks: ' Columbus, when he first spied land, the ten thousand Greeks when they first spied the sea, and roared Θαλαττα, enjoyed a burst of happiness; but our joy when we entered the deserted house at Karasjok was not equalled by that of Spanish mariner or Hellenic soldier. To be able to sit and write and talk and smoke in comfort, without dread of mosquitoes; to be able to sleep as long as one pleased without a check, and then to wash and cook unveiled, with a change of clothes; to discharge all the obligations of our present life in peace, irrespective of mere pleasure, were blessings only to be appreciated by men who had plodded on foot across 120 miles of desolate fjeld within the Arctic Circle, and that under the broiling, plague-breeding sun of July.'

We determined to stay at Karasjok for two days, until the Tuesday, with the intent of recruiting our mangled and fevered bodies, of strengthening our defensive armour by converting gloves into gauntlets and sewing up veils behind, and of cleaning the guns, which sadly needed the hot water and thorough scrubbing exacted by the old muzzle-loader.

The house, being furnished, as I have said, with an eye to the strictly useful, contained a good supply of cutlery, crockery, and glass, the latter comprising wine-glasses of various shapes and sizes. These were suggestive, but the question was what to drink out of them. Now, on exploring the kitchen, which, as housekeeper, caterer, head-cook, and kitchenmaid to the expedition, I justly regarded as my special department, I found that the floor sounded hollow under my feet, and, searching, discovered a trap-door with a ring attached. This was too important a find to be kept to myself, for visions of a cellar at once flashed across me. I therefore summoned John and lifted the trap, revealing, as I expected, a flight of steps leading into darkness.

Lighting the only candle we could discover among Fandrum's goods, we descended into what John called ' a charnel house of dead men—empty bottles —from which the spirit had fled.' Thirsty souls had been in that house before us. But, to our satisfaction, there were a certain number of survivors of different nationalities; as it proved, champagne, port, claret, Madeira, and Curaçoa. We were grate-

ful, but would willingly have exchanged them all for
a few bottles of native beer. Having scruples about
appropriating any of this treasure-trove, we inter-
viewed the steward, who assured us that it was all
at our disposal, and we agreed to leave behind us
the price of what we took, according to the tariffs
of the hotel at Trondhjem and the steamers.

It was agreeable to meet afterwards at Alten,
where he had a store, Herr Fandrum himself, and
to find him quite content with the arrangement.
Karasjok being a station for travellers, he was
bound by law to provide them with shelter, but I
have great doubts whether he was under any com-
pulsion to part with the contents of his cellar.

The village of Karasjok, standing, like Assebakte,
in a level meadow, at the time of our visit a sheet
of rich grass, on which the mowers, with their short
scythes and double right and left sweep, were busily
at work, consisted of a small and rather graceful
red-roofed wooden church, closed in summer-time;
about twenty wooden houses, only the priest's and
merchant's being two-storied; a number of quaint
outbuildings, all on four legs; a conspicuous grindstone and trough; and a deep well, with a gigantic
crane supporting rope and bucket. At the bottom
of this well the water was surrounded by ice 3
feet thick. It was an excellent place for cooling our
milk, bottles of which we used to lower into it for
the night at the end of salmon lines, and haul them
up at daybreak before the village was astir. The
common meadow and the private paddocks belonging
to each house were enclosed by uniform palisades
of sloping stakes. Nothing excited the admiration
of the villagers more than the way in which, in those

days of youth and activity, we used to spring lightly
over these formidable fences. Behind the village
woods of rich green rose on broad, flat terraces,
which clearly marked the old-time levels of water
or ice, until stopped by a barrier of rugged cliff,
which was in its turn dominated by mountain slopes
streaked with snow, beyond whose skyline lay the
ghastly fjeld.

During the great heat of mid-day and early afternoon, for the weather was magnificent, when we
remained indoors, having for the time ample occupation, we were favoured by the inhabitants with
more than one visit. A timid tap usually preceded
the entrance of a dozen men, women, and children,
who arranged themselves in a line across the apartment, and for some moments there was the silence
of wonder. Then some bold spirit would advance
with a gentle ' weh, weh !' expressive of admiration,
and begin to examine the many articles of our kit
littered about the room, whereupon we felt it
incumbent on us to invite inspection, to exhibit, and
to explain.

I think that, on the whole, the revolvers, which
we had thought fit to bring with us, excited the
greatest interest, but it was of a serious kind, and
not unmixed with trepidation. The explosion of
five caps on the Dean and Adams—for in those
days revolvers were not breech-loading—startled
the company greatly, and only Amut, our pedagogue
boatman, who had but one serviceable eye, at last
found courage to handle the weapon himself. The
exhibition of indiarubber bands, on the contrary,
and the demonstration of their power of elasticity
and recoil, excited positively childish delight; and

when Amut, again the bold experimentalist, in
stretching one to the utmost, let it escape from his
fingers, to strike a bystander on the cheek, the glee
became uproarious. I have no doubt that had
there been anything worth buying a good business
might have been done with indiarubber bands as
a medium of barter and exchange. The third
place in popular favour must be accorded to the
spirit-lamps, and the fourth to the brilliantly
illustrated cover of Soyer's cookery-book! This
admission may possibly gratify the shade of the
gifted author of 'A Culinary Campaign,' if, indeed,
anything short of a first place could content the
master-mind of the great Alexis, saviour of the
British army in the Crimea.

On one occasion, when the length of an interview
had outlasted our patience, the intruders being all
males of the loafing, unintelligent, loutish kind, John,
with great presence of mind, seized a revolver, and
playfully snapped the five caps rapidly round the
room. They took the hint, hastily retreated, and
we were left in peace. What might a black-
bearded Englishman not do, one of that race who
only the year before had lowered the pride of
Russia, whose empire extended to their immediate
neighbourhood?

In the cool of the evening we strolled out on to
the green, and I began a water-colour sketch of
the village, at once attracting a number of garrulous
and doubtless critical spectators. But John, who
was also provided with paper and pencil, relieved
me in some degree by actually persuading a highly-
picturesque man, a nice-looking young girl, and
several children to group themselves as he wished on

the grass; the interest of the bystanders was thus
divided between two artistic efforts. John's sketch
was very successful. I abridge some of his remarks
anent it and its execution: 'With their long hair,
red caps, reindeer-skin and wool-embroidered pesks,
belts, and quaint komagers, they made a gay party.
The drawing involved a slight sacrifice of truth, for it
was as unnecessary to depict the triple layer of
dirt as it was impossible to reproduce the fidgety
motions, involuntary sighings, and unsuppressed
scratchings. The girl was very shy, but instinctively not indifferent to the appearance she
made in a picture. With Eve-like simplicity,
she wetted her fingers in her mouth, and smoothed
her tresses down to the standard of Finsk neat-
ness.'

During our short stay we had no time to try
the fishing in the river. Had we done so, we should
probably have caught a number of the ubiquitous
trout and grayling, but nothing else. Amut assured
us that no salmon lay in the purely sandy bed of
the Karasjok; he even insisted that they never
came up it, which seems open to doubt; but at
any rate by the village their existence was ignored,
and no one caught or tried to catch them. The
only salmon we saw was an 18-pound fish, which
was offered to us for sale by a Finn, who had arrived
in a canoe from the lower waters of the Tana.
Strange to say, it was one, according to Amut's
interpretation, of a number taken by a party of
Englishmen who had fished for a few days and then
left the river, driven away by the 'slemme myg.'*
These could be no others than our friends, and it

* Bad mosquitoes.

was sad intelligence. In the first place, it annihi-
lated all hopes of that jovial meeting to which we
had looked forward, and, secondly, seemed to prove
that the mosquitoes were as bad as ever nearer the
sea. But as the fish was in good condition we
bought it, and at the very next meal, having
plenty of pickles, I served up a dish of *côtelettes de
saumon à l'Indienne*, which provoked the hearty
appetite and elicited the loud approbation of the
other half of the expedition.

Before entering upon the details of our descent
of the Tana, I may make a few general remarks
regarding it. We had not been a week on the
river before we realized that we were a good deal
too late for the best fishing, that what rise there was
only came on as a rule at certain hours, and lasted
but for a short time; again, that the upper waters
were not likely at any time to be much good for
salmon-fishing, although they swarmed with trout
and grayling. There were but few streams or pools,
and the frequent long still reaches were hopeless,
especially in bright, breezeless weather; there might
be a chance of picking up a fish here and there, but
no more. It seemed also probable that the salmon,
when they had passed the rapids and lower pools
of which our boatmen spoke, and where they would
be sure to dwell for a time, would at over a hundred
miles from the sea become stale and sulky. One
at least of our men had some practical knowledge
of rod-fishing in the river, for he had been boatman to the expedition of two years ago, and from
his account, as far as we came to understand it,
the wisest plan was to make for the lower waters
as quickly as possible, especially after the report

that our friends had departed, a report confirmed beyond doubt at our first camp.

The mosquito question did not trouble us as much as might have been expected after our terrible experience on the fjeld. Shelter, repose, sound sleep, and regular meals—if at irregular hours—had restored our shattered nerves; we had become in a great measure callous to the continual presence of the insect host, and with gauntlets, improved veils, and underclothing, were better protected against its attacks.

There is little doubt, I think, that we had also been so thoroughly inoculated with venom that fresh bites caused less irritation. My long experience has convinced me that such inoculation is a certainty after sufficient endurance of the plague; it is not absolutely a preventive, but a great mitigator of the evil. For many years past I have not positively suffered from mosquitoes, although sometimes greatly annoyed by them. I detest them as much as ever, particularly the venomous pipe with which they herald their attack; but when bitten I do not swell, and in an hour all irritation has passed, except the bite happens to be just under the wrist or ankle-bone, or between the fingers, when its effect lasts rather longer.

I shall try in my account of our tent life on the Tana to mention the pests as little as possible, but it must be understood that, except in very heavy rain or a strong breeze, when we were out in the boats or under canvas, and not always in the latter case, and until the sharp night frosts came, we were never free from them; but for every million on the fjeld there were perhaps a thousand on the river. That

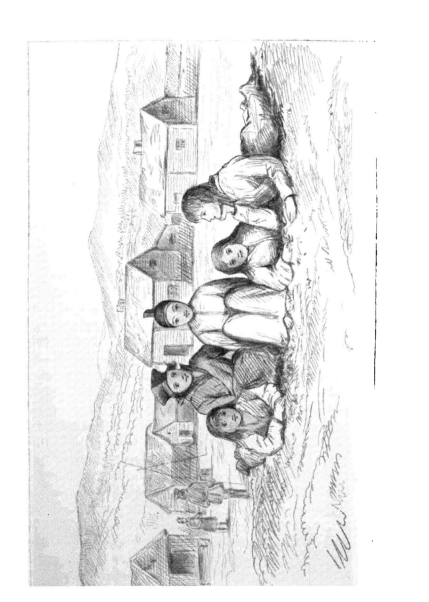

John and I felt equal to coping with them is proved
by the fact that the very next year after our visit
to Tana we undertook an exactly similar expedition,
entailing three days' march across an Arctic fjeld,
ourselves on foot, with horses for the baggage, to the
Staburs Elv, a then virgin river that runs into the
Porsanger Fjord. We pitched our tent on a flat
close to the mouth, where there was a small village;
but the men were all absent at the fisheries, and
three women were the sole occupants of it. We
had sent back the horses; neither boats nor boatmen
were procurable, and the river ran through an
absolutely uninhabited country, so that when working up it we had to sleep out in the woods, carrying
ourselves whatever was necessary for the bivouacs;
but neither there nor on the fjeld did the mosquitoes
seriously interfere with our enjoyment.

I am bound to say that, from what we heard,
1857, our Tana year, was acknowledged to be the
worst, or in sporting phraseology best, mosquito
season within the memory of man up to that date.

Before leaving Alten we had ascertained on which
days the fortnightly steamer called at Stangenæs,
in the Tana Fjord, and it will be seen, after what I
have said, that the question now was whether
we should hasten to the lower water, try it, and
get away, or take it easy all down the river.

Now, we had not travelled the long distance from
England to Alten, and crossed the fjeld, to hurry at
the last, and therefore decided to stick to as long
and enjoy as much as possible our novel mode of life,
regarding sport as a pleasant accessory to it. It was
true that the idea of salmon-fishing had induced us to
come to the Tana, but the idea of camping in the wilds

had been an equally strong inducement. We were
neither of us gluttons in sport, for the simple reason
that we had not learnt habits of gluttony. Of
salmon-fishing we knew next to nothing, having
taken only a few small fish in Ireland, but two
fine old precepts relating to it had been duly impressed on our minds : ' Always cast whenever you
can,' and ' Show 'em the butt.' To this sound
doctrine I have endeavoured to adhere all my life,
and for the last five-and-twenty years at least have
seldom caught a salmon in Norway or elsewhere
except by wading or bank-fishing ; but, then, my lines
happen to have been cast in pleasant places, which
admitted of it. The modification of the ' always '
by the ' whenever you can ' is fair enough ; it is
sometimes next to impossible to continue casting
with any hope of success, and I hold that he is the
best fisherman who adapts his style of angling to
circumstances in all ways, and thereby makes the
best bag.

It appears to me that there is a great deal of
false sentiment talked and written about the use
of the fly in salmon-fishing. By speaking of wings,
body, tail, and so forth, you can keep up the fiction
that the feathered hook is a fly, but you might as
well call it a bird ; it is simply a scentless and
tasteless lure, like nothing in nature, and no one
knows for what the salmon takes it, certainly not
for a flying insect. A beautiful object it is, no doubt,
requiring much skill and possibly some judgment
in its manufacture, and a considerable amount of
cash, which in the eyes of some people may add
to its merit ; but it is the casting only which
ennobles the use of the fly beyond that of other

lures. When salmon are really on the rise and
mean business, the veriest duffer who can sit in a
boat and pay out line, leaving his skilful boatman
to do the rest, can hardly help hooking them.
Whether he can play them properly when hooked
is another matter, depending a good deal upon
his knowledge of how to show them the butt and
let, even when the line is running free, the splendid
elastic curve of a well-made salmon-rod exert its
utmost power, like the quivering muscles of a living
thing. When the fish do not mean business, it is
the artistic caster who entices them into a fatal
momentary impulse, and who enjoys the practice
of his art whether he catch fish or not ; but that,
in such a case, he might be wise in resorting to
other methods I will not deny.

For there are other styles of angling, less com-
mended than fly-fishing, which are, to my mind,
quite as legitimate on occasion, and quite as artistic.
For a hundred men who can throw a fly decently
there is not one man who knows how to handle a
spinning-rod on a river-bank overgrown with rough
herbage, coiling the line with deft manipulation in
his left palm so that it can be released between the
thumb and forefinger for another cast or when a
fish is struck, or if needful be reeled in through the
hollow under the bent little finger. I learnt this
trick in my youth from an old Thames fisherman,
and have never forgotten it; it demands long
practice and a fairly strong current.

Then, the correct working of that deadly lure the
prawn, which is, after all, only a so-called salmon-
fly in the flesh, appealing to the piscine senses of
smell and taste as well as vision, is no mean art.

A young friend of mine, after three times rising with the fly a salmon that would not take, cast over it one of Farlow's single-hooked hog-backed spoons, rather over half an inch in length, and at once hooked and eventually killed it. Its weight was 23 lbs.

Fly-fishing for trout, of course, stands apart. In its highest phase it is a real science, based on the study and exquisite reproduction of Nature. The coarse, undiscriminating voracity of uneducated trout in parts of Norway and some other countries does not detract from its credit or fascination.

One of the higher flights of piscatorial art is attained in the capture of salmon in very low, clear water by wading with a 12-foot rod, backed line, fine gut, and small trout-flies—claret body and mallard wing for choice—a style of fishing in which I and my friends have occasionally been not unsuccessful on the river which I now rent in Norway. I once had the good fortune, when angling alone in this way, to gaff a 16-lb. salmon on the dropper, after luckily losing a heavy sea-trout which had simultaneously taken the tail-fly, and on the same day caught another salmon of smaller size, two grilse, and a number of nice sea-trout. And this performance was soon after eclipsed by that of a friend, who took a 19-pounder on a fly that might have reasonably been used in an English trout-stream.

But all this is by the way. To return to Tana: we, then, two inexperienced salmon-fishers, determined, after our first week on the river, to take out our full month on its banks; to enjoy, in defiance of mosquitoes, our camp life to the utmost; to act

according to circumstances, collectively or individually, just as we pleased; to be as energetic or
lazy as we liked; not to be slaves to the rod or
oppressed by the incubus of making a big bag; to
fish, shoot, explore, sketch, write, loaf, or sleep, as
inclination prompted. All this I gather from our
journals, and the result seems to have been, on
the whole, satisfactory. It is true that while the
physical barometer remained at steady, the mental
mercury vacillated between stormy and set fair,
between periods of depression and jubilant exultation, but this was only to be expected. It is not
given to all young mortals to preserve the equal
mind in adversity, nor to abstain from insolent joy
in prosperity. But in the end we came out of our
little unpretentious campaign better men than we
had entered upon it, having learnt, in a small way,
certain lessons which travel and the pursuit of adventurous field-sports always bring home to young
men; lessons of self-control and self-reliance, of
belief in the silver lining of every cloud, and in
the satisfaction of doing everything for one's self,
from acquiring sufficient mastery of strange tongues
to pitching a tent, cooking one's own meals, and
greasing one's own boots. It is certain, however,
that the day we left Karasjok our minds were
occupied by two dominant ideas, those of possibly
great sport and possibly intolerable mosquitoes.

Very early on Tuesday morning we and our
baggage were ready for a start down the river, but
that which happened at Alten with regard to the
horses was now repeated at Karasjok in the matter
of boatmen; at the appointed hour no one appeared. After waiting a considerable time, it struck

me that, the part being included in the whole, the
best thing to do was to rouse the entire village, and,
loading my revolver with powder, I went out on to
the green and fired several shots. The effect of this
reveille was magical.

In a few minutes the whole population came
tumbling out of their dwellings, and the majority
followed the boatmen into our house, where another
half-hour was consumed in unexpected wrangling;
for the spirit of mutiny was abroad, its chief
instigator being without doubt a hard-faced, disagreeable woman who had annoyed us greatly
during her visits by the most obtrusive and inquisitive handling of our kit. Encouraged by her evil
influence, and the presence of all their relations
and friends, the men we had engaged tried to back
our of their engagement, and one of them, by
name Mikkel, absolutely refused to go. But, as luck
would have it, this very man had already drawn
some of his pay in advance in order to purchase, as
he said, provisions for the journey, had, in fact,
accepted ' arles,' and after that his present conduct
put him hopelessly in the wrong. Amut, the one-
eyed schoolmaster, although he showed evident reluctance to start, did not venture on decided speech.

The position was rather serious, but John rose to
it nobly, and under emergency exhibited a miracu-
lous gift of tongues, which astonished me, and, I
believe, himself. Whilst I got part of the baggage
outside the door, and urged the two Assebakte men
to carry it down to the boat, my comrade harangued,
expostulated, and threatened in a manner somehow
intelligible to the crowd, and at last gained the day.
The reluctant Amut and the contumacious Mikkel

gave way, and a general move took place to the
river bank, where the boats lay. John had with
great presence of mind introduced the name of the
Foged, a magistrate invested with ample authority
to inflict severe penalties on those who attempted
to delay or impose on travellers, and this master-
stroke, all the more admirably audacious because
we had not the faintest idea where the Foged lived
or how to get at him, turned the scale of victory in
our favour. My impression is that the objection-
able female had suggested to the men that by refusing to go they might obtain higher wages from
the Englishmen, who could scarcely be expected to
know how much they ought to pay ; but it so happened that Thomas had given us particular instructions on this point.

After all, I may be wronging them. To judge
merely from the affectionate farewells, tender em-
bracings, and lingering handshakes that preceded
embarkation, it may be that, when the moment
came for leaving their beloved home, that little
paradise Karasjok, their hearts had really failed
them. As John noticed, not Regulus himself, when
returning to Carthage, with a certain prospect of
torture and death, received a more sympathetic
demonstration from the populace opposing his
departure than did those egregious exiles who
were bound for the remote regions at the mouth
of the Tana, with which it proved they were well
acquainted.

After seeing the baggage-boat well out in the
stream, with Mikkel as one of the crew, we stepped
out into our own canoe and pushed off, amid the
mournful adieux—not directed at ourselves—of the

crowd, which lasted, signal-wise, until we were out of sight.

I may say at once that, as soon as the two men got out of the atmosphere of their native village, their good-temper and high spirits returned. They took the greatest possible interest in all our proceedings, learnt after a few instructions to help us in everything, and parted from us with sincere regret. The honesty of all four was unimpeachable. Amongst our belongings scattered about outside and inside the tent must have been many articles invaluable in their eyes, but we never missed a single thing, and at times their scrupulous zeal in restoring odds and ends that we had tossed away caused us positive annoyance, but this we took care to conceal.

We were not long in running down the smooth stream of the Karasjok, the high banks and bed of which consisted of pure ivory-coloured sand, glittering in some places, especially beneath the clear sunlit current, with minute scales of mica. It did not look the least like fishing-water, and we were willing to credit Amut's statement that salmon seldom lay in it. But our progress was several times delayed by the alarm of ducks. At this season most of the broods were in the flapper stage, and as our guns lay beside us in the boat, we seldom lost an opportunity of replenishing the larder. There are few things better for breakfast or supper than broiled flapper, especially when slightly devilled with French mustard and cayenne, although the tender innocent may not come of a stock the most esteemed as food. Our plan was to stop the baggage-boat, and, guided by Amut's skilful and silent paddling to drop down upon our natant prey. In this way we secured during the first morning three golden eyes,* as many tufted pochards,† and a couple of teal, the latter full grown.

Similar episodes occurred repeatedly during subsequent water-stages, to the great joy of our boatmen, who always kept a sharp look-out, and not seldom roused us from quiet reveries during that most delightful of all modes of travelling, slipping downstream, by their excited whispers of 'Fugl! fugl! Bisso! bisso!'‡ and showed much disappointment when, having as many ducks as we wanted and not recognising through our glasses a new species, we refrained from firing and left the anxious old birds and broods in peace. To the Finns all ducks were, of course, alike, and comprehended under the term 'chooaveekee,'§ just as the word 'lax' among Norsk peasants includes several species of fish besides salmon.

Before noon, when the scenery has become much more rural than we expected, with low, rounded, birch-clad hills and park-like stretches sloping to green lawns sprinkled with innumerable flowers, we are aware of another valley opening on our left, through which comes rolling silently a second river, exactly similar in character to the Karasjok. This is the Anarjok, and by the junction of these two is formed before our very eyes the majestic Tana. It is a thrilling moment. At last, on August 4, a

---

* *Clangula vulgaris.*
† *Fuligula cristata.*
‡ 'Fowl! fowl! Gun! gun!'
§ Written phonetically; I cannot find the word in the lexicon.

month and a day out from England, we are looking
upon the broad, glistening flood, the glory of Nordenfjelds. From where our boat lies to the sea, 140 miles,
we are masters as far as any enjoyment is to be
reaped by land or water; no fear of trespass,' no
need of licenses, no rod to anticipate us on the best
pools, no compulsory reliance on rascally guides or
extortionate innkeepers. Our own inclination shall
be our law, the tent our portable castle, the boundary
of empires our silent highway. Wherever we tread
our feet shall be, as it were, upon our native heath,
and whether our names be Macgregor, or Briggs, or
Sahjunt, or Poteenjur, or Yahnee, or Haree, is to us
immaterial. We are monarchs of all we survey,
and as kind Tana, in recognition of our homage, sends
us a pest-dispelling breeze, we forget for the moment
all about the winged aborigines of the land.

The converging streams are separated by a grassy
promontory, with a beach of clean sand. On this
we land, and, preparatory to sitting down to lunch,
shake hands and raise a two-man-power British
cheer. The occasion seems worthy of a special
toast, and we accordingly open a bottle of sherry
from Fandrum's cellar, and drink ' skaal' to the
Tana.

Before eating, our men cut branches of willow,
which, peeled, supply both wood and binding,
and busy themselves by erecting three strange
devices on the promontory, close to the water's
edge. As this savours of sorcery, for which in old
days both Finns and Lapps were notorious, we playfully accuse Amut of dealing in the black art; but
the Arimaspian—as John, student of Herodotus,
whose works are among his baggage, has, with regard

to his one eye, christened him—wrinkles his ugly face
into a knowing grin, and informs us that they have
only established signals, intelligible to any of their
compatriots who might pass, that they were on their
way down the river. Much in the same way does
the Red Indian convey to those who might be interested intelligence of his route and other valuable
information.

Having eaten, the Finns lie down to sleep for
a couple of hours, while John and I are content
to smoke our pipes in the sun, wander about the
shore, and find plenty to talk about. When the
men wake we give them each a dram of cognac, for
which they shake us warmly by the hand, and intimate with hideous grimaces their appreciation of its
strength and flavour.

Once in the boats again, we are in a minute on
the Tana, and for the rest of the afternoon paddle
quietly down it through charming scenery of the
same half-pastoral character. At times the banks
close in until the river is scarcely wider than the
Karasjok, but much deeper, and again recede,
forming lake-like expanses, where the strong breeze
meeting the current raises waves high enough to
overlap the low gunwale of our canoe, obliging us
to spread over the whole boat one of our large
waterproof sheets. We lie, as usual, on a similar
one face to face, with shoulders supported by our
‘ round-bottomed sailor's bags ’—so described in
Edgington's account—and dovetailed legs.

I have always noticed that in every small gathering
of boatmen, bearers, ghillies, or any other analogous
retinue, there is sure to be one who is the humorist
of the party. On this occasion the *rôle* of wag is

played by a cheery young fellow, not tall but
sturdy and active, one of the Assebakte men, by
name Johannes, but who, tapping himself on the
breast, smilingly explains that he is 'Leet'l Savvitch,'
an alias bestowed upon him, as it appears, by
Campbell, a member of the last expedition. He
evidently has no idea of the meaning of the appellation, but we accept it, and 'Little Savage' he
remains during our stay on the Tana. He is very
proud of the title, and also of a few sentences of
English that he has picked up like a parrot, and
introduces abruptly either into conversation or to
enliven silence.

The first of these that he favours us with
is rather startling and of bad omen: 'Notta da-
am-feesch to-dai-yee!' It shows that there were
occasional blank days for someone when the Tana
was last prospected. But it is neutralized in a small
degree by another utterance: 'Tomas kitch beeg
feesch, teventee poond'; and perhaps by a third
which clearly reflects on himself: 'ga-affeem, yuda-
amfool!' Many chances of using the gaff there must
have been before that vigorous exhortation was
impressed on Little Savage's brain. The fourth
man, Clamek, is also an Assebakte Finn, a quiet,
rather reticent man, who does his duty well and
cheerfully, but, on the whole, keeps in the background.

Towards evening, to our great satisfaction, the
sand begins to disappear, and rocks to show themselves here and there both on the banks and in the
bed of the river. It is time to think of camping,
and we remember that there is before us the task of
erecting the tent for the first time since we saw it

accomplished by professionals on the floor of the warehouse.

And now at last we come to broken water and an actual pool, a likely place enough for salmon, and catching sight of a few beehive-shaped huts under a wood which indicate a level spot for camping, direct our men to row to the eastern bank. But to this they strongly object, and implore us not to land on the Russian side of the river, adducing arguments which, if not altogether intelligible to us, are so evidently earnest that we consent to prospecting for a landing-place on the Norwegian bank, and, as it happens, find one a few hundred yards below, where a kind of terrace abuts on the river, dry and clear of trees, with a spur of hill behind it.

The tent which has now to be erected is nine feet square, with what I may call two laceable canvas porches at opposite ends of the main edifice. The latter is supported by three poles, the central one being the tallest, and has a green and white striped lining, which can be used or not according to fancy, but we decide never to omit it. This is also supported by the poles, there being between it and the outer canvas an interval of about three inches. I shall let John describe the first erection of our home in the wilds.

' We chose a site with as much care as if we were going to found a city. Several spots were rejected for the sake of the view ; one on account of small dips in the ground, ominous of pools if the weather should prove rainy. At last we lighted on an even square of smooth turf, flanked by the river and a little brook on two sides, and on the others by the forest. As this was our first essay in tent-pitching,

we spread out the printed model, and followed the
directions which accompanied it with blind faith.
There was a great deal of land-surveying, followed
by assiduous hammering; but somehow either we
or the directions were wrong, for after pinning down
the whole affair with sightly rows of pegs, we found
it impossible to erect the pole. Harry crept underneath, and performed unimagined feats of strength
in trying to raise the canvas, to no purpose. Atlas
came forth, and Hercules took his place, but with
like want of success : we had not measured our
ground according to our cloth. The next failure
was that the door fronted the wrong way, and the
pegs had to come out again, so fastidious were we.
By the time that we had turned the little meadow
into arable land by loosening every sod our white
cottage was erected, and its emblazoned flag floated
gaily on the breeze. The Finns enjoyed this triumph
of architecture as much as we did, although they
had looked on open-mouthed, without offering to
help us. However, as spectators, they saw most
of the game, and were competent to take a hand in
it next time, after which we used to entrust the
whole erection to them as soon as a good site had
been selected.

'My friend marched up and down the main
chamber, nine feet square, with the air of a master
builder, whilst I lit a pipe, and felt the satisfaction of a humbler mason after his day's work is
done. We then formed a committee for settling
the internal arrangements. The back porch was
to be turned into a pantry, wherein to stow the
barrel of biscuits, the groceries, and the spoil of
Fandrum's cellar ; the central compartment was,

of course, the sleeping-room and general resort;
the front porch was dedicated to implements of
the chase. The beds we laid on waterproof sheets
parallel to each other, leaving a walk between, and
erected on either side a row of birch branches to support the mosquito-nets. Leathern straps with brass
hooks attached encircled the central pillar, on which
to hang clothes and the utensils of a simple toilet.'

And now that the responsibility of house-building
was off our minds, they at once turned to thoughts
of sport, and we opened the rod-boxes and tackle-
cases. I was going to use for the first time my
brand-new big rod, made for me by John Macgowan,
an Irishman who had migrated from the banks of
the Erne to London, and started a shop in Bruton
Street, where for a good many years he did an
excellent business. He had accompanied anglers
more than once to Scandinavia, and was in all ways
a practical man. His work would nowadays be
considered lamentably old-fashioned, but I still use
one of a pair of trout-rods he made for me at the
same time, and prefer it to the many I have since
handled, whether cane-built or otherwise. My
friends call it heavy and clumsy, but I love it, and
should know the feel of it in the dark amongst a
hundred others.

I was looking the other day at my Tana salmon-
rod, and the very sight of it made my lumbar and
humeral muscles ache. I took it out into the
garden, and could scarcely believe that there was
a time when I could wield it, casting day after day
from morning till night, and feel no distress; but it
was as grand a rod as ever, still bending evenly from
the hand to the top ring with magnificent power

and elasticity. It is twenty feet long, in four joints, made of hickory; the butt is at the grasp five inches in circumference; and the total weight, without reel, by no means excessive considering its size, is five pounds. With this Titanic rod I now prepared to flog the Tana.

As fly I selected a ' colonel ' in splendid uniform, gleaming with gold, John a truculent - looking 'butcher' splashed with blood. They were both just three inches long, a size to be noted with regard to results, and attached to casting-lines of the strongest treble gut. Such was the style of fishing practised in those days, when Norwegian salmon were uneducated, and recommended to us both by Macgowan and the anglers at Alten. I now believe that they were all wrong, and that with finer tackle, say, the strongest single gut, with which the heaviest fish that ever swam can be killed, we should have done better.

Concerning the size of the fly I will say nothing; but the most unsophisticated salmon of mature age cannot surely help being surprised that the strange creature or insect—call it what you like—on which he casts a curious and longing eye should in some mysterious way be attached to a miniature cable; it must be contrary to his experience in the sea and elsewhere. We know but little about the intelligence of fish, but that they can become in some way educated, and can impart the lessons of that education to their offspring, we do know, the proof being that in almost every river it has become necessary nowadays to use comparatively fine tackle and smaller flies. Granting, then, the fact of education, the probability of original intelligence is undeniable, and there appears to be no reason why the untutored monsters of the Tana should not have had the instinctive faculty of suspicion.

It was, I believe, that great angler Mr. Corrance who first recognised the fact that in order to best lure the big old fish of Norway you must risk the chance of occasional breakage and use fine tackle; such, in any case, was his practice for a number of years. It is true that when, in the height of the season, that madness known as ' the rise ' comes upon salmon they are not particular, and it does not require a great deal of art to hook them; but when they have been a long time out of salt water, have lost whatever appetite they had, and are beginning to dispense with digestive organs, it seems but natural to suppose that they require to be coaxed into taking by superior artifice.

Be that as it may, one thing I can firmly declare, that the above arguments were in no way applicable to the permanently resident denizens of the Tana, who never went to the sea, and who exhibited at mealtimes such astounding blind voracity and such reckless confidence in their powers of digestion that without the testimony of my own eyes I would not have believed it.

John and I tossed up for boatmen and choice of stations. Fate ruled that Mikkel and Little Savage were to pilot my canoe, Clamek and the Arimaspian his; he was to go to the head of the one pool, I lower down the river.

I began to cast in very likely-looking deep water at the head of a swirling eddy produced by a rocky projection. The ' colonel ' had not completed his third swing through the current before there came a

tug, and putting a slight strain on the twenty feet of
hickory in my hands, I dragged to the surface and
along the water a grayling of a little over a pound
in weight ! When lifted into the boat what a pitiable
object was he, with the huge gaudy fly stuck in his
baby mouth ! How it ever got there was the marvel.
But it was no unique miracle : a couple more casts
and I was obliged to treat one of his relatives of
rather larger size in the same unceremonious fashion.
A third tug, soon after, was followed by a certain
amount of futile resistance and a deal of splashing,
when the victim to the 'colonel's' gay seductive-
ness proved to be a fat trout of over 2 lbs. And
so it went on. I shifted quarters, dropped downstream, cast carefully the whole time, and always
with the same result, grayling and trout, trout and
grayling.

I was a young fisherman, to whom it was agreeable to catch fish in any way, and such a supply of
grayling, averaging 1½ lbs., and of trout running
from that weight to 3, 4, and once even to 5 lbs.,
had never come in my way before; but I was
vexed at the absurdity of the position; and then to
think of the pity of it ! Here was fishing enough
to have satisfied the wildest dreams of any number
of home anglers, and made the reputation of a
dozen piscatorial clubs, positively thrown away on
a man who had come over 2,000 miles to catch salmon
with a rod like a weaver's beam, and a machine for
weighing them up to 50 lbs.

As I was paddled and poled up the river again,
for the Finns employed both methods of locomotion,
according to the depth and strength of the current,
I saw John being taken to land with his rod steadily

bent in a fashion which showed that he had got hold of something of rather more importance than grayling or trout; and, sure enough, in a few minutes Clamek, who had the gaff, hooked on to the beach a 10-lb. salmon, as ugly a stale fish with a beak as ever was seen, but a salmon for all that. I then returned to the tent, and busied myself with preparations for supper until joined by John, who produced besides the salmon a 5-lb. grilse and a few good trout and grayling. Our combined catch of the two latter fish would, if carefully weighed, have amounted to about 60 lbs. The Finns were delighted, for we allowed them to carry off as many as they pleased, as well as the ugly salmon.

We then had a high tea with grilse cutlets and rashers of ham, and prepared to turn in, after a very long and, on the whole, very tiring day, but were disturbed by Amut, who put his head into the tent with the magic exclamation, 'Fugl!' As John's boots were already off, I crept down to the river and shot a goosander,* useless for food, but a fine specimen. The Finns, after their supper, retired, in spite of all they had said to us, across the river to the Russian huts to pass the hours of rest. As they did this more than once during our descent of the river, I suspected that they had, in their simplicity, agreed that it was wiser to prevent Englishmen, who were, of course, haughty and irascible, and possessed revolvers, from meeting Russian subjects, the two nations having concluded peace only the year before. This is mere conjecture, but it seems not improbable. And so ended our first day on the Tana.

* *Mergus merganser.*

CHAPTER VIII

DOWN THE TANA

ALTHOUGH, while there is still sufficient light during the whole of the twenty-four hours to fish or shoot, read or write, or to do anything that one pleases which is dependent on eyesight, one does not feel bound to truckle to the arbitrary routine of daily life that obtains in countries recognising a distinct line between daylight and darkness, nevertheless, Nature refuses to be cajoled into foregoing her rights. The man who persists in jumbling up the past, present, and future, in confounding yesterday, to-day, and to-morrow, will be driven in the end to confess that he is only mortal, and must conform in some measure to the laws that govern ordinary human existence. It is in vain that he who has pursued his sport until past midnight and dined in the small hours declares that he means to be up early and out fishing; Nature puts in her veto. When the time for rousing comes he will refuse to listen to the voice of the rouser, and in the end regard with complacency the idea of an anomalous meal, which may, according to fancy, be called breakfast, lunch, or supper.

So it was with us at Akko Guoika, for thus the Finns called the scene of our first camp, and on

several subsequent occasions. Guoika means
'broken and swiftly-running water,' in short, pool,
stream, or rapid; and half of the few names given
in Professor Friis's chart of the Tana, published in
1888, and the only one I know of, have this termi-
nation, suggesting, of course, a good locality for
salmon-fishing.

I took some pains to study this chart by the
help of the same Professor's 'Lexicon of the
Lappish Language,' in the hope of finding out
some meaning in the names of places, and my
philological researches were not altogether encouraging. When I discovered, or thought that I had,
that Akko Guoika meant 'The Old Woman Rapid,'
and that Galggo Guoika, lower down the river,
where we had our best sport, had exactly the same
meaning, I began to think that there was not only
as much tiresome repetition about Lappish appella-
tions as obtains in the rest of Norway, where the
country bristles with Langvands, Storvands, Krok-
vands, and the like, but even more crass stupidity;
nevertheless, although I write Akko and Galggo
with their meanings just as they appear both in
chart and lexicon, I will allow that the words can
possibly, in a circuitous fashion, be connected with
running water, in which case tautology is the only
charge to which they are open. Otherwise, who
was the old woman thus immortalized? Could she
be Thana herself, whom I have seen mentioned in
some mythology or other as the goddess of water?

The name is not uncommon elsewhere in Norway.
For instance, when in 1889 we were circumnavi-
gating the great lake Rösvand in Helgeland, at that
time unexplored by Englishmen, there was an im-

posing mountain which plagued us with repeated storms; it turned out to be Kjærringtind, 'Old Woman Peak,' and in the same region, but remote from the mountain, we came across a separate lake, Kjærringvand, 'Old Woman Water.' Again I ask, Why this ubiquitous crone ?

I regret that it is no longer possible to refer the point to Professor Friis, who was, as well as a man of great learning, a keen sportsman, and absolutely devoted to his native fjelds. In a delightful volume entitled 'Tilfjelds,' translated by Mr. W. Lock, he gives an account of his youthful rambles and sport in that elevated region. When I last saw him, many years ago, in the Christiania Club, he shook me warmly by the hand, and exclaimed in English : ' Ah, you are just from the fjelds ! how beautiful you are to look at !' expressing by this apparently fulsome compliment his satisfaction at my appearance of health gained on his favourite playground. One of his hobbies in after-life was always to carry a monstrous umbrella on his up-country expeditions, and he told me that once, when on the point of starting for the mountains with a friend, he noticed that the latter was not provided with the same portable shelter, and accordingly addressed him thus : ' If you do not at once fetch an umbrella I will not go with you, for I know that if it comes on to rain you will want to share mine, and that I swear you shall not; it will be as unpleasant for me as for you.' His friend accordingly forthwith purchased a ' gamp,' and the Professor was satisfied. Fancy an English mountaineer or sportsman equipped in the same fashion ! Nevertheless, a big umbrella does afford protection from rain both in walking or when used as a small tent to sit under ; there was practical sense in the professorial idea.

When we emerged from the tent at Akko Guoika after a sound morning sleep, for our night had been a good deal disturbed by the mosquitoes, which we had not succeeded in excluding from the nets, the forenoon was well advanced ; it was intensely hot, without a breath of air, and that peculiar sultriness which portends thunder. The men had brought back from the Finlandic huts a plentiful supply of milk and butter, and we had a sumptuous breakfast, in connection with which I will note that fillets of grayling fried to a delicate brown and garnished with pickled onions, of which we had a huge bottle, make an admirable dish. The same fillets have, besides, a distinct affinity with tomato sauce, also among our stores. Whilst we were smoking the after - breakfast pipe, and lazily discussing the weather, which seemed to take all energy out of one, a man appeared poling a canoe up the river, and presently landed on catching sight of our encampment. He explained that he had been one of the crews retained by ' Ambroo, Smeet, Gis', and Klova,' who, after catching in a week many 'stuora luossa,'* about seventy miles down the river, had been driven away by the mosquitoes, thus confirming the report we heard at Karasjok.

Later in the day, as fishing in such sultry heat seemed to be absolutely useless, I left John to his own devices, and went for a ramble with a gun through the woods, in the hope of finding some ryper ; but my only victims were a cat-owl,† a handsome bird of tawny plumage and fierce expres-

* Big salmon. † *Strix Lapponica.*

sion, peculiar to the sub-Arctic regions, and a long-billed, shrill-voiced fowl of the air, which I later ascertained to be a spotted redshank,* a rare visitor to England. Just as I got back to camp a tremendous thunderstorm, which had long given warning of its approach, burst upon us in all its fury. The men had already retreated to the huts across the river, while John and I were driven into the tent. The thunder roared, the lightning played all round us, and the rain came down in torrents; but our little refuge stood its first ordeal magnificently. Now and then we had to rush out and ease off a straining stay-rope, but not one drop of moisture penetrated into the canvas sanctuary either from above or below; within a granite fortress we could not have been more secure. And now I will audaciously declare that this was because we had *not* (italics, please) cut a trench round it; had we done so, we should have been standing in water. 'Which the same I take leave to explain.'

The red-tape theory which governs, or used to govern, the pitching of all military and other tents of small size is that by cutting a trench you will isolate the tent on a right little, 'tight little island,' which will be nicely drained, and that by further digging a channel from the said trench to the main conduit or any natural outlet for overflow you will carry off any water which may collect therein. The theory is perfect, and as long as there is only a slight fall of rain acts to perfection. Watching the trickle of the artificial brook down the ditches you may be tempted to say, 'How well that drain is working!' and may go to bed with the same serene

* *Totanus fuscus.*

sense of security as did the Wimbledon Volunteers
in the days when I was young. But in the middle
of the night comes the real storm and the unceasing
torrents of rain, and, like those unfortunate
Volunteers, the description of whose woes furnished
much copy for the daily papers, you may get out of
bed to find yourself up to your ankles in water, and
all your belongings which are not hung up soaked.
The why and wherefore are simple.

The narrow ditches, which do their duty well in
moderate rain, become filled under a heavy, con-
tinuous downpour or the burst of a thunderstorm;
the water falls far faster than they can carry it off,
while the trench kindly does its best to drain what
I may call the mainland as well as the little island,
and the result is a small flood, which, in accordance
with the laws of Nature, spreads out on either side
of the trench, submerging superficially part of the
mainland and the insular floor of the tent, and
causing much discomfort, as well as, in all probability, much bad language. If it rain hard enough
and long enough, any barrier that you may have
tried to raise with the sods and soil cut out becomes
sapped and demoralized, and the water that per-
colates it is only the dirtier.

And now take the case where neither trench nor
drains have been cut. I, of course, beg the question
that the tent must be pitched on a fairly level area
of grass, without any actual holes or depressions,
especially such as begin outside the canvas and lead
inward under it, forming channels for water; on such
grass, in fact, as may be seen all over Wimbledon
or any other common. Now, did anyone ever notice
surface-water produced by rain alone lying on flat

11—2

grass ? Every golfer knows that hollows or indentations in the turf mean pools after heavy rain, but, in the absence of these, when was casual water ever seen on the level course, there being no other agent except rain to account for it ? So with the lawn of a country house; whether it be flat or rolling, so long as its surface be unbroken no water will be visible upon it, even after a month's rain or the most violent storm-burst. In these cases the turf may be soaked through and through, and the moisture may penetrate a foot or more into the soil, but the rain will disappear as it falls, and if a sheet of tarpaulin had been previously laid on course or lawn the ground beneath that would be comparatively dry. Even in the driest weather when you lift your tent-sheet you will always find the under-surface damp, although no moisture can penetrate to the bed above.

One more illustration. In any of the level districts of England may be found a grass field, without furrows or hollows, through or along the side of which trickles an innocent-looking rivulet, which has perhaps in the course of time cut itself a channel of considerable depth, bordered with coarse herbage. There comes a long spell of really bad weather; the brook swells until its banks will no longer contain it; it spreads over them into the field, and the passer-by remarks, 'See how the floods are out!' Had there been no rivulet there would have been no flood, and that is what happens when you cut a trench round your tent; you create a circular brook, fed by drainage and rainfall, which under extreme elemental pressure is incapable of disposing of its superfluous water except by flood, and you suffer in consequence ; and it must be noted that the heavier the rain, the more certain the flood.

I have been tempted to discuss this matter at some length, because I used to be so often asked the questions : ' Of course you cut a trench round your tent ?' and ' Isn't it dreadfully damp and uncomfortable in wet weather ?' I could but say that I had never in my life cut the suggested trench, and that, although I had been for weeks together under canvas in the same spot and sometimes in shockingly bad weather, never did a drop of actual water find its way in. In weather when the external atmosphere had become saturated there might be the same sensation of dampness inside as outside, but no tangible or perceptible moisture have I ever seen on anything; and when at night the tent was closed you could lie as warm and snug as in a house, provided always that you had proper night-gear and plenty of blankets.

In every tent there is a flap of loose canvas pendent from the lower selvage of rope, to which are fastened the loops for the small pegs. Now, when in pitching the tent the selvage is being strained tight to the ground, pull the loose flap inside and spread it flat ; then on it lay the edge of the waterproof sheet, raised about three inches against the internal canvas. It can, if necessary, be kept in place by stones or pieces of wood, or by ties sewn to the canvas inside and passed through the eyelets of the sheet. This will render it impossible for the wet which streams down the external canvas to cause any inconvenience. On that foot or eighteen inches of waterproof sheet between the edge of the bed and the side of the tent may be deposited all articles susceptible of injury by damp, watch, paper, note and sketch-books, colour-box, knife, ammunition, and what not, they will lie there as safe and uninjured as upon a dressing-room or study table. On the Tana we did not at first discover the merit of these small arrangements, but later and in subsequent camping expeditions we brought them to perfection. Guns should also be brought inside the tent; ours suffered from standing in the porch, and in those days of muzzle-loaders a few snaps were the result.

There can be no doubt that the lining is a most luxurious addition to a tent, it precludes the possibility of a chill striking through the wet outer canvas when one is asleep with one's head within a couple of feet of it, and imparts a delightful sense of comfort and security. Moreover, in dry weather it need not be packed in the tent-case, and makes when folded an excellent covering for the bottom-boards of a boat, or softens the asperities of a bed of twigs. I have one capital tent with upright sides and an extra roof of canvas which spreads from a ridge pole into very broad eaves, so that unless the rain is positively horizontal it cannot touch the inner fabric thus protected; but the false roof is apt to be obstreperous in very windy weather.

For a good many years past I have during my sporting excursions occupied a series of specially built wooden huts instead of a tent, and cannot deny that the little permanent home of logs has some great advantages over its nomad cousin of canvas. When the gale is roaring outside there is no anxiety respecting its steadfast walls, independent as they are of rope and peg. When the snow has

fallen and the frost is sharp there is either a small
stove with a metal flue passing through the roof, or,
far better, a hearth on which to kindle a glorious
blaze, and a stone chimney built into the timber.
At such times one realizes the force of Macaulay's
lines :

> ' When round the lonely cottage
> Loud roars the tempest's din,
> And the good logs of Algidus
> Roar louder yet within.'

But, for all that I cannot say of the hut what I have
said of the tent, that no water has ever entered it ;
for I have several times heard the drip of the rain
which had found its way through the roof, and more
than once, to escape the same, have had to leave my
bunk and make up a hay bed on the floor. The
most careful inspection cannot always detect and
remedy this insidious leakage. But tent or hut,
either or both, the angler and hunter will always
regard with affectionate remembrance his pigmy
places of habitation in the wilds.

Late as it was when the storm had passed away,
we determined to shift quarters. The Finns, who
had evidently been having a carouse with their
Russian hosts, were very dull and apathetic, and
the packing of the wet tent was not effected without
much trouble ; but at last we got all on board and
dropped eighteen miles down the river, passing on
the way through an enormous fence of salmon-traps
built up of stakes, stones, and wicker-baskets, and
known in Norsk as ' stængsler,' in Lappish as
' stanga ' or ' buoddo,' and by British anglers at
Alten and elsewhere as ' stengles.' They stretched,

as usual, in two wings slantwise all but right across the stream, leaving a small opening, which they told us at Alten the Kvæns who occupy the valley of that river were in the habit, unless carefully watched, of illegally closing, and thereby entirely blocking the upward passage of the salmon.

In the gray light of a chilly dawn we arrived at a place which the men called, as far as we could make out, Taula-Vados. I have tried to discover a meaning for this name, which is not in the map, but can only hazard a wild conjecture, based, of course, on Friis's lexicon, that it might have been Tóle-Vadas; and as the former word means in dialectic Lappish 'fire,' and the latter 'a little dry place,' the whole might signify a clearing caused by conflagration. But I feel that I have small right to air these amateurish philological efforts.

It was anything but a little dry place now, for the grass was soakingly wet, and the prospect of erecting our tent, wet also, on such ground was not cheering. But as we landed and approached it, there was not a sign of human occupation, and in the end it proved that the settlement, which as far as appearance went might have been a smaller Karasjok, minus the merchant's and priest's houses, was deserted. John, always classically minded, compared our position to that of the ten thousand Greeks as described in Xenophon's 'Anabasis,' who, progressing by regular stages of so many parasangs, with the territory of the great King on the other side of a river, always lighted upon convenient quarters in the shape of an abandoned village. Our course was therefore clear: following the precedent of the Grecian mercenaries, we advanced and took possession of the place in our own names. Our skirmishers, Little Savage and Clamek, found in one of the huts the sole inhabitant, an old woman, who offered no resistance.

We selected as our own residence the best mansion, which clearly belonged to a carpenter, for in the centre of its single room was a planing-table with a vice, and the floor was littered with chips. The place was soon swept and made fairly comfortable, and as there was a fireplace with a chimney, well adapted for cooking, and a mass of collected birch-twigs on which to spread our tent-sheets and mattresses, we had reason to congratulate ourselves on having found such quarters, fairly free from mosquitoes, which were swarming in the clearing and along the river bank.

During our voyage down the Tana we stopped at or passed a dozen villages, all deserted except by an old woman or two, and were never able to discover what had become of the rest of the inhabitants. It is possible that they had joined their nomad brethren, the herders of the deer, and gone with them to the seaside, or that, like the tribe at Assebakte, they were fishing in some of the neighbouring fjeld lakes, where a plentiful supply of trout and char would be sure to reward them, and the capture of fish by nets might be easier than in the Tana. In any case, their absence remained to us a mystery, which our men could doubtless have cleared up, had we been able to understand their explanations.

We stopped at Taula-Vados three days. The weather was again hot and breezeless, and the first morning we both toiled with the rod for three hours, and never moved a fish except the usual trout and grayling. This was terribly disappointing, and we began to think we had come a long way for very little.

As I was returning in my canoe upstream I saw in the water a strange figure in something like acrobatic costume engaged in energetic action not unbefitting the dress. It proved to be John, who, in defiance of mosquitoes, was washing himself and his undergarments at the same time. This struck me as such an excellent idea that I ran up to the hut, partially undressed myself, collected everything that required washing, and returned to join my companion in his double *rôle* of aquatic gymnast and laundry-man. We had a delightful and eminently useful frolic in the clear, cool stream, and then ran madly up and down a convenient stretch of sandy beach, protected by two gray blankets which I had also brought from the house. It was on this day that Herr Barth passed us on his way downstream, but would not accept our invitation to land. A second visit to the river in the evening was slightly more encouraging, as John pricked a heavy fish and I killed two grilse.

About this time I find myself accused in John's journal of strange conduct, not recorded in my own pages. He charges me with repeatedly vociferating my farewells, in a foreign tongue, to a person of the name of Leonora, and my intention of sealing with my blood the love that I had reposed in her; of endeavouring to entice him, or the Finns, or the old woman—for there was none other to entice—to follow me over the downs, on horseback, too! with the absurd aim of winning a blooming bride; of declaring in the very teeth of the Tana that to me

there was no pastime in life to be mentioned with hunting the fox; and, as a climax of audacity, of coolly
requesting that shining river to call at Ella's bower
on its way to the sea, and deliver to her certain
wreaths which I pretended to have flung upon the
stream. And he further asserts that I was guilty
of these extravagances at all seasonable and un-
seasonable times, except when, to use his very
words, I was 'perspiring with serious face over the
frying-pan.'

If these accusations were true—and, as I have
remarked before, the evidence of contemporary
manuscript, especially of one which I have so
often quoted, is indisputable—I can but say that
it must have been well for me that neither Foged
nor lunatic asylum were handy; but in reading
them I derive some satisfaction from the thought
that I must have in a great measure emancipated
myself from the thraldom of the Gray Terror, and
have been, on the whole, despite my vocalized
anguish on the subject of Leonora, in fairly good
spirits. I know that I was so on the second morning
of our stay at Taula-Vados, for I sprang lightly
from my lowly couch of twigs, and was sustained
during my arduous duties with frying-pan and
gridiron by a strong presentiment that I was going
to catch fish. It was a delicious balmy day, with a
light breeze and alternations of cloud and sunshine.
I have reason to believe that I prepared a meal of
more than usual merit, and did not hurry or perspire
unduly over its preparation.

The Finns had lately, in obedience to that spirit
of dogmatism that seems to be instinctive in all
boatmen or other attendants on sportsmen all over

the world, taken upon themselves to assert that our only chance of sport lay in fishing early in the morning or late in the evening, and therefore when, after a quiet pipe and stroll in a lovely birch-clumped mead that we called our park, we sauntered down to the river not long before noon, they were not in a hopeful mood. I do not suppose that they knew much about it, but had probably evolved some theory out of their previous experience with the last expedition. I may point out that time had now become with us a mere matter of conjecture, regulated only by the sun, for John's watch had struck work altogether, and I had forgotten to wind mine up, and started it again according to fancy.

The boatmen also contended, for some reason best known to themselves, that the salmon must be lying in a deep reach with a gentle, swirling current above the place of embarkation, while we were determined to try some broken water which we had caught sight of on the previous day a long way below it, and whither we accordingly went. There were three good pools below the rapid, and on reaching them the men went round like weathercocks, and allowed that our predecessors had killed some good fish there.

Luck in fishing is a theme that has been so often treated of by others that I need not enlarge upon it, but never was there a more astonishing illustration of it than on August 7 at Taula-Vados. The river was broad, and we agreed to fish the same water, I beginning at the first pool and John at the second, and to pass and repass each other as best suited us. I had not cast for ten minutes before there was a plunge and boil in the current, and, to my joy, I was at last fast in a salmon, which Little Savage succeeded

in gaffing, after several futile attempts that made
me fully understand the reason of the forcible
British exclamation impressed on his memory.
The fish weighed 15 lbs., and before long I laid
alongside of him a second of 13 lbs. A third, an 18-
pounder, whose weight, from inexperience, I overestimated, took me down to the lower pool, but was
eventually stretched in his beauty on a sandy beach,
where John joined me, and we compared flies.

There is no note, nor have I any recollection, of what
flies we were respectively using, but it is certain that,
whilst I killed three salmon and rose three others,
John had been so worried by trout and grayling that
no salmon seemed to have had an opportunity of
laying hold of his fly. Whether he rose any or not I
cannot say, but he did not catch one. It must have
been pure luck. Possibly, as I have since found to be
the case, the salmon lay on one side of the pools,
which side I had been fishing, and the inferior fish
on the other, for I rose but very few of the latter
myself; but whatever the cause, the division of labour
and its results were most unfair, and John's disgust
thoroughly justifiable. Finding that his luck did
not change, he went in soon after, and I followed him,
after catching in the lower water a little 7-pounder
and two grilse; then, as always happened, the rise
stopped abruptly. Nothing is more remarkable than
the unanimity with which, as a rule, fish, either
salmon or trout, begin or cease to take over a large
area of water. Here it was that one of the delighted
Finnish boatmen bestowed upon me the distinctive
appellation of ' Luossa Olmai,' which Amut inter-
preted as ' Lax Mand,' or Salmon-man, a sobriquet
which I naturally accepted with the same modest

dignity as did Cooper's hero scout that of Deer-slayer, Path-finder, or Hawk-eye.

In the evening I was out alone for a short time, and must have just missed the rise : one salmon I lost, which appeared to be very heavy, but that is often the case with lost fish, and killed a 12-pounder. John seems out of curiosity to have weighed his catch, unsatisfactory as it was, although several of the trout were from 3 to 5 lbs., and I find the total recorded at 73 lbs., just a pound less than my take of salmon and grilse. Mine was but inferior sport ; the average of the fish was far below what I had expected from the Tana, but at the same time I had caught more of them in a single day than in my whole previous life ; nevertheless, John's bag was certainly the more remarkable.

The next morning we were late in rising, and sent off two of the men to obtain a fresh supply of cream and butter from settlements that they knew of on the Russian side of the river, the store of the solitary local inhabitant not being equal to the demand upon it ; now that our oil-bottles were empty, we used a good deal of butter in cooking.

By the failure of our biscuits we were introduced to rye-meal dampers, baked by the men. This is not a kind of farinaceous food that I should recommend to anyone in training for athletic sports, nor to a dyspeptic subject, but, eaten hot with plenty of butter, we thought it excellent. Of its exact specific gravity as compared with that of lead I am not certain, but should say that it must be slightly heavier than the metal ; when cold and dry it would not be out of place amongst a collection of mummy relics in an Egyptological museum, or it might, perhaps, be cut by a lapidary and polished in slices. Nevertheless, in its warm condition, fresh from the baking-pan, we continued to eat it with much relish all the way down the Tana.

Here also I brought to an end my scientific experiments with our little keg of English pickled pork. I have heard of mountaineers boiling thermometers or barometers—I am never quite sure which, but I believe the former, although I would often have gladly boiled, or roasted, or grilled my own barometer—but I feel sure that boiled thermometer could sooner be reduced to palatable and digestible food than the contents of that keg which had been recommended to us as such delicious eating. I wonder that the waters of the Tana, in which it was so often soaked, did not become brackish in consequence. I will allow that I have since frequently eaten pickled pork which was really excellent, but that which we had with us was a barrelled practical joke. What the Finns did with it I am unable to say ; if they succeeded in consuming it, the ' *dura ilia messorum* ' must beside theirs have been those of a delicate invalid.

We spent a good part of the day wandering about in the woods in search of game, but picked up only an old rype or two. Without a dog it was next to impossible to find or flush the young broods. They were at the best only three parts grown, but excellent eating when obtained, and of that we had to think, now that our purchased stores were nearly exhausted. The sausages were all gone, of the ham only half remained, and of portable soup a six-inch roll ; in condiments, however, we were still affluent. I used subsequently to go regular rounds near the tent

morning and evening, the latter for choice, when the
ryper ran out into the clearings to feed, and in this
way managed to add considerably to our stock of
provisions. There must have been a fair supply of
birds somewhere in the woods.

In the evening we again went a-fishing, and this
time John had the luck, for he caught, besides trout
and grayling—whose capture must in future be
taken as granted—two salmon of 17 and 16 lbs.,
whilst I bagged only a single grilse. The rise was a
very short one, for John persevered for three hours
longer without seeing a fin, nor did my trial of an
artificial spinning-bait in the deep upper water meet
with much success.

On Sunday afternoon we packed up and departed,
leaving the old woman alone in her glory, and on the
carpenter's table a sufficient recompense for our
arbitrary occupation of his house.

On our way to the next camp, after falling
in with a large brood of pintail ducks * and
bagging six flappers, we passed a village of three
or four huts on the Russian bank rejoicing in the
euphonious and disproportionate name of Para-
sooalook. Then, a little farther down, as our
men told us that there would be no houses at
all near our next halting-place, and that there was
a farm or settlement on the Norwegian side some
little distance from the river, called, as far as we
could make out, Lauta-Guaipa, where we could get
more milk and butter, we agreed to lie under the
bank whilst Amut, taking with him a wooden butter-
keg and a couple of bottles, disappeared into the
forest, and in half an hour returned with the supplies.

* *Anas acuta.*

The names of the above places, like those of several others which we passed or stopped at, were not given on Munch's excellent map, which we had with us ; but as it notices only six settlements along the whole course of the Tana on both banks, this was not to be wondered at. Friis's chart of forty years later marks about three times that number ; ' javre,' ' jokha,' 'njarga,' 'suolo,' 'gædge,' and 'giedde,' go for nothing, being only lake, stream, point, island, rock, and mead.

Never was wanderer's tent pitched in a lovelier spot than at Vuovde Guoika, 'The Wooded Stream,' which we reached about ten o'clock. Here was such a bewildering choice of sites, each more attractive than the other, that we spent, as before, a considerable time in selecting one, although conscious that it would not be occupied for more than forty-eight hours at the outside. But one of the delights of life in the wilds is to be, when possible, fastidious in such matters. It was not only a youthful fancy, at least, not with me; it has lasted all my life. I can, moreover, say with truth that I have seldom been out in the forest for the day after elk or other game without being as particular as circumstances would allow in my selection of a spot whereon to pass the one hour devoted to rest, lunch, and a single cigar or pipe. Pages upon pages might be written about the charm of halts in the forest or in the fjeld, always stipulating for the absence of mosquitoes, which, after all, in September, the hunter's month, have ceased to be worthy of regard. Even in the worst weather a great deal can be done towards lessening discomfort by judiciously chosen shelter and a good fire, so that one might be tempted to say with the immortal Dundreary, 'This is snug.'

At Vuovde Guoika our camp was pitched on a
grassy terrace about twenty yards from the river,
which there swept round a rocky point into a
deep, quiet bay with a beach of yellow sand, on
which grew masses of bluest harebells and fragrant
wild thyme ; our tent was also carpeted with these
flowers. Behind it the green slopes of higher
terraces, dotted with clumps of birch, alder, and
mountain-ash, formed the foreground to a wide
glen, which trended gradually upwards between
steep wooded hills capped with buttresses of gray
crag, and, narrowing as it ascended, became merged
in the shadow of a huge mountain that loomed
purple in the dusk, with splashes of cold gray snow
near its summit.

A great beauty of the little park round the tent
was its astonishing trimness. There were no plots
of coarse herbage or tangled weed, the grass was like
that of a well-kept lawn ; no unsightly withered
branches or fallen trunks ; the trees, all in their
prime, were grouped as if planted by a landscape
gardener ; the flower patches spruce and orderly as
the parterres of a London park—can I give them
greater praise ? It is impossible to ignore the
natural artificiality of the scene : the very rocks
that protruded from the soil amidst an undergrowth
of berry-bearing shrubs and ferns had arranged
themselves with an eye to effect. And it was all
Nature's exquisite handiwork. One might imagine
that at her bidding the ' Hauge-folk,' the trolls and
elves of wood and mountain, had been betrimming
the spot against our arrival.

About midnight there came floating down the
river and through the wood ghostly shapes of

THE CAMP AT VUOVDE GUOIKA.

white vapour, which lingered round our tent like
the evil mist-shrouded warlocks that encompassed
the camp of King Olaf; but they worked us no
harm, and at break of dawn were forced to curl
upwards, until, transfigured by the rays of the
rising sun into phantoms of rosy light, they melted
into upper air.

Beautiful as it was, Vuovde Güoika did not appeal
to the soul of the mere angler; there was but little
likely-looking water, the greater part of it being a
long reach without much current, and a sandy bed,
which we used always to consider unfavourable for
salmon. The weather, moreover, continued during
the day very hot and breezeless. However, by
rising tolerably early, John killed a fine salmon of
23 lbs. the morning after our arrival, and I one
of 11 lbs.

About two miles below the tent the Tana received
a tributary, the Levvojok, which we visited the
next day, and which, after catching a small fish
of 8 lbs. off the shingly bar at its mouth, I explored rod in hand; but it proved to be more of
a mountain torrent than anything else, impossible
for salmon to get up. In some of the larger pools
were fish which I took to be char. During my
absence John got a 9-lb. salmon.

On returning to camp I spent an hour or two in
sketching our camp and its surroundings, and then
took a stroll in the woods, where I bagged a couple
of ryper. Towards evening clouds worked up, and
there was a heavy shower, but directly it cleared
we packed up and got off, leaving lovely Vuovde
Guoika in the undisturbed possession of the ' Hauge-
folk.'

12—2

It was but a short stage to the next fishing-station, which the men called Puakko-jallabi; but there is no such name in the map, nor can I conjecture what it means. Beyond the mouth of the Levvojok a splendid snow-fjeld, Rasta-gaisa, came into view, and lower down another barrier of stengles and a village that was positively occupied, for some of the inhabitants, women, children, and dogs, stood on the bank and silently stared at us as we glided by. There was also a beach, with several boats drawn up and nets hung out to dry.

Our camp was established, for a change, on the Finlandic bank of the river, which appeared to offer the only level site for a tent, but its flatness was nothing to boast of ; only by filling up depressions in the turf with birch-twigs were we able to elaborate an area nine feet square on which to lay our waterproof sheets, and even then there was an unreduced monticle just in the small of my back, which greatly interfered with my comfort in bed. The men may have selected this place on account of a rather dilapidated and half-subterranean cabin which gave them shelter, for it was now growing very chilly after sunset, and the two previous nights they had slept in the open. The nearest farm was two miles distant. A plentiful supply of firewood was at hand, the proceeds of tumbledown fences, and before long glorious twin blazes were announcing to the neighbourhood that the ancient encampment was reoccupied.

There was some excellent fishing-water at this place, as good as we had seen. The river was contracted and deep, with a rocky, boulder-strewn shore on the opposite side, and within a mile were two short rapids, each with a large pool below it. Nevertheless, our sport was not remarkable ; it was too late in the season for the fish to be otherwise than capricious in their rise, and we were possibly not persevering enough in our efforts to entice them. There are anglers who will work from morning till night on the chance of a fish, but for John and myself three or four hours of unproductive casting were quite sufficient. It sometimes happened that for that length of time not even trout or grayling would rise, and when they did, we were pretty well sick of them. The trout never appeared to exceed 5 lbs. in weight. The notion of using trout-rods on the Tana was ridiculous. I know now that on its broad flood,. had we oftener resorted to harling we should in all probability have done much better ; but we seldom tried it, it was not as yet in our experience, and we were rather bigoted novices about casting.

But salmon, and good salmon, too, were occasionally willing to take our flies, although they were but few and far between. My sustained efforts on August 12 at Puakko-jallabi resulted in three rises, the first of which proved fatal to a grilse, and the second to a noble 20-pounder, which in the rough water gave my big rod plenty of work before he succumbed to its steady strain and was guided to land, where Little Savage, who, at my suggestion, had been practising on dead trout laid in shallow water, put the gaff in very cleverly and hoisted him out.

The third rise was that of an enormous fish, which rolled up like a porpoise in mid-stream and swallowed my ' butcher,' eliciting from the boatmen by his huge dimensions a murmur of awestruck astonishment. As I have said, lost fish are always

the biggest, but I fully believe that particular salmon
might have tested my weighing-machine to something
like its utmost capability. I never saw him again,
although I had him on for a quarter of an hour. After
running out to begin with some forty yards of line,
he did not rush madly about the pool like smaller
fry of 10 or 12 lbs., but lay boring in the current,
immovable and heavy as a rock, and then—I
know not how it happened, whether I was showing
him the butt just a shade too much, or whether, as
is more probable, the casting-line, which I had not
examined too closely, had become frayed in previous
encounters—there came a short rush and struggle
on the part of the salmon, a boil visible on the surface of the stream, and finally that sickening instant
when the line flies back and the bent rod resumes
its straightness. The Finns uttered a groan, and I
could have plunged overboard after the fish. The
treble gut had parted just above the fly, and the
monster was gone with the ' butcher ' in his mouth.
He must have been well hooked, and would have
been a prize worthy of the big rod.

Meanwhile John, having killed two minnows of
10 and 8 lbs., had returned to the tent, where
I joined him a couple of hours later and told
the sad tale of my lost giant. As he puts it, the
boatmen, in corroboration of my story, ' could only
convey a notion of the fish's magnitude by stretching
their arms, eyes, and mouths to the widest, all the
while ejaculating intensive adjectives.'

The next morning, eager to redeem my misfortune or mismanagement by some real success, I was
up early and down at the pools by six o'clock; but
John, who apparently had not much faith in the

adage that the early bird picks up the worm, and
improvised for the occasion a humorous counter-
maxim of his own, not discreditable to a man disturbed at such an hour, that, although it might be
orthodox to fast on fish, it was quite a mistake to
fish fasting, refused to leave his warm blankets, gave
me his blessing, and sensibly went to sleep again. It
being understood that we were always to act exactly
as we pleased, I did not rail at him for a sluggard
and Sybarite; and when, five hours later, I returned,
weary, hungry, and disappointed, he did not jeer at
me for a misguided zealot, and say 'I told you so,'
but earned my deep gratitude and restored my
equanimity by setting before me a splendid breakfast
of fried fish, broiled ryper, and ham, which he had
cooked himself.

Such was the truly Christian spirit by which,
despite sundry passages of playful chaff, our relations
on the Tana were characterized. In the evening John
had his reward, for whilst I took in the upper water
a single salmon of 12 lbs., he brought back from
the lower pools three, of 18, 17, and 13 lbs., and
several trout—such fine, handsome fish as to be
worthy of special mention.

CHAPTER IX

On August 15 we leave Puakko-jallabi in heavy rain,
and before reaching our next destination have to
pass a long series of formidable rapids. Here the
skill of the Finns in using the 'staggo' or punt-
pole is severely tested, and they reveal themselves as true artists in that line. I will quote
John's sketch of their method during the descent:
'When we hear the roar of the rapids, and are
gliding down the curve of smooth water that over-
hangs them, the steersman rises, laying aside his
paddle and taking a pole instead. Now the little
shallop begins to dance like a cork, and the waves
try to seize their moment for jumping in upon us. A
black reef is seen jutting out of water right across
our bows, and while we hold our breath and prepare
for a jolt or a capsize, behold it gnashing its teeth
and foaming several yards astern. The Arimaspian
is all eye. We are on the brink of a long babbling
slope that looks more like a stony lane than a river,
and I begin to think that our very best way will be
to get out and walk. By a well-timed movement of
the pole the boat is brought up short, and rides
quietly in some log water, while the mariners re-
connoitre. Clamek has relinquished the sculls, and

stands at the bows armed with a pole, and double
punting commences; both men remain perfectly
still, and "stack" together as evenly as if they were
parts of one machine. We creep down the deepest
part of the channel, only grating here and there,
until we see the stones shelve off and become dimmer
as we gaze over the gunwale; we are once more in
deep water.'

These manœuvres are repeated until we and
the baggage-boat are clear of the dangerous rapids,
and then follow a couple of serene hours between
shingly and sandy bars, high rocks, and overhanging woods, until we land, about midnight, at
a spot on the Norwegian bank opposite the Russian
settlement of Utsjoki.

The long grass is very wet, and we decide to defer
the erection of the tent until morning, but no shelter
presents itself except a wretched half-ruined shanty,
which Amut sarcastically terms a 'svinesti,' or pig-
sty; it is certainly not an attractive residence even
for a single night, and therefore we follow his advice
and cross the river in search of something better.
Here is a small village, deserted as usual, the omnipresent old woman and a child being the representatives of the absent population.

As Utsjoki proper—in Finsk Ocjok—the most important Finlandic settlement in the Tana district,
boasting a church and parsonage, lies on the
Mandojavre, a lake some miles from the river,
we do not see it, and the hamlet in which we
find ourselves, called also Utsjoki by the boatmen,
must be a suburb of that capital. The old woman,
who occupies the biggest house, places a room in
it at our disposal, but the sight and smell thereof

are sufficient. With hasty thanks for her proffered
hospitality we withdraw and recross the river, determined to do the best we can with the despised pig-sty.

It was evidently once the habitation of human
beings, but is now tenanted by a colony of rats, whose
runs lead through the rank herbage in all directions.
The roof is of turf, overgrown with moss and matted
vegetation, through which protrude the remnants of
a stone chimney; the single window has fallen out
and the door dropped from its hinges, but there is still
standing a rather curious external porch, with a dome
of turf and rafters supported by dead birch stems,
and beneath its shelter we stow our baggage. The
interior conveniences consist of a fireplace, with
a heavy, serviceable hearthstone, and a long row
of stout pegs, on which we hang our wet garments
and the smaller articles of baggage. Our first
care is to light a big fire, and, to our surprise and
joy the chimney does not smoke. We then, all using
our knives assiduously, cover the entire floor with
a layer of damp birch twigs a foot thick, and over
these spread the canvas lining of the tent. A couple
of logs found outside are brought in and judiciously
disposed as chairs and tables, and our apartment is
furnished.

Our men then bid us good-night, and once
more cross the river, to take possession of the
odoriferous room which we had declined to occupy.
Left to ourselves, we cook a good supper of broiled
flappers and preserved peas, and what with the blaze
of the fire and the simmer of the kettle, attain almost
domestic comfort, for the mosquitoes are demoralized
by the wet and cold, and we have hung nets over
door and window. The occasional rustling of the

rats imprisoned under the birch twigs and canvas is of little consequence. It is morning before we fall asleep, and mid-day before the Finns return to rouse us.

The weather being fairly warm and sunny after the rain, we have a bath in the river, and then get the tent up in a spot that almost equals Vuovde Guoika in beauty, although it lacks its complete seclusion and freedom from signs of man, as well as the background of crag and lofty mountain; the birch-clad hills are lower and more undulating in outline. But there is the same trim lawn with a profusion of flowers, the same prospect through the tent door of the clear blue river, the same leafy shadows playing on the canvas, and as yet the same tranquillity, broken only by the gurgle of water and the susurration of foliage.

It is therefore with no small surprise that, when on this 16th of August, after spending a quiet Sunday afternoon in or about the tent and enjoying the summer-like weather, I go out to fish at seven o'clock in the evening, I find it become of a sudden so bitterly cold that I cannot sit in the boat any longer, and am obliged to land and run back to restore the circulation to my numbed limbs. I have caught a salmon of 10 lbs., and find that John, who has also been driven in by the cold, has another about the same size.

I regret that we have no thermometer to register the degree of frost; it must be intense, for in that short time the water in can and kettle has been masked with ice nearly an inch thick, sundry articles of clothing which were washed and hung out to dry are as stiff as boards, and all objects are covered with white rime. It is one of the so-called 'iron nights' of occasional occurrence, when in these high latitudes the breath of winter strikes into the heart of autumn and foretells the approach of the pitiless tyrant. Strange it is to reflect in how short a time the flower-besprinkled lawns, the broad green woods, and even the blue current of Tana itself, will be covered by a uniform mantle of snow, and the reindeer sleigh of Finn and Lapp glide beneath the Aurora over the sunlit pools where we have been casting our lines.

There is one great good in an 'iron night': it routs the mosquitoes with enormous slaughter. That any of them should survive it is the wonder, but that they do I can testify; and a far greater marvel is their infernal power of protecting their eggs and imparting to them such vitality that their venomous broods can laugh at the terrible might of the Ice King, and be ready to emerge unscathed with the leaves, the grass, and the flowers—the eternal evil with the eternal good. This night we require our warmest coverings, and before creeping under the blankets put a brazier inside the tent for half an hour, and to be in keeping with this unusual luxury put a cup of hot grog inside ourselves after we are in bed, and so, with a final pipe and a chat over plans for to-morrow, go comfortably to sleep. The Finns have long ago returned to their lodging in the Utsjokian suburb.

The morrow finds us oppressed by sundry cares. To begin with, our stock of tobacco is so low that, after anxious consultation, we feel compelled to restrict ourselves to a single pipe each per day, which may be consumed either after breakfast or the last thing at night, according to fancy; it is hard, but unavoidable, self-denial. Then the supply of extra

wicks for the spirit-lamps, our only means of lighting
the tent at night, seems to have been left behind or
lost, and our ingenuity is sorely taxed in providing
a substitute for the real thing. Of spirit we have
plenty in a huge metal flask, but, as John humorously
remarks, it is unluckily not a wicked spirit. After
several abortive experiments, the brilliant idea strikes
me of utilizing part of the bandages which we have
brought with us in case of accidents, and have happily
not been obliged to use. Cut in strips and rolled
they are found to answer admirably, and our minds
are at ease on the score of illumination and the means
of boiling the kettle in the tent.

And now comes a much more serious question,
that of flies. It is always difficult for beginners to
harden their hearts in the purchase of an inexhaustible stock of those very expensive items in an
angler's outfit which the Americans call ' dollar
bugs.' The huge plethoric volumes of later life are
often the result of sad experience and perhaps more
ready cash. But our store of flies would, I dare say,
have been amply sufficient had it not been for the
havoc wrought among them by the trout and grayling, and on this contingency we had naturally not
reckoned   It is pitiful to see the condition to which
many of our choicest and largest specimens of the
fly-tyer's art have been reduced by the persistent
attacks of the rapacious pirates ; and the large flies
are those that we particularly want, for our next
halt will be at Galggo Guoika, where, the boatmen
assure us, we are likely to have better sport than
hitherto.

It behoves us, therefore, to make an effort,
and devote some hours to the reparation of our

lures. Silk thread and cobbler's wax we have, and by dissecting some flies for the benefit of their brethren, and adding feathers from duck and ryper, we succeed in constructing a few insectile phenomena that are, at all events, likely to make the salmon stare. This afternoon they do not get beyond staring, for our attempt at fishing does not produce a single rise, and we return to camp much disgusted.

I have mentioned that Little Savage was a humorist. About this time his sense of humour nearly got him into serious trouble. It so happened that the fancy took John to cook for himself a salmon cutlet, using for that purpose the gridiron belonging to our camp-kettle. Now this was a treacherous implement, with a tendency to revolve on its handle, which vicious propensity had to be checked by the insertion of a nail or wedge of wood. Whether this precaution had been neglected, or whether the wedge, either of metal or wood, had fallen out, I know not, but it is certain that when John's well-buttered cutlet was just done to a turn, to that delicate pinkish-brown which is so appetizing, it was suddenly deposited in the embers by a cruel revolution of the gridiron. Little Savage, who was standing a few yards off, watching the cookery with eager eyes—for he was greedy as well as humorous—was so tickled by this lamentable catastrophe as to indulge in a loud chuckle, and—it was then as well for him that he was young and active, and understood the art of ' ducking and avoiding.'

Lever, in his immortal novel, ' Charles O'Malley,' makes Count Considine remark that he has seen ' a cut-glass decanter, well aimed and low, do effective service.' I would humbly submit that, regarded as a missile, a hot gridiron is even superior, and has the merit of being less commonplace.

That Little Savage realized the impropriety of his ill-timed mirth was evident from the penitent air with which he recovered the volant and errant gridiron, and carefully replaced it among the cooking utensils.

He had previously received a lesson in the matter of inquisitive greediness. One day he was audaciously watching us eat our supper, and could not repress his curiosity at the sight of the bottle of cayenne pepper, the vivid hue of which appeared to fascinate him. So evident was his desire to taste the contents that I resolved to gratify it, and emptied into his outstretched palm a small spoonful of the scarlet condiment, which, with a triumphant glance at his less fortunate comrades, he immediately licked up.

I need not go into details of the result. Luckily for him the water-can was handy. We were never troubled again by inquisitive supervision during meals.

In the evening, after our meal, we are visited by a party of Russian Finns, two of whom are remarkably handsome, one a very tall, dark man, and the other a youth of about seventeen, with a really lovely girlish face; if he has a sister like him she must be one of the belles of Finland. Another of the company is an angler, and, to our surprise, exhibits with much pride a fly, if I may so call it, of his own making. It is tied on a huge hook, the body of red cloth, and the wing a single brown and white feather nearly erect; two large shining beads form the eyes. He tells us that with this monster he

yesterday caught a big salmon, and that he takes a
good many in the course of the season. There is
clearly hope for our own monstrosities; but we cannot
pretend to imitate the glaring, beady eyes, which may
exercise on the fish the same fascination as those of
the serpent on its prey.

Our guests are very curious and inquisitive, and
hearing from the boatmen that we have revolvers,
are anxious to see them. So we set up the lid of a
keg as a target at 25 yards, and make good practice
thereat, the Finns shouting with delight and astonishment each time the bullet strikes. To further im-
prove the occasion, I get out the rifle, and cut over
the same mark three times in succession at 150 yards.

The news that Englishmen are on show having
spread, we are favoured the next day with more
visitors, who are rather in the way while we are
packing, but by three o'clock we are able to bid
them good-bye and drop down the river to Galggo
Guoika, a stage of only twelve miles, broken halfway by a halt at a beautifully - situated Russian
village, whence we obtain a good supply of milk and
butter.

Here, at Galggo Guoika, called in Norsk ' Kone
Fos,' 'Woman Fall,' which seems to confirm the
meaning of the Lappish title, we find at last traces
of our friends; the marks of three fires, a stand for
rods, and scattered about the grass a number of
rejected scraps of rubbish, which have doubtless
already afforded an interesting field of research to
the local children.

In my journal I record my opinion that Galggo
Guoika is by far the best fishing-station on the Tana,
there being a good deal of splendid water, with ample

room for two rods; that it is a charming place, with a choice of excellent sites for a house; and that stores might easily be brought up from the mouth of the river. The correctness of this opinion has been proved by the fact that the Englishmen who have for a number of years fished the Tana have made it their headquarters, and there built their house. Whether other stations have been occupied I am not certain, but both at Utsjoki and Puakkojallabi (if the latter be really the correct name) sport might doubtless be had. A good deal must, I think, depend on the present position and condition of the stengles; but the magnificent Tana has always proved to be an uncertain river.

While the Finns, who are now quite competent to do the work without instruction, are putting together our pavilion, we are informed that the headman of the neighbouring village, whoever he might be, objected to its erection; but of this we, of course, take no notice, and neither does the objector appear in person, nor is any subsequent attempt made to interfere with us. It shows, however, how soon native simplicity is corrupted by contact with aliens ; it is possible that the so-called headman may have thought the occasion good for mulcting the strangers. I have known similar instances in other parts of Norway where we as first-comers were welcome and free to do as we pleased, but from those who followed in our footsteps payment was demanded, and allow that it was natural and not unfair. I may notice that the tax imposed of late years on anglers in the Tana by means of a license was not in force in our time.

From the large number of mosquitoes which have

survived the 'iron night' at Galggo Guoika, we can
well understand that the plague must have been
terrible earlier in the season, although it can scarcely
have equalled its incredible development on the fjeld.
I conclude that those who fish the Tana nowadays
must have studied the science of self-protection by
suitable clothing, gauntlets, hats, and veils, and
possibly by the use of some of the many preparations
which have been recommended as rendering the
human cuticle distasteful to the bloodthirsty insect ;
but on this point I have no authentic information.

On the morning after our arrival I am out alone
on the river by seven o'clock, and going upstream,
begin fishing at the head of the highest pool, where,
to my great annoyance, I hook and lose two good
fish one after the other, and then a third, which has
taken my fly under water, expresses his surprise or
exultation by jumping a clear yard out of it, so that
I strike him in mid-air, and this time get the hook
well home.   After a gallant resistance, the 20-pounder
is coaxed to the bank and neatly hoisted out by
Little Savage, who is becoming quite an expert with
the gaff.   Dropping down to the next pool, I take
another fish, of 13 lbs., and return in good spirits
to camp and breakfast, almost regardless of the mosquitoes, who do their best to spoil a hungry man's
meal.

About noon, finding John inclined to be physically
lazy and mentally energetic over the Lappish vocabulary which he is compiling, and feeling restless myself,
I take a gun and start on an exploring expedition.
In crossing the first hill I discover in a soft spot the,
to me, unknown track of some large animal, which I
suspect to be a bear, and accordingly load the right

barrel with ball. My wanderings bring me to a lovely stream, abounding in clear, rocky pools, but too precipitous in its course to allow the salmon to ascend or me to follow it down to the Tana without infinite trouble. The banks are in several places formed of low cliff and piled-up boulders overgrown with birch, and appear to my eyes to afford ideal dens and lairs for wild beasts; but the heavy bullet destined for big game is eventually expended on a solitary rype, at which I fire the wrong barrel, a mistake revealed to me by the lead cutting in two a small branch half an inch from the bird's head.

Towards evening there is a change in the weather; a violent wind gets up, attended by torrents of rain, which do not prevent our going out on the river, clothed in waterproof. I begin fishing, as before, at the highest pool, John some hundred yards lower down. After casting in vain for nearly an hour, I get a rise in a deep reach with a slow but eddying current, and find myself fast in a big fish. Owing to the rain pelting in my face, and the raging upstream wind, which affects the movements of the light boat and the handling of the heavy rod, it takes me a long time to get on terms with my vigorous captive, who keeps far out in the stream, while there is no suitable place for me to go ashore. But at last, on a convenient bar of shingle, I have the satisfaction of seeing the *coup de grâce* administered to a splendidly-shaped hen fish, which pulls down the indicator to 26 lbs., the heaviest we have yet taken.

After the success comes disaster, for while casting, rather savagely, I fear, in the teeth of the baffling gale, snap goes my mighty rod at the slenderest part of the third joint, and my fishing is over for that

evening at least. As I drop downstream towards
the tent I pass and give a cheer of encouragement to
John, who is holding on to a good one, with which he
not long afterwards makes his appearance, of 22 lbs.

It is a terribly wet, windy night. The men seek
shelter in the village, and we, after a not too comfortable meal, are glad to close the tent and go to
bed, where we smoke the one pipe of the day and chat
for some time before falling asleep. John reveals to
me his discovery in the pages of Herodotus that the
hyperborean races of the Budini and Geloni mentioned by that historian are respectively the Lapps
and Finns, and adduces sundry unanswerable arguments to prove it. For the Geloni, or Finns, are
described by the father of history as foreigners,
husbandmen, dwellers in wooden houses, and eaters
of grain, who have settled among the Budini, or
Lapps, whose language they speak as well as their
own; whereas the latter are autochthons, nomads,
and the only people hereabouts who eat sawdust.
Their country is shaggy with forests, in which lie
large deep lakes and immense reedy fens, whence they
procure the skins of beasts with which they clothe
themselves. The two races are different in language,
appearance, and habits, but the Greeks called them
both Geloni, just as the Norwegians of to-day include
both tribes under the comprehensive term Finn.
They are devout worshippers of Bacchus, and get
roaring drunk in his honour; and of this we ourselves
have ample proof within the next twenty-four hours.

John's discourse is very interesting, but my chief
desire is to know where we can find any of the ' beasts
with square faces ' mentioned by Herodotus as supplying the Budini with part of their furry clothing.

Could it have been the track of one that I came across to-day ? And whilst speculating on this I am overtaken by slumber.

When we wake, very late, the weather is worse than ever ; it is blowing a gale, and at intervals there are tremendous rainstorms. We feel very averse to leaving our warm blankets. A water-ouzel, which has somehow got inside the tent, probably overnight before we closed it, sits for an hour on the keg in the corner and on my knee-boots, bobbing and chirping very pleasantly, and not in the least dismayed.

The Finns, doubtless as unwilling as we are to leave their shelter, do not arrive until nearly noon, but as a peace-offering they bring with them a huge ' melke-bunke,' a wooden dairy-pan filled with curds covered with half an inch of slightly sour coagulated cream, and on this we feast at breakfast. They declare that it is too rough to go on the river, but as the weather temporarily improves in the afternoon, we take to the boats.

My big rod not being provided with a spare third joint, as it ought to have been, and was by the next season, I have to fall back on what I call my little seventeen-foot Irish rod, in reality big enough for anything, but feeling like a wand in the hand after the disabled giant. Within the hour I extract from the upper reach two salmon, of 17 and 16 lbs., and then the gale recommences with such fury that I have to give up, and reach camp just in time to escape being swamped. John, who has gone down to some better sheltered water, returns later, weather-beaten and streaming, but in excellent spirits, with four fish, of 19, 20, 23, and 7 lbs., so that we feel altogether

well satisfied with the results of our afternoon's
fishing.

The next day is almost as stormy and rainy, and
being determined to give the weather a chance, and
the water a longer trial before evening, we spend the
morning in the tent in various occupations, including
that of patching up more flies. At four o'clock we
go out, I up to the old reach, John again to the lower
water. The experiment of a longer trial is not successful, for I flog perseveringly for more than two
hours, fishing all my water twice over with a change
of flies, without getting a rise from a salmon; but the
weather meanwhile improves so much that before
the evening the sun puts in an appearance, and at
last rests on the crest of a rather peculiar hill of
conical shape, thereby marking the hour of seven or
thereabouts. This appears to be the signal for the
rise to begin, and for me to have a merry time.

I first prick a good fish, which rolls away with a
boil and a plunge; a couple more casts and a sudden
check on the line like that of a sunken log announces
something out of the common. For a few seconds he
lies stationary, and I show him the butt and hold on
for all I am worth to get the hook well in; then he
runs for a clear sixty yards out into the deepest water,
rises to the surface and shows his tail, to my excited
vision as broad as a boat. A change of tactics takes him
to the bottom, where for ten minutes he bores motionless, except for a series of horrible jerks, very trying
to the nerves. Perhaps he knows of a stone down
there which may assist him in his efforts to escape.

His next move is to press slowly but irresistibly
upstream, and we are obliged to follow until he
alters his mind, and, running out more line, nears

the opposite bank and begins to float slowly
down again. An anxious minute ensues when he
finds a rock and lies up behind it, so that I have to
get below and put on a slanting strain to dislodge
him. Evidently infuriated by this artifice on my
part, he makes a sudden rush, causing the reel to
whizz, and ends by apparently turning a somersault
on the surface. But the gallant fish is past further
serious resistance. For nearly half an hour he has
fought against the constant strain and sinewy play
of the rod, and must now yield to the inch by inch
drag of the pitiless reel. When I have recovered
most of my line and see the broad silvery side roll
over in the water, I know that he is beaten, and that
I may venture to search for a landing-place; it
has become simply a question of whether the hook
will retain its hold.

In playing a salmon there is no more critical time
than when he is being brought up to the gaff. But
now all goes well; my captive makes his final
instinctive effort when he catches sight of the Finn
crouching on the shingle, but cannot sustain it. He
is carefully but firmly checked and towed back, the
steel flashes, and in a minute all is over. I find that
I have overestimated his weight. I thought he was
the 'vog,' or 40-pound salmon, of my dreams; still,
he is a grand fish of 34 lbs., and very handsome,
despite his partially developed beak.

There is no time to lose; I know that the rise
will soon be over, and must to work again. Beginning once more at the head of the reach, I hook
and lose in half a minute a nice fish, then kill two
of 17 and 11 lbs., miss two others, pricking
one of them, and wind up with a 19-pounder just

before the shadow of the conical hill darkens the whole water, when the rise stops as if by magic ; not another fish will stir. While we paddle quietly down to where the white tent glimmers like a phantom through the dusk, I reflect with satisfaction that our friends have not caught all the salmon at Galggo Guoika, and that those which survive have a fair chance of taking our flies, for we have not been pestered to any extent by trout and grayling. There are either fewer of them or they have adopted separate hours of rising.

I find John, who, after killing a small fish to begin with, had become weary of fruitless casting and gone in, great on the subject of wolves. A hundred yards behind our camp there is a very small rushy pond surrounded by a thicket of birch and alder, where we killed a couple of ducks the evening of our arrival, and since then one or the other of us have bagged several more by sneaking up to it whenever there was an odd ten minutes to spare ; we began to regard it as a certain draw for a duck.

Accordingly, John, as soon as he had got rid of his rod, took his gun and made the usual cautious approach to the thicket. Peering between the bushes, he spied lapping the water exactly opposite to him on the other side of the pond, which was not ten yards wide, an animal which at first he took for a huge dog, and then it flashed across him that it was a wolf, a beast which Amut had mentioned only the day before as not being uncommon in these parts. Taking careful aim at its lowered head, he pulled the trigger, and the treacherous gun, which had gone off freely enough at ducks, snapped on this important occasion. In half a second the wolf was round and

lost in the thicket, into which John pour d the
second barrel without effect.

Shortly afterwards the beast must have been
seen by some Finns who were haymaking not far
off, for raising a shout of 'Gumpe! gumpe!'* they
all began running down the river bank as hard as
they could. John at once joined in the race, and
would doubtless soon have gone to the front had he
not been arrested by a sense of the absurdity of
trying to catch a wolf on foot, a task more hopeless
even than that of Leech's 'distinguished foreigner'
who declared to the indignant whip that he would
try to catch a fox on horseback; and so he left the
remainder of the field to pursue their wild career,
strolled back to camp, and took a ramble over the
hills, in the hope of meeting some beast, square-
faced or otherwise, but with a total want of success.
We vow, nevertheless, that we will have a private
wolf-hunt before leaving Galggo Guoika.

Another cold, rainy morning finds us occupied in
or about the tent, after a very late breakfast, and in
the afternoon we both go to the upper water. Halfway up I get out of my canoe and walk, being in no
hurry to begin before seven o'clock, which is undoubtedly the hour when the rise comes on. On a
strip of soft beach I discover the tracks of two
wolves, which seem to have swum over the river the
night before, eight impressions as large as a man's
hand spread out; the trail continues upstream
beyond the spot where I am obliged to re-embark.
It is quite clear in which direction we must pursue
the chase to-morrow.

As an angler, I am again doomed to misfortune,

* 'Wolf! wolf!'

for the first fish I get hold of, a very heavy one,
manages to snap my casting-line at the knot above
the fly, and departs with my choicest lure and a
couple of feet of treble gut. Meanwhile John has
gone to land with a fish of 18 lbs. He gets one more
of 12 lbs., and I three, of 16, 13, 8 lbs., and a grilse.
My lost fish was worth the lot put together. I also
get a thorough ducking, for in stepping out of the
boat my foot catches on one of the sculls, and I fall
flat on my face in a foot of water. I therefore walk
home again at a rapid pace. It is bitterly cold, with
a sharp shower of sleet.

It is just as well that we have no intention of
going on the river the next day, for when we come
out of the tent we find all our Finns more or less
intoxicated, in company with a strange party of their
compatriots. On going down to the beach to wash,
the secret of their inebriety is revealed by a small
keg of strong-smelling, ardent spirits standing in the
bows of one of the newly-arrived boats. Little
Savage and Clamek, the least drunk, go at our
bidding with reeling gait to fetch ' buttes chaccé '*
and ' muorra dollé,'† and clean the cooking utensils.
Amut and Mikkel are incapable of doing more than
stagger round the fire, occasionally addressing us
with absurd solemnity by our full names for the
benefit of their friends ; they are all quite harmless
in their cups.

Breakfast over, we lace up and peg down the
tent porch, take with us lunch and flask, gun and
revolver, and start on our expedition up the river.

Nothing ' rues the hunting of that day ' except a
few duck, teal, and ryper that we pick up on our

* Clean water.   † Firewood.

way home. But we have a long and interesting ramble in the wildest possible country, and are not greatly troubled by mosquitoes.

It is not difficult to follow the trail of the wolves from the spot where I found it for about a mile up the bank, but when it turns off into the forest it baffles us; no eyes except those of a Red Indian or an Australian black could detect it on the firm soil beneath the trees. A considerable distance inland from the river there is, however, a deal of broken ground, backed by a low cliff. We agree that if 'gumpe' has a residence in these parts it is pretty sure to be thereabouts, and after a long, patient search, actually find it, a snug lair enough, well sheltered by an overhanging bank and the gnarled roots of a tree. Although the proprietor is unluckily absent, there are signs of quite recent occupation.

An exploration of the neighbourhood failing to reveal fresh traces, we climb to higher ground and vainly search the country, as far as possible, with our glasses. Then, after a rest and some food, we arrange to separate and meet again at a conspicuous knoll not far from the river, communicating with each other by our whistle signals. I arrive at the rendezvous without seeing or hearing anything of John, and sit down on the crest of the knoll to enjoy the magnificently wild prospect around me. At my feet is a park-like expanse of grass and many-coloured moss, diversified with copses of birch and underwood, through which a small stream winds like a silver thread to join the Tana. The great river itself sweeps on in splendid curves between its shoals of shingle and clean yellow sand, and beyond it lies an interminable green wilderness of rolling woodland, broken here and there by a cluster of sombre pines or a rocky bluff towering above the level tree-tops. I sit for some time watching the fish rising in the deep reaches below and listening to the far-off crow of the ryper, until roused by John's shrill whistle call, 'Where are you?' to which I immediately reply, and descend to join him. Working slowly home, we fire a few shots and make, as I have said, a small mixed bag.

Strange as it may appear to say so, we were during this and other similar rambles exposed to the chance of a terrible danger, of which we took not the least account at the time, nor was it brought home to me until some years later, when I read Herr Barth's account of his visit to Tana in his capacity of inspector of forests. I will quote the passage in which he alludes to this danger.

Some way above Assebakte the monotony of the birch forest gives place to a long stretch of valuable pine-wood, which it was his duty to examine, and he had landed for this purpose, luckily in the company of one Anders Johnsen, a headman among the Karasjok Finns. I must mention that Herr Barth had shortly before had a narrow escape during the passage of a rapid, when his canoe stuck on a rock, happily near shore, to which he and his companion scrambled with difficulty, while the rush of water cleared all their effects out of the boat. This is what he says:

'While we strolled along a small sandy path running through the wood, I in front and Anders behind, with a step between us, suddenly I was dragged back by a strong pull on my shoulder.

" Ulvesax !"* said Anders, when he had stopped me, and at the same time showed me sticking out of the sand in an expansion of the path a little bit of a single link of the chain to which the trap was fastened. My next step would have been right into it. But my guide, suspicious of such a danger, had the whole time kept his attention fixed on the path, and so perceived it, mercifully before it was too late. I would far sooner have perished in the rapid, bad though that would have been, than have been caught and mutilated for life in the horrible wolf-trap, and it gave me such a turn to think how narrowly I had escaped as I have never in my life felt before or since in the presence of personal danger.'

Now, it happened that on this very occasion when John and I were following the wolf tracks up the river bank we noticed a portion of some iron apparatus projecting from the sand ; but as the wolves had passed clear of it, or, as is probable, it had been laid only overnight by some of the local Finns who had heard of my discovery, and we were intent on their trail, we neither meddled with nor examined it, and in the end forgot all about the matter, but I find a note of it in my journal.

At that time it was customary and permissible to use, besides the steel-traps, every kind of detestable engine and contrivance for the destruction of wild beasts and big game all over Scandinavia : the ' selv-skud,' an arrangement of heavily-loaded spring-guns round the carcass of an animal killed by a bear ; the ' grop,' or covered pitfall, for wolf or elk, sometimes furnished with sharp spikes to impale the fallen animal ; the ' led,' or wicket, generally set for elk,

* Wolf-shears.

an opening in a fence commanded by a spear, which was driven horizontally with terrific force by a bent sapling fastened in proper position and released on touching a wire; the 'rev-krok,' or fox-hook, in which a young upright tree, curved into the form of a bow with a stout cord and big hook attached, also played its part, and several others. But those mentioned were the most dangerous, because they were so well concealed that it was next to impossible for human beings, unless previously warned, to detect them, especially in the dusk, and many terrible and often fatal accidents were the result. My Lapp elk-hunter who attended me for several years was in his boyhood seriously injured in a pitfall, and one of his relations was killed by a 'selv-skud.'

Lloyd, in his 'Scandinavian Adventures,' gives a detailed account, with illustrations, of these deadly devices, except, I think, the 'selv-skud.' To the success of the latter in killing bears I can bear witness, for when we returned to Alten we were informed that the gentleman in the brown cloak had been recently very active in the neighbourhood of Raipas, and killed several cows within a radius of ten miles, which induced us and Honywood to spend a couple of nights in the forest by two of the carcasses, in the hope of getting a shot at the murderer when he returned to his feed. Had we been posted, after the manner of Indian sportsmen, and as recommended also by Lloyd, in the pine-trees, we might have had a chance, but as it was, no bears to my knowledge came near us. I will allow that one night, after some hours of intense watchfulness, I fell sound asleep. The beast no doubt prowled around, detected the presence of Englishmen, and resolved to defer his meal. But no

sooner had we got back to Raipas than the farmer
arranged their ' selv-skud,' and in this ignominious
way were two bears bagged within the week. Nothing
was left for us but to ride up and mournfully inspect
their dead bodies.

It used to be customary in the old days to post on
the church doors notices of the localities in which
spring-guns, pitfalls, traps, and the like were set,
which was all very well in districts where there was
a resident priest and service all the year round; but
in remote regions like Finmark, where churches were
few and far between, and open only in winter, such
a safeguard against accident was inoperative.

For many years now, however, all lethal devices of
the kind have been abolished by law under heavy
penalties ; the use only of poison is permitted, and
that in all conscience is bad enough, but some allowance must be made for the farmer desirous of protecting his flocks and herds from evil beasts. The
sportsman is, at any rate, safe from such a disaster
as threatened Herr Barth.

I have often thought what a dreadful fate it would
have been when on a solitary ramble far from camp
to have been pinned through thigh or knee by the
horrible spikes of the wolf-trap, and be held to pass
a night of agony, with the chance, if an artery was
pierced, of dying of loss of blood before morning, and
the certainty, if one survived, of becoming a cripple.
To be impaled in a pitfall would be as bad, and the
' selv-skud ' by comparison a happy release.

On reaching camp, we found Little Savage and
Clamek penitently lighting the fire ; the other two
were still incapable, and we indignantly ordered them
off to their lodging. But they returned later, for

when we had closed the tent and were in bed, the last sounds that reached our sleepy ears were those of drunken shouts and laughter and staggering feet; the orgy had recommenced.

We had decided to leave Galggo Guoika the next day, as the weather seemed to be rapidly breaking up, and we could not tell what obstacles there might be in the way of our catching the steamer in the Tana fjord. That day, too, the Storfos would have to be negotiated, by all accounts a tremendous rapid, requiring a long and difficult portage, and much care in taking down the boats. So we were astir in good time, and, to our delight, were greeted by a bright sun and a warm breeze when we opened the porch of the tent. The strange canoes and the keg of spirits had departed— the latter was probably empty—and our men were all sober again, but, to judge of their repeated applications to the water-can, afflicted, as John observed, by what the faculty call crapulousness and the vulgar hot coppers.

While they were taking down the tent, a number of the villagers came to see us, and a woman applied to me for some remedy for a bad scythe-cut on the palm of her very dirty hand. The wound was not fresh, and quite healthy without any inflammation, but had never closed properly, and caused her, I dare say, a good deal of pain and inconvenience when at work. I first insisted on the hand being thoroughly washed in warm water from our kettle, and then closed the cut with common sticking-plaster which I overlaid with strips of diachylon, and finally bound up the whole artistically with one of my brand-new bandages, putting in a stitch or two to keep it in place. The bystanders murmured their applause at this wonderful surgical feat, and as for the woman herself, she regarded the damaged member and its clean white wrappings with the same pride and delight that a new bonnet or dress might excite in more civilized lands, and exhibited it to all her friends in turn, positively cooing with satisfaction. It was as well that we were leaving, otherwise I doubt not that I should soon have been overwhelmed by an extensive practice. It has since been my lot to treat various injuries and ailments, and to put on a good many bandages, but amid much gratitude I have never met with delight to equal that of my first patient, the Finn woman on the Tana.

I utilized the last five minutes while the baggage was being carried to the boats by rushing off to the little pond, where, as usual, I bagged my duck, a pintail, and returned at the same pace, to find all ready for a start.

We were sorry to leave Galggo Guoika. Considering how late we were, it had served us well in the matter of fishing, and we knew that it was the last camp into which we could settle down for awhile before leaving the Tana altogether. Amid the kindly farewells of the inhabitants, we took our departure on a most lovely afternoon, and in a couple of hours, after calling at a Russian village, where our men borrowed a long light rope, to be returned on their home journey, reached the head of the mighty Storfos rapid.

Here we and all our heavy baggage were deposited on the rocky shore, and the men proceeded to take down the boats one at a time. It seemed incredible

that they could ever arrive safely at the broad pool
which was just visible at the bottom of the half-mile
hill of raging water and foaming reef ; but they did
their work splendidly.   Little Savage, springing with
wonderful steadiness from boulder to boulder along
the shore, paid out or held on to the rope, which was
attached to the stern of the canoe wherein Amut and
Mikkel, both standing up, handled their poles as
calmly as they did on the quietest reaches of the
river.   The collaboration of the three men was
perfect; peril after peril was mastered without any
apparent sign of nervousness or misunderstanding.
Who would suppose that they had all been more or
less intoxicated for twenty-four hours ?   As the
descent of the rapid had to be accomplished twice, I
had plenty of time to try and sketch the scene, which
was very striking.   It was just sunset, and the wild,
rocky shores, the rushing river, the bold hills, and
overhanging woods, were lit up by a strong yellow
glare, amid which the figures of the Finns in their
picturesque costume, with touches of bright colour,
stood out with great effect.

The safe passage of the rapid by both boats
was followed by a most laborious portage, for
the shore consisted entirely of boulders of every
size and shape, from a block as big as a house
downwards.   This occupied a long time, and as it
was getting late, John and I went forward, and after
a short climb entered an enclosure, where some
Russian Finns were haymaking.   They welcomed us
civilly, and we tried to explain who we were and
what we wanted, permission to erect our tent on
their grass.   This was readily accorded as soon as
the men arrived, and being able to obtain from the

Finlanders plenty of fladbrod and curds and cream, we had quite a feast before turning in.

There was a magnificent pool below the rapid, in which we caught during the short time we tried it two fine fish of 25 and 21 lbs., and in the evening I shot a brace of ryper out of the brushwood on the edge of the clearing; but it was so dark that, had it not been for the white pinion feathers, I could not have seen the birds when they rose.

The next day we were in the boats by noon, and on our way to Polmak, ten miles down the river, the first settlement on Norwegian territory on the east bank, where we were told there was a merchant's house with a resident proprietor. Another long rapid had to be passed, but it was nothing like so dangerous as the Storfos, and there was no need for us to land or to unload the boats. The Finns exhibited their usual skill with the pole, but owing to the low gunwale, we took in a certain amount of water, which interfered with the comfort of our bed on the bottom boards. Once through, the river became broader and shallower, with but little current, until we sighted the merchant's yellow-ochre-coloured house at Polmak, and fired a volley to announce our coming. This brought out a jolly-looking bearded Norwegian to greet us heartily as we stepped upon the beach. He had expected us, and as soon as we were seated in his comfortable parlour, with a bottle of sherry before us, handed me a letter from Hambro. It was dated Hammerfest, August 1, and I extract from it the following passages :

'We left the Tana on the 29th, driven away, I confess, by the mosquitoes, after a week's fishing, that is, Clover and I fished three days, Smith and

14—2

Guest six, in which time we took 650 lbs., the
fish running from 12 to 31 lbs. Polmak was our
headquarters, whence we went twenty-one miles
up the river, and pitched our tent near some good
pools. No longer than a day after we had left
we heard that you had landed at Alten to cross the
country, and we felt more disgusted than I can
describe at having left so as to miss you. We had
a long discussion about going back, but have given
up the idea, as the chances are so great against our
meeting. I hope you have had a pleasant journey,
but fear not. . . .'

To think of it! 650 lbs. in the week, only
50 lbs. less than we had taken during our month,
and to be driven away in the midst of such grand
sport by the curse of Finmark, the Gray Terror!
But I can quite understand it. If the mosquitoes
were only half as bad at Galggo Guoika in July of
that year as they were on the fjeld, I believe, when
I remember my own feelings in the log-hut at Assebakte, that we should have been driven away too ;
we could not escape, and they could, which makes
all the difference.

That night in the house of Skanker, for such was
the merchant's name, we were treated to the
almost forgotten luxury of sheets, and in the morning
to coffee and cakes brought by handmaidens to the
bedside, according to the good old Norwegian
fashion. It is surprising to find that after this
brief relapse into Sybaritism we retained sufficient
insane energy to start in the afternoon with our tent
and all the men up the Polmak River to the great
lake of the same name, where we camped, and
tramped laboriously over many miles of forest and

fjeld in search of a bear, of which we found no traces.
We had for a guide a local barbarian of repulsive
appearance and an unpronounceable name, whom
we christened Bonthron. He had a hut on the lake,
and was said to be a mighty hunter, having killed
in that district fifteen bears to his own gun. I
expect that he had exterminated them, for he failed
to show us the faintest sign of one, and a snarling
cur which at the start he tried to coax into following
us had sense enough to have important business
in the opposite direction, and ran off to attend
to it.

I will not go into the details of our wanderings in
that wild region ; we saw a considerable number of
ryper, which probably showed themselves because
our guns were loaded with ball. Several things
remain impressed on my memory without the aid
of journals: that Polmak-vand—Buolbmag-javre in
Finsk—is a splendid sheet of water amid grand
surroundings ; that there ought to be good fishing in
it, for there is nothing to prevent the salmon
running up from Tana, and we noticed many
trout rising ; that on it we saw, out of shot,
a flock of splendid long-tailed ducks ;* that no
stream, I believe, in the world, not Mæander itself,
has so many maddening windings as the Polmak
river ; and that on a sticky flat left by receding
waters we picked up a number of garnets : they and
their clay-bed were probably the result of disinte-
grated mica schist. No, there is one thing more,
that John let fall his favourite cutty-pipe on the
stones and broke it, and that his temper was in
consequence for some time affected by the incident,

* *Anas glacialis.*

which last reminiscence may I hope be forgiven me.
I did my best that evening to mend it with a cotton-
reel and indiarubber bands, but the pipe then required such powerful suction to extract smoke from
it that its use was more of a penance than a comfort
—so hard, too, when we had obtained a supply of
good tobacco from Skanker !

We got back to Polmak on Saturday evening,
and passed a luxuriously quiet Sunday, disturbed
only by necessary business, for the men had to be
paid. They received eighteen dollars each, inclusive
of what they had drawn from time to time. Mikkel,
who had an alarming predilection for a dram, had
recklessly expended four dollars during the voyage;
Little Savage only had left his earnings untouched.
We gave them besides two old hooks—I hardly dare
to call them salmon-flies—apiece, the remnants of
our stores, and a dollar each for 'drikke-penge.' Of
the last gift they made immediate use, getting well
drunk within the hour, and in that condition attended
Skanker's family prayers. I fear that in the end
a great part of their earnings found their way into
the merchant's pocket, for he kept a store. The
last that I saw of Little Savage was in a huge
square cap of green velvet with a resplendent red
border, a pair of richly embroidered woollen gloves,
and brand-new komagers. Was this gorgeous attire
designed to melt the heart of some fair Chloe of
Karasjok or Assebakte ?

I regret to say that our plausible host proved to be
like one of those extortionate innkeepers who excel

'In robbing with a bow
In lieu of a bare blade and brazen front ';

for he presented us on the morning of our departure
with one of the most exorbitant bills for board and
lodging that it has ever been my ill fate to look over,
and all extras were charged for on the same scale.
The item for washing three or four flannel shirts, as
many undergarments, and a few pocket-handker-
chiefs, was five dollars, or £1 2s. 6d., and the bottle
of indifferent sherry which he produced, without its
being ordered, when we entered his house, was valued
at two dollars and a half, or 11s. 3d. As we left a
few small articles behind when we went up to Polmak-
vand, he had charged for our rooms all the time we
were away. We were in his house just three nights,
and had but two hot meals ; we might have lived
for a week at the best hotel in Norway for considerably less than the total of his account.

Although the merchants of the out-of-the-way
stations in Norway were bound by law to provide
accommodation for travellers, they were not really
innkeepers, and one felt some delicacy, perhaps mis-
placed, in discussing money matters with them, but
on this occasion we were obliged to remonstrate
strongly, as far as our Norsk permitted, with Skanker.
He was in no way disconcerted, took off two dollars
with a rather contemptuous air, and assured us that
Hambro, Guest, and party had paid in just the same
proportion without a murmur, in which case he must
have made a small fortune out of them. The worst
of it was that one was completely in his power, for
he alone could supply boats for the journey to
Guldholmen, at the mouth of the Tana, where, as
Hambro's letter informed us, another Skanker lived.
The man was a humorous dog in his way ; some very
vivacious young friends who, at our recommendation,

visited Tana the following year found in their bill
an item, ' fifteen dollars for noise !' I felt some
satisfaction in hearing that three or four years later,
when the river had become well known, his career of
extortion had been cut short ; for an angler of sterner
mould, having previously made arrangements with
the Foged, refused to pay his bill, delayed his journey,
and summoned that functionary, who made things
rather warm for the Barabbas of Polmak. It is
only fair to say that during my many years' experience of Norway I have never known a similar case
among the mercantile gentlemen to whom I have
often been indebted for comfortable quarters on the
most reasonable terms.

Monday, August 31, was a disagreeable day, with
a constant drizzle, and, all things considered, it was
not surprising that we left Polmak in a bad temper ;
nor was there much to enliven us during the voyage
downstream. Although the banks were in places
rather fine, the river was very broad, shallow, sandy,
and uninteresting. It took us eight weary hours to
reach Guldholmen, a little rocky islet with several
store-sheds, an enormous copper for boiling cods'
livers, and a comfortable house, which we entered
with some misgiving, especially as the proprietor
was the very image of his brother. But a capital
supper of reindeer steaks and claret restored our
good-humour, and we lay down early, it was no use
undressing, as we heard that the steamer would call
at Stangenæs, some miles distant in the fjord, at or
before five o'clock the next morning.

We left Guldholmen in a large sailing-boat laden
with casks of cod-liver oil. Rather to our surprise,
our host refused payment for what he called mere

hospitality due to wandering strangers. Could he
have been aware of the very different sentiments of
his brother in that respect ? But, after thanking
him for his courtesy, we felt it our duty to privately
present his sister, who acted as housekeeper, with
a donation for the purposes of 'local charity,' and
this she smilingly accepted.

Our boat was rather late, and the impatient
steamer fired a gun before we got within a mile of
her. We learned afterwards that she was nearly
leaving us to the terrible fate of a fortnight on
Guldholmen ! But we did get on board, and were
soon gazing from the deck, not without some sadness,
at the rapidly receding mouth of Tana, who relapsed
for a brief space into his mystery, and rolled down
between his silent woodlands and yellow sands untroubled by the echo of the gun or the strange
accents of the Britishers, with which he has of late
years become so well acquainted. As we rounded the
Nordkyn, the most northern point of the mainland
of Europe—for the North Cape is on an island—we
had terrific weather, but the little steamer behaved
gallantly, and we were luckily not affected by the
tremendous tossing, being both born sailors. In
due time we reached Hammerfest, and thence
returned to Alten.

CHAPTER X

AN APPRENTICE TO ELK-HUNTING

‘ An elk looked out of the pine forest ;
He snuffed up east, he snuffed down west,
Stealthy and still !’

So sang, according to Charles Kingsley, Wulf the
Goth, warrior, hunter, and woman - hater, pining
for fight and chase, and reluctantly compelled by
fidelity to his chief to idle away his valuable time
in the court of frail Pelagia’s Alexandrian mansion.
In writing this chapter I have no desire to work
myself into the sort of frenzy that the sound of his
own voice kindled, after supper, in that grim old
pagan ; nor to horrify my—may I hope numerous ?
—readers as he horrified his solitary auditor, the
young monk Philammon, with the concluding stanza
of his ferocious hunting-song :

‘ I sprang at his throat like a wolf of the wood,
And I warmed my hands in the smoking blood.
Hurrah !’

If we make allowance for all circumstances, including supper and compulsory inactivity, still this
was going a little too far. Prince Wulf was, as he
tells us, a keen and successful hunter. Armed with
bow and arrow in lieu of express rifle and cartridge,

218

he had matched his human stealthiness and stillness against the elk's, had made a clever stalk, and hit the big bull exactly in the right place. His exultant recollection of the feat was pardonable, but he might have spared sensitive Philammon the final wolf-like worry and the sanguinary remedy for cold hands. I here enter a claim for keenness myself, but I confess that even in chilly weather I prefer to put on my gloves and let someone else do the ' gralloch.'

While touching on personal experience, I may observe that when Prince Wulf speaks of the elk as snuffing up east and down west, there I am with him : I fully corroborate the snuffing ; the animal still retains the cautious and inconvenient habit. I will go further, and say, what would certainly be troublesome to explain in verse, that he actually boxes the compass with his confounded ugly long nose, every point of it up and down, and that such persistent all-round snuffing too often results in his detecting the presence of an Englishman in his immediate neighbourhood, and in his forthwith making tracks for the ' next parish,' or maybe for the one beyond that. And when this happens for the twentieth time, that Englishman's philosophy is apt to fail him, and he waxes mad, and would perhaps do all that old Wulf did, and more, could he but out-manoeuvre and turn the tables on that wisely fugitive elk. But now, as I sit, pen in hand, by the fireside at home, pledged to avoid undue excitement, and calmly considering my subject, there comes to me a faint aura from the far-off wilderness, a phantom breath of the Scandinavian air, which exhilarates like sparkling wine and brings no re-action ; a vision of the vast silent forest stretching

away from the dense pine-brakes which clothe the
banks of the rushing river, up to where emerges the
treeless, rocky waste of the higher fjeld.

ὁ μέν πόνος οἴχεται τό δ' εὖ μένει,
'The trouble passes, the good abides.'

I forget fatigue and failure, remembering only the
charm of forest life, which, once realized, never
vanishes ; and I whisper to myself a hope that before
the inevitable day which cannot now be far distant,

'When all the sport is tame, lad,
And all the wheels run down,'

I may once more and again find myself in fact instead of fancy stealthily following the broad cloven
'spor' among the close pine-stems, or toiling, if
somewhat breathlessly, yet with sanguine expectation, up the mountain slopes, or prone on mossy
couch at the summit, carefully searching the expanse of subjacent forest. It will be observed that
I do not, as I might just as easily while I am about it,
wish to find myself with my rifle-sight on the right
spot behind the elk's shoulder, nor lighting my pipe,
after long abstinence from tobacco, in contemplation
of the mighty dead ; and for this reason, that to
enjoy elk-hunting one must come to regard the
necessary toil as a pleasure, to love the woods and
woodcraft for their own sakes, and not only with an
eye to a result.

If the sport does not entirely fulfil the definition
of the 'real' so well opposed by the late Bromley-
Davenport to 'the artificial,' in his article on
deer-stalking, inasmuch as the whole of Scandinavia
is certainly ' annexed and appropriated by man,'

either king or subject, with the result that game-laws, close times, and proprietary rights have to be studied, it does, nevertheless, belong essentially to the former class, inasmuch as it is beyond doubt ' the pursuit of a perfectly wild animal on its own primeval and ancestral ground.' In such sport it may well be that a single success must last the sportsman a long time ; meanwhile he must be capable of deriving almost as much satisfaction from his surroundings and mode of life as from his anticipation of ' more blood.' I fancy I hear someone remark, ' This is a fine theory, but will it hold water ?' Well, human nature is frail ; there are moments, as I have already allowed, when equanimity and philosophy are scattered to the winds ; we may be wroth even with that which we love. The test is, how often and how thoroughly do we make up the quarrel ? Does the good abide when the trouble has passed ?

I have somewhere above used the expression, ' the big *bull*,' although the elk belongs to the Cervidæ, its specific name being *alces*, the Latinized form of the Teutonic elk or elch. In Scandinavia the male is always spoken of as ox—we say bull—the female as cow, and the young as calf. A certain number of people know well what an elk is like ; a larger number have only a vague idea of a huge brute resembling a misshapen cart-horse with horns—old Pontoppidan, once Bishop of Bergen, tells us that in former times it used to be termed by some naturalists ' equicervus,' the horse-deer—and, finally, a great many people know little or nothing about the animal, its appearance, or its natural history.

It may be questioned whether even those who are most familiar with the animal ever saw a full-grown

male elk, either alive or dead, or even the head and
horns, without some renewal of original astonishment
at its uncouth appearance, amounting almost to
monstrosity.   Take the size and bulk to begin with.
These, of course, vary considerably even in animals
of the same age ; but a ' stor oxe,' eight or ten years
old, will stand in equine measurement upwards of
eighteen hands at the withers; his weight may be
from eighty to ninety stone.   Then regard the immense hump-like development at the shoulders, and
the comparatively slender quarters sloping away
towards the tail ; the massive shaggy throat and
gigantic head, the latter out of all proportion in
length, terminating in a huge hooked nose and projecting lip, and crowned with long ears and heavy
palmated antlers ; the wicked-looking eye, placed
near the top of the skull ; the wiry mane and hair of
the hide ; the elongated legs, clean and steel-like as
a thoroughbred's, with elastic ten-inch hoofs, cloven
into acute lobes, like twin daggers, and as weapons
not less dangerous.   Was there ever a more pro-
digious, ungainly, antediluvian-looking monster ?

It may be asked—indeed, I have already heard the
question—Why elk-hunting ?   Why not elk-stalking
or shooting ?   We may summarily dismiss the last,
it implies a great deal too much.   The shots which
the sportsman obtains, in even a successful season,
are few and far between ; he has to make the most
of his opportunities.   But if he be ' one of the right
sort,' he will not grumble over his small expenditure
of ammunition after he has once gone through the
excitement of the chase and seen the magnificent
quarry stretched at his feet.   Referring to the dic-
tionary—let it by all means be the grand old two-

volume Johnson—we find ' to hunt,' from the Saxon
' hund,' a dog, ' to chase wild animals,' and to
' search for.'   Now, in the chase of that wildest of
animals (the elk) we use dogs; and all who have
tried the sport will, I think, be willing to concede
that a searching for the object of it constitutes its
main characteristic. That same searching, continual and laborious, has, I am bound to confess,
proved a cause of backsliding in some who have
fallen away from the select band of elk-hunters.

As I shall show, the dog is used in two distinct
fashions, the one being Swedish, the other Norwegian.
In the latter he is led, or rather leads, in harness, and
his *rôle* is simply to assist the sportsman in finding
the elk ; in the former he runs loose, has to find the
deer himself, to chase and yet to delay it, until the
guns arrive within shot.

In the present chapter, the bulk of which, like that
of several others in this volume, has already appeared
in print as an article in the *Fortnightly Review*, I
record the adventures of a novice in elk-hunting a
good many years ago ; it will serve as an introduc-
tion to other chapters on later sport of a similar kind,
and readers will, I dare say, readily understand that
the sketch is based on personal experience. With
these remarks, I think it best to let the pages stand
as they were originally written, some alterations and
interpolations excepted.

My friend Brown, then, who is certainly no longer
a young man, but who comes of a hardy and sports-
manlike family, has received a double invitation to
visit Scandinavia. The first comes from his old
friend Jones, who has discovered a retreat to which
he can periodically escape from the care of business

and society in the heart of the Swedish Norland. The second is from his younger acquaintance Robinson, who also conceals himself at intervals from the world in the mountainous forests of Naemansdal, in Norway. I propose to attach myself to Brown, who accepts both invitations, and see what comes of them.

The intelligent reader will gather from the insidious and highly original nomenclature which I have adopted that my selfish purpose is to mask, not only the personality of the sportsmen whose doings I record, but also the whereabouts of their Scandinavian retreats. I will go so far as to say that the latter are somewhere between the Skager-Rack and the North Cape, which statement opens out for the curious a tolerably wide field of investigation. I do not feel in the least bound to imitate the open-heartedness of many who, having somewhere discovered a secluded corner where they can enjoy themselves after their own fashion, forthwith invite all mankind through the medium of the *Field* to share their seclusion and their joy. Such public-spirited generosity is beyond me; I applaud the discreet aposiopesis of the twin authors of 'Three in Norway,' who, when on the very brink of revelation, exclaim, 'No; philanthropy has limits. No man can expect to be told patterns of flies!' And therefore I hope that the reader, kind as well as intelligent, will pardon my reticence, and suffer my trio to remain *incogniti* in a *terra incognita.*

Brown, as I say, readily accepts the invitations. His holiday commences in August; he must return to England by October. In Sweden elk-hunting begins and ends with September; in Norway it is permitted from the 15th of that month to the same date in the following one.* He will, therefore, first visit Jones, and look up Robinson on his way back to England. He meets with some discouragement when he declares his plans to a few friends. 'You may as well,' says one, bound for Scotland, where he hopes on the 12th to assist in slaying some hundreds of young grouse, 'go into the fields and pot a bullock as a big brute of an elk.' Says another: 'My dear Brown, you will break your heart over it and never get a shot ; you are not young enough, and, forgive my saying so, too stout for that kind of work. Come with me and have some quiet trolling in Wales.' 'Norway and Sweden are small places, and there are too many people in them,' remarks a third ; 'they are played out. If you want wild sport, why not run across the Atlantic, take the Canadian Pacific rail for a couple of thousand miles, and work up the Kicking Horse River ?' But Brown is not to be disheartened or deterred from his purpose ; he wishes his friends good-bye and good sport in their respective lines, and one fine morning in August takes his ticket for Hull by the 10.30 train from King's Cross, and is off. A week later he jumps out of bed at an early hour, opens the window of an upper room in a comfortable Anglicized farm-house, and gazes eagerly at the prospect before him.

The foreground is a gentle descent of greenest grass, beginning to sprout afresh after the removal of the hay-crop. At its foot lies a broad reach of river sweeping round the sharp curve of the opposite beach, where the steep sand and gravel glow richly

* It was so at the date ; since then the law relating to close time has undergone several alterations.

in the morning sun, and gliding thence with gradually widening channel and decreasing current until, a quarter of a mile below, it is merged in the placid expanse of the blue lake. The near shore as far as the mouth of the river, a sunny slope facing the south, is cultivated in alternate strips of oats, barley, and potatoes, and, with this exception, nothing is visible except forest, unbroken, rolling forest, until at the extremity of the lake rises into air above the mists at its base the bare, snow-patched cone of a noble mountain.

Brown's eye follows the range of pine-clad hills, and he wonders which point of that interminable woodland conceals the doomed elk, who is quietly breakfasting unconscious that the bloodthirsty gaze of an airily-clad Briton is on his hiding-place. There is a stir about the farm ; an old woman and a comely, bare-legged damsel pass the window laden with pails of milk ; the farmer and his youngest son have been to take up the nets in the lake, and are bearing between them up the grassy slope a basket filled with fine trout and char ; one elder brother is busy chopping wood in an outhouse, and another sharpening an axe, assisted by a very buxom, yellow-haired young woman, who chatters merrily as her stalwart arms turn the grindstone.

Brown dresses himself, and takes a stroll before breakfast. A quiet path down a glade bordered on either side with densely-set birch-trees and an undergrowth of bilberry and juniper brings him to the pebbly margin of the lake. The tranquil sheet of water is completely encircled by the endless forest ; only here and there above the dark mass of pines rises the paler edge of the open fjeld. A brood of

red-throated divers is splashing and diving and
calling at a safe distance from shore ; a family of
cinnamon jays comes jerking and flitting through
the wood to inspect the stranger, and as he subsides
on to a boulder and lights his pipe, fearlessly
surround him, and comment in musical whistles on
his appearance ; above the tree-tops a huge buzzard
sails past on motionless wings. Brown thinks to
himself that after all there is some refreshing sense
of the primeval about this played-out country.

His glance falls upon a flower nestling under the
boulder on which he is seated ; like many who love
field-sports, he has a smattering of natural science,
including botany, and he examines it.   It is a butter-
wort, with its star of curled green leaves and rich
purple blossom ; and surely the delicate fern-like
fringe of that turf hummock is Alpine rue, and just
beyond are groups of the minute Scottish primrose.
He is encompassed by floral rarities.   In returning
to the house, he quits the path, and takes a short cut
through the wood.   He finds the delicate *Linnœa
borealis* trailing over every decaying stump, the
single-flowered winter-green with her one pure
blossom, more fragrant than was ever lily of the
valley, and her taller sisters with their clusters of
wax-like bells.   As he stoops to gather a specimen,
he is startled by a rush of whirring wings, and from
the brushwood close at hand a dozen ' hjerper,' the
smallest of the grouse tribe—otherwise known as
' gelinottes ' or ' hazel-hens '—scatter into the
neighbouring trees, where they sit motionless, and
render themselves all but invisible.   Brown returns
to breakfast in an enthusiastic frame of mind, partly
owing to the exhilarating air and partly to the varied

interest of his stroll, with a magnificent appetite, and
with a bouquet of flowers such as no wealth could
have purchased for him in Covent Garden.

I need but glance at his occupations and amuse-
ments during the next few days. He is allowed to
shoot a few black-game and hjerper in a part of
the near forest where he is not likely to scare the elk.
He and Jones make an expedition up the river,
combining boat and bank fishing. A series of waterfalls below the lake bar the ascent of the salmon,
but there are plenty of trout. Although it is rather
late in the season, they have a good day, a day, in
fact, that astonishes Brown. He uses the fly only,
his friend fly and spoon alternately. They return
with forty-seven fish, which weigh 51 lbs. The
largest, of 7 lbs., succumbs to Jones's spoon, and is
by him termed a decent fish; but Brown, less accustomed to such victories, exults in the conquest of
one of half that size, lured with a big 'March brown.'

The next day, however, this success is altogether
eclipsed by his capture, just above the rapid where
the river runs out of the lake, of a glorious 9-pounder,
who falls a victim to the attractions of a big phantom
minnow. When he exhibits his prize to Jones, the
latter, without other comment, says: 'It is a pity
we haven't time to work the "sound" properly; the
big trout are just running in out of the lake. About
this time last year Smith took out of that bit of water
six successive fish which weighed 79 pounds; the
largest went over 19.'

Brown is inclined to think this anecdote somewhat cruel and ill-timed. And after his 'crowning
mercy' of the 9-pounder, the rod is laid aside for
the rifle, for the morrow is the first of September

—'the glorious first!'—and a thirty days' war is declared against the elk. As Brown selects the cartridges for his pouch, about enough, by the way, to last him half a dozen seasons, and handles his double-barrelled express, he thinks with some compassion and contempt of the crowd of stay-at-home sportsmen who are similarly engaged, all eagerly bent on the slaughter of the poor ' little brown bird.' It is true that last year he was himself as eager as any, but what a despicable thing is a field of turnips compared to that illimitable forest whose recesses he is about to explore !

He has been duly instructed by his host in the theory of the chase. On the opening day they are to hunt together, just to see that Brown is properly entered, and after that they will go singly and take separate beats. Brown rejoices to hear that in Sweden you may kill as many elk as you please— or can—on the same farm, while in Norway a man is meanly restricted to one for each holding. What a pitiful restriction ! thinks he, as some vague fancy of having half a dozen elk to gather flits across his mind.

They make an early start and form a party of four. Nils, the boatman, has changed his occupation to that of hunter, whilst overnight his friend Johan, a well-known local Nimrod, has arrived from the other side of the lake. These two men have charge of the dogs, Pasop and Huy. The latter appear to Brown to be a variety of the breed very popular some years ago in England under the name of ' Spitz.' Huy is a small hound ; his coat of soft and erect ash-coloured hair is especially long and thick about the neck and shoulders ; his eyes are bright and keen, but his expression is generally mild. Pasop is a good deal bigger, with coarser hair of a dark, brindled gray. His yellowish-brown eyes glare habitually, and he wears a perpetual frown, expressive of deep thought and latent ferocity. Both have acutely cocked ears, and their bushy tails curl to that degree that they seem to lift the hind-legs off the ground. Huy testifies his delight at the commencement of the annual campaign by many lamb-like gambols and short, quick barks, but Pasop, after a single caper, sternly represses his emotion and settles, perhaps somewhat prematurely, down to business.

And now, while the party are preparing to start, I may say a little more on the interesting subject of these dogs. They are undoubtedly of one and the same race as the Arctic dog, from time immemorial the dog of the Lapp, the Esquimaux, the Samoyed and the Chukche, the dog of the Arctic explorer, the sleigh drudge. This dog, descending from the extreme North, in the natural course of events became distributed over the whole area of Sweden and Norway, it is the aboriginal dog of the land ; and owing to the scarcity of dogs of other breeds it has, to a considerable extent, remained to this day unchanged in its general appearance and natural qualities.

Although not unfrequently cunning, surly, and even savage, it is, on the whole, docile and tractable, and has many characteristics which render it of great value for sporting purposes, strength, activity, an excellent nose, keen sight, sufficient stanchness and endurance to stay with the object of the chase, and at the same time sufficient instinctive caution to avoid danger by not ven-

turing into too close quarters with anything that
stabs, strikes, bites, or scratches.   Nature has provided it with a coat capable of resisting the often
intense cold of northern latitudes, and the preservation of this coat depends almost entirely on constant
exposure to the elements in winter as well as summer.
A Lapp will refuse to admit his dog to the shelter and
warmth of a hut, and leave him to lie outside all
night in the snow, on the ground that it is cruel, by
a mistaken show of kindness, to enervate the dog
and weaken his power of resistance to extreme cold.
' What,' he will ask, ' will the dog do, if he now lies
by the fire, when he has to watch the reindeer under
the Northern Lights ?'   A large percentage of farm
dogs in the north of Norway are treated in the same
way, and left to find, like wild beasts, what shelter
they can.   But a relaxation of this rule in many
cases is one great cause of the production of a great
number of dogs differing so far from the true racial
type as to appear mongrels.

In default of other breeds, the employment of
this dog of the aboriginal Arctic race in the chase of
the elk has become established and habitual.   With
careful training it can be taught to recognise the
great deer as its special quarry, and not to turn
aside on other spoor or scent ; but it can be and is
educated equally well for several other distinct
purposes: as a bear-dog, who will not be tempted
to stray after elk-spoor ; as a reindeer-dog, either
to track the wild or to guard and collect the tame
herds ; as a cattle or sheep dog, to assist in their
recovery from the woods ; as a mere farmhouse
watch-dog.   It is of great use to the tracker of
the marten-cat, whose pelt is so much esteemed by

ladies, and of the fox.   If left severely alone without
education it will run wild on the scent of anything,
and amuse itself by baying treed squirrels or hunting
lemmings.   Lastly, it can be employed with great
success as a bird-dog.   There is no more deadly way
of approaching capercailzie, black-game, and other
forest birds than with a dog of the breed under discussion, held or fastened to the belt by a long leash
and allowed to precede the shooter.   But a dog so
trained becomes after a time quite spoilt for elk-
hunting, as he will take the wind from birds at a
long distance, and lead up to them, to the great
disgust of the sportsman who hopes to come on
fresh spoor, or the mighty deer himself in the
flesh.

After this, I hope, pardonable digression, I must
follow the fortunes of my friends Brown and Co.

The party take boat across the river, and for
some distance follow the rough main-road through
the forest, from which they branch off by a narrow
path that plunges into the depth of the woodland,
after which all conversation is carried on in whispers.
By this and the serious countenances of his companions Brown is much impressed.   They march
in single file; Johan and Nils go first, each with a
dog, the Englishmen following; Pasop has the post
of honour.   The end of the long leader attached to
his collar is twisted round Johan's hand, and Brown
admires the harmonious adroitness with which, when
at last they quit the path also and turn into the track-
less wilderness, the pair work their way among the
trees, through the occasionally dense covert and over
the bristling chevaux-de-frise of fallen trunks.   The
dog instinctively selects the easiest passage, never

strains inconveniently at the leader, which, nevertheless, he keeps taut, never goes the wrong side of
a stem, and in an instant obeys the slightest motion
of his master's wrist, and shifts his line accordingly.
Huy, who wears a kind of harness passing round the
chest and under the belly, behaves with equal dis-
cretion, guiding, and yet guided by, Nils.   But it
strikes as much sense of the ludicrous as still remains unevaporated in Brown that the general
effect is decidedly that of two blind men with their
faithful canine conductors.

And now, as they reach the foot-hills, the ground
becomes gradually steeper, and Brown begins to
wish that there was a view to admire.   The fallen
timber on the slopes presents continual obstacles,
which have to be negotiated with some care to avoid
being spiked by the sharp dead branches, and
making undue noise.   When Brown, who is bringing
up the rear and trying all he can to imitate the noiseless progress of the van, causes by his awkward
clambering or treading a loud crack or crash, Jones,
who is long and spare, and going well within himself,
half turns and looks back at him with a frown and a
reproachful shake of the head.   The fact is that the
pace is too good for Brown on this his first essay and
over such a country.

It is not much relief to him when they emerge
occasionally into the open, and have to wade across
swampy upland meadows, or to labour through
morasses up to their knees in spongy moss.   He had
no idea until now that his rifle, which he gallantly
refused to let Johan carry for him, was so heavy.
However, he struggles on gamely, streaming with
perspiration, and after a couple of hours of mute

endurance, Jones mercifully guesses at his friend's
condition, and with the faintest of whistles brings
Johan to a halt. Brown tries hard to conceal his
distress, and with the air of one who is luxuriously
enjoying his outing, stretches himself on the elastic
couch beneath the pines, whilst the other three hold
a whispered conference.

But in ten minutes they are off again, and the
monotonous march continues without a break and
without much change of scene or incident. Whilst
on the lower level and following the path, always
an attraction to game, they had disturbed several
broods of black-game and hjerper ; but now they
are penetrating into the solemn depths of the forest,
where bird life seems to die out altogether, to be
resuscitated on the open fjeld above, the favourite
haunt of the ryper or willow-grouse. Only now
and then the sudden loud flapping of a wary old
cock capercailzie, the feathered anchorite of these
sombre solitudes, makes Brown start and grasp his
rifle nervously.

He is fast arriving at the same point of exhaustion
as before, when of a sudden, see ! what is Pasop
about ? The hound is slightly straining at the
leader, with his head thrown up and his pointed
nose snuffing energetically, and behind him Huy is
repeating the performance with improvements of his
own, until his ears almost touch the centre of his
spine in his exaggerated anxiety to catch the wind,
and the curl of his tail tightens until it seems likely
to fly in pieces. This time Jones looks over his
shoulder, and without even a whisper rolls his eyes
towards the dogs with expressive indication of what
is taking place.

In an instant Brown is another man ; his distress
leaves him, and his heart throbs only with excitement ; his shooting-boots no longer feel like clogs of
lead, and he forgets the burden of his rifle.   ' What
is the meaning of this ?' he thinks.   ' Are the elk
close ahead ?'   And he makes sure that his cartridges
are in, and wonders how on earth he is to shoot with
those fellows meandering about in front of him.
Another hundred yards, and down goes Pasop's
head, and the party comes to a sudden stop, Brown
in his excitement blundering into Jones before he
can pull up.   Patience, good sanguine Brown ; you
will be a wiser and sadder man before you have
half ended your apprenticeship to elk-hunting.   Here
it is at last ! the fresh ' spor ' at which the dogs are
snuffing eagerly, thrusting their noses into the mighty
footprints.   Johan stoops, and with his first and
second fingers extended draws two lines and makes
two dots which trace the impress of the hoof.   ' A
bull, cow, and calf,' he whispers, after carefully
surveying the ground, ' and moving quietly.'   The
tracks are clearly those of last night or early morning ; they cross the line of our hunters at an angle
of 45° up wind.   Nothing can be better, and the
pursuers advance with extra caution.

At this critical juncture, whether from excitement
or from the effect of his forgotten toil, Brown's throat
begins to tickle, and he is afflicted with an irresistible
desire to cough.   Jones, to his disgust, hears in his
rear sundry choking sounds, and, looking over his
shoulder as usual, discovers Brown purple from re-
pression.   A single smothered explosion, however,
relieves the sufferer, and Jones foregoes his intention
of sending him home at once to shoot hjerper

for to-morrow's dinner, and gives him another
chance.

And now signs dear to the hunter multiply themselves. The dogs repeatedly rise on their hind
legs and snuff intently at the bushes tainted by the
passage of the mighty deer, and even at the long
pliant grasses which here and there bend unbroken
over the trail. Nothing escapes Johan's eye; it
is as perfect as his dog's nose. Here a scattered
leaf or two shows him that the tall cow has cropped
the foliage from the top of a slender sapling; there
the calf has nibbled a single twig on a low bush;
while the bull, taking a line of his own at some little
distance, has blazed a tree by rubbing his horns
against it, to get rid of the velvet, and farther on
has playfully sparred with a young fir and left it
a wreck, the bark in tatters, and every branch
broken.

All this time Pasop has been doggedly pressing
forward, and Huy straining more and more upon
the scent, and when the passage of a deep ravine
and small stream has been cautiously effected, the
leading hound stops, raises his head, and with his
fierce frown gazes intently at a long, low eminence
covered with thick wood, and separated from the
spot where the hunters stand by a strip of bare
morass. Johan at once turns in his tracks and signs
to them to descend again into the ravine. Then, by
working up this and employing his perfect knowledge of the ground, he makes a kind of half-circle
and gives the dogs the wind off the said eminence
from several different stations. In each case Pasop,
with working nostrils, repeats his concentrated stare,
and Huy more demonstratively, but as mutely, cor-

roborates the opinion of his elder. 'The elks are there,' whispers Johan, and Brown realizes that the critical moment has arrived at last, when the hunter stoops and commences to loosen the leader from Pasop's collar, while Nils does the same by Huy.

It is grand to see the way in which the old dog, after one long, deliberate shake, goes off with flashing eyes at a steady, wolf-like gallop, quickly overhauling the apparently faster Huy, who has snatched a start in the first few moments of his release. Johan has carefully selected the spot for loosing the dogs; it is a knoll, fairly clear of trees and fallen timber, close to and nearly opposite the centre of the long wooded slope towards which the pair are now racing. It commands a partial view into a broad valley beyond, wherein lies a considerable sheet of water.

As the dogs disappear into the dense timber immediately opposite, there is perfect silence among the group upon the knoll. All are listening intently; every ear is straining to catch the first welcome note that shall proclaim the finding of the elk. It is long in coming, evidently longer than Johan had anticipated, for he mutters something to Nils, and his rather stolid face looks for a while positively anxious. Jones begins to fidget, and Brown fears a fiasco, the elk must have moved farther. No! there it is! at last! The stillness is gloriously broken by Pasop's deep, angry bay, followed by Huy's excited treble barking. 'They have him!' exclaims Jones, as he dashes down the declivity in front and covers with long strides the flat below. Johan sticks close to him, and Brown follows as best he may; Nils has his orders, and remains on the look-out where he is. The dogs have evidently found on the crest of the hill, and are running the elk along the ridge.

Brown at once bears away to the right, hoping to avoid the steepest part of the ascent in front, and to take the rise at an easier angle. He confesses to himself that for a man in his condition, fresh from England—of course the condition, not the age, is to blame—to think of running for any distance uphill is supremely absurd : on fairly level ground he can do as well as others ; and at the instant he demonstrates this fact by catching his foot in a root and coming down on his face, extended in a particularly moist spot. He is soon on his legs again, but the fall has knocked the remaining wind out of him, and he subsides into a walk. On reaching the belt of wood he discovers that the hillside, which looked fairly practicable from a distance, is broken up into deep gullies, and, of course, barricaded with dead timber. For some time he becomes engaged in a terrible obstacle-race, and makes little progress ; then it occurs to him to descend again and keep along the edge of the swamp, where he is able once more to get up a kind of jog-trot. He can still hear the dogs above him on the left, but their cry is becoming fainter and fainter, and he realizes the hopelessness of trying to come up with them. He begins to think that his trolling friend in England had reason, and that this sort of thing is better suited for younger and slimmer men.

Nevertheless, in one fashion or another, he ' keeps wiring away,' stopping now and then to listen as well as his throbbing pulses will allow. Oddly enough, yet as often happens in similar circumstances, some

lines of an old song that he used to sing in his Oxford
days flash into his head :

> ' Behind them, but far in the rear,
>   Come the welters who won't be denied ;
> Like good uns they still persevere,
>   And they all take the brook in their stride.'

But there is little stride about Brown when he
does encounter a brook ; in he goes with a splash,
stumbles through, drags himself up the opposite
bank, and, with the words of the song buzzing in his
ears, struggles on, he has little notion why or whither.
The dogs are now out of hearing ; no doubt they have
sunk the hill, and are away into the forest on the
opposite side.   At last he reaches a spot where the
shoulder of the ridge which he has been following
dips to the slope of the valley, and he can see the
lake glistening through the trees.   Here he halts.
What is the use of his going farther ?   Where are
Jones and Johan ?   Where the dogs ?   And where,
oh where, is the elk ?   He takes off his cap and
turns his face to the breeze.   Surely it has shifted still
more, is shifting even now, and blowing in stronger
gusts on his right cheek, in which case—— Hark !   A
faint note comes from the woodland below, another,
and another, each more distinct than the last.   By
all that is lucky, the chase is turning his way !   Jones
told him overnight that elk generally feed and run up
wind.   His hopes and excitement revive, and he
continues listening, motionless as a statue.

There is no doubt about it now : Pasop's deep
note and Huy's shriller bark are clearly audible.
The sounds approach but slowly, and then it flashes
across him that the dogs have stopped the bull ; he

is certainly no longer running. Brown dashes on
his cap, snatches up the rifle which he had laid down,
and goes headlong at the steep descent before him.
If he could be taken quietly over the ground
that he covers during the next ten minutes, and
be shown the obstacles that he surmounts in
reckless haste, I doubt his believing in his own
performance.

Suddenly, through a break in the forest, he sees a
glorious, a maddening, sight. Some three hundred
yards away, on a patch of open ground, a long-
legged, hunchbacked, horned monster, more huge
and uncouth than anything he had dreamt of, is
slowly gyrating and yawing from side to side, while
in front of him, wherever he turns, and keeping just
beyond reach of his terrible hoofs, Pasop and Huy,
their jaws white with foam, wheel and bound and
rage with incessant clamour.

For an instant Brown is so astounded as to
forget that he has a rifle, then he clutches and
throws it half up to his shoulder. No ; the distance
is too great; he must try to get nearer. He has
been told that a bull elk when bayed by dogs,
whom he no doubt despises, and regards merely
as noisy nuisances, is always suspicious of real
danger at their back, and strains his senses to
detect it. Brown, therefore, for all his unnecessary
hurry, advances as noiselessly as possible, and, to his
delight, comes suddenly upon a small tract of grass-
land, with a tumble-down fence and two or three
ruinous wooden buildings, a deserted ' sæter,' or
mountain dairy. The ground dips abruptly at the
opposite side of this, and he will not be visible to the
elk as he crosses it. Now at last the game is in his

hands !   It is simply a question of how he shall make his attack.

Oh that some sylvan deity, patron of the chase, would now inspire Brown with venatorial craft, even as Pallas was wont to breathe wise counsel into the ear of warlike Tydides ! or, to speak practically, oh for five minutes of Johan !

But neither deity nor mortal comes to Brown's assistance, and, left to his own devices, he commits —alas! that I must record it !—a horrible, a fatal blunder. In the sheltered hollow where he now is there is no breath of air to remind him, and he forgets *all about the wind !* The elk is working slowly along the slope below the sæter, so slowly that at times the baying of the dogs seems all but stationary. Instead of waiting patiently and stalking him from the rear, Brown slips across the grass-land and over the steep brow into the forest, until he judges himself to be in exactly the right line ; and then, with a certain sense of pride— misguided man !—at being alone and at last ahead, casts about for a place of ambush.

The covert is very thick down there, but he finds a narrow green glade, which was perhaps at one time a road to the sæter, and with a beating heart there awaits the elk. He cannot be more than a hundred yards distant now. At the end of the glade is a dense clump of young pines, forming an impenetrable screen right across it. The elk advances as far as this, Brown expecting every instant to see him round it on one side or the other and afford a shot. But he waits and waits, and still there is not a glimpse of him. The dogs are baying furiously ; they will surely move him into sight. Brown begins to sneak up

the glade, when he is conscious of about six inches
of an enormous black hooked nose protruding beyond
the edge of the fir-screen. Now he is coming! Not
a bit of it; the nose is withdrawn, only to reappear
on the opposite side.

Brown meditates how he can approach with least
noise. On the right hand two or three large trees
have fallen one on the other, forming an almost impassable barrier; on the left he cannot see three
yards into the covert. There is the nose again!
He raises his rifle and covers it, almost inclined to
shoot a foot behind, on the chance of hitting the
invisible head; but just then he detects a spot where
the screen of trees is not quite so dense, and behind
it what appears to him a patch of the elk's hide
about as big as his hand; it cannot be far from the
right place in the body. He raises his rifle again,
takes careful aim, and fires. For a few moments
there is a dead silence as the smoke hangs in the
glade. The dogs cease baying; then they recom-
mence, but, to Brown's horror, the sound recedes
rapidly, until it is far down the hill. He dashes forward, forces his way through the thicket in the faint
hope of getting a long shot with the second barrel,
sees at once that there is no chance, and as the dogs
come slinking sulkily back, sits down upon a fallen
tree, as miserable a man for the moment as could be
found in the North of Europe.

When Brown is discovered by the other three he
is outwardly in so wretched a plight that even Jones
cannot be cynical or stern, and does his best to console him. His face is scratched, he is soaked to the
skin, and covered with mud from his fall in the
swamp; his clothes show ghastly rents, and through

one can be seen on his thigh a long tear, happily not deep, but gory to behold, inflicted by a tree-spike. But he has pulled himself together, has emptied his flask, and is consuming the pipe of comfort.   With a good deal of grim humour he narrates his adventure.   Johan's keen eye finds the mark of the bullet : it has cut a groove in two sprays of a pine-branch just where they join and form an angle, and was probably deflected; but Johan, after careful measurement, pronounces the shot too high.   Nils follows the track of the elk for a long distance into the valley, but finds no traces of blood, and a verdict of ' miss, with extenuating circumstances,' is recorded against Brown.

' Never mind, old man,' says Jones heartily ; ' you got up to him and let off your piece—that is something.   I assure you that I ran that bull for a couple of miles, but the dogs couldn't hold him at first, and the turn up-wind beat me.   Better luck next time !'

But Brown did not have better luck next time, nor for a good many times after that.   I have followed him through his typical Swedish elk-hunt, and am loath to leave him before he has achieved some sort of success to console him for its disastrous finish, and has tried the Norwegian method of hunting also. I need not describe in detail how he fared when out alone with Nils and Huy, especially as, though they found and ran several elk, he never succeeded in getting up to a bull before his departure for Norway; repeated records of similar chases cannot fail to be monotonous.   I will, therefore, conclude with an extract from a letter which Brown wrote to a friend in England from Robinson's quarters in Naemansdal :

' When I last wrote I was suffering agonies of mind from the recollection of my idiotic blunder over that bull. You remember how sometimes your uncle George, haunted by the image of a particular bunny which he had missed, could be heard muttering to himself at intervals all the evening, " Damn that rabbit !" Well, intensify his self-reproach fifty-fold, and you have my feelings. I could think of nothing else for a week, day or night. I used to lie awake and go through the whole thing again, and see exactly what I ought to have done, and how easy it was to do it. You will be glad to hear that I am better— I cannot say cured—and have, in a mild form, been " blooded." My bespattered conscience, like the toga of the Roman envoy at Tarentum, will take a good deal of blood to " wash it white," but it is a shade cleaner already.

' I used to think the Norland ground rough and steep and wild when I was there, but it is level and smooth and highly cultivated compared to this region. The hills here run up in terraces, and each terrace is faced with cliff; consequently, one has the choice between tremendous climbing or long circuits. I prefer the latter, but I can tell you that the change in my condition since I left England is remarkable. I believe I am a stone lighter, and certainly feel ten years younger. The farms are miles upon miles apart, and there is nothing but desolation between. The natives do not appear to make hayfields out of mountain swamps, or to leave a few thousand trees lying about as recklessly as they do in Norland. The timber is almost entirely Scotch fir, which is, to my mind, a much grander tree than the spruce, and easier to see under, which recommends it to the

hunter. Excepting the thick belts near the rivers,
the forest is tolerably open, and one can frequently
spy the elk from the heights with a glass, as they spy
red-deer in Scotland. The dogs here are practically
used only for stalking, but I will not declare upon
oath that no one ever runs a dog at an elk. The
farmer who hankers after the flesh-pot will wink at
an occasional breach of the law in his favour. The
usual plan is for the shooter, when it is certain that
the elk cannot be far ahead, to go forward alone and
try a stalk. It is impossible to take too much care
or time over this, and there is also great art on
occasion in waiting for the elk to move.

' Robinson, up to date, has killed three fine bulls.
Personally, I have been out three days, have seen
or had glimpses of four elk, and heard the crash of
others which I managed to disturb only. And I
have fired two shots : the one a snap, very difficult,
and a miss ; with the other I bagged a cow. Do not
be alarmed. I have not been imitating the hero of
Nils's tale, who, while lunching near the sæter,
pointed his rifle at one of the cattle, with the remark,
" Now, if only that was an elk !" Somehow it went
off, and killed the best milk-giver in the herd. I
shall tell you no more about my failures, you have
had enough of them ; for the future, " Horas non
numero nisi serenas."

' I will give you a sketch of my solitary success.
Robinson and I arranged a little " drive," or, as
they call it here, " klap-jagt," from the noise made
by the beaters. The familiar English translation is
" slap-jack." We posted ourselves near the only
two passes by which elk could descend from a very
precipitous hill, and sent three or four beaters round

to drive the said hill towards us. The men, for some
reason best known to themselves, insisted on carrying
axes instead of sticks, as though they intended to
cut down the trees instead of tapping them. There
was a wide and perfectly level swamp running under
the base of the mountain, and on the opposite side
of this lay the forest. Consequently, I had a long
stretch of flat in front of me, on which, while waiting,
I amused myself by judging distances. In the end
this proved useful. When, in about half an hour,
I began to hear the sound of the axes on the trees
and no elk had appeared, I made sure that all chance
of one was gone; but the dog which the man with
me was holding began to throw up his head and try
to catch the wind off the hill. I have noticed more
than once that the breeze will bear down a scent
from a great height. Then I heard a couple of shots
from Robinson's pass, and soon after an elk made
his, or rather her, appearance out of the narrow belt
of wood below the cliff. The misguided animal, instead of crossing the swamp at once into the opposite
forest and safety, came slantwise down it towards
my station.

' It was a long shot, and the creature was feminine
and hornless; but meat was badly wanted, and the
orders of my superior officer were to slay, regardless
of sex—as a rule they spare women here, and children
always—so when " she," evidently demented to her
perdition, arrived at a point which I had judged to
be about four hundred yards distant, and was nearing
the wood opposite, I put up the corresponding sight of
my rifle, took careful aim, and let fly. I hit her—how
disagreeable is the use of the female pronoun in such
a narrative !—far back above the hip, and reduced

her long swinging trot to a lame amble ; then I held
well forward with the second barrel. The bullet ·
from this struck the base of the neck just above the
shoulder, went clean through, and she dropped on
the spot. I am bound to record the surprise and
delight of the natives when they came up, for seeing
where the spor crossed the swamp, they had judged
her to be in no danger whatever from me. I
confess I was much of the same opinion just before
firing. She was a very fat barren cow, and supplied
us with as delicious steaks as I want to eat. It
appears that Robinson had a very difficult shot
running downhill, and, as his hunter phrased it,
" shot boum, boum !" which is the local expression
for a double miss.

'And now I must conclude this letter. Leaving
the "slap-jack" out of the question, I have had
some trial of both the Swedish and the Norwegian
style of hunting. There is no doubt immense
occasional excitement in the former, but to the
latter belong, I think, the greater niceties of woodcraft and the greatest exercise of patience and skill.
In both the chief responsibility rests on, and the
utmost admiration is due to, the dogs. I may
mention that Huy is now my own property, that I
have my eye on a forest, and am in danger of becoming, for the short term which my age will allow,
a confirmed elk-hunter.'

CHAPTER XI

A HANDFUL OF LEAD

On the table before me stands a small silver cup, or 'quaigh,' filled with misshapen lumps and fragments of baser metal. It is of Scandinavian workmanship, and roughly engraved with devices emblematical of the chase. In the middle of the last century, as the date and name scratched upon it prove, it was owned, and in all probability fashioned, by one Thor Thorsen, some peasant hunter of the northern wilds, by whom also, we may fairly suppose, it was often drained to celebrate the death of the elk, the bear, or the wolf, or, which is quite as likely, by way of consolation for their escape.

Its present contents, themselves once liquid, form when emptied into the palm a small handful of lead, and are the mutilated remnants of modern rifle bullets, which, after finding their billets and fulfilling the purpose of their creation, have been released from active service. Originally the uniform offspring of one mould, they now vary considerably in size and shape. Some appear to have met with but little resistance in penetration, and although bruised and blunted, still retain in a great measure their cylindrical form; others bear the strongest

miniature resemblance to a battered Tyrolese hat
with the crown knocked out. There are flattened
fragments like chips from the edge of a broken
plate, and vicious-looking deformities, twisted and
crumpled out of all recognition, the veritable
'ragged lead.' So tightly clinched in the cruel
amorphism of one of the latter as to have survived
the thorough cleansing which it has undergone are
two or three long brown hairs, significant of the
missile's passage through the hide of a bear.

Meditating, as I sit in my chair, on these relics, I
am transported in mind across the rolling billows
of the North Sea, and far up the coast of Norway,
to a grand region of fjeld, forest, and lake, now
lying silent and desolate beneath the white mantle
of winter, to be traversed only by the runner on
snowshoes, and happily at all seasons impenetrable
except on foot. For there, over a couple of thousand
square miles, are found neither inns, nor stations,
nor roads, nor vehicles, nor horses, nor any convenience whatever whereby the ordinary tourist
and scenery-seeker might be assisted in his intru-
sion. Half a dozen small homesteads, buried in the
wilderness, and accessible only by long boat voyages
on the larger lakes, or weary travel across the fjelds,
contain the inland population, and, together with
the same number of private huts, specially built in
sequestered glens, afford temporary resting-places to
the wandering hunter, whose entire kit and outfit
must, in shifting quarters, be carried on the backs
of men. There I was fortunate enough to secure for
myself on lease some years ago a hunting-ground, the
respectable size of which—about that of the county
of Surrey—insured me against any immediate danger

of being crowded out.*   There, during one season,
that handful of lead was expended and recovered,
and it is my purpose in this chapter to take it as
my theme, and to try and sketch the circumstances
under which some at least of those now 'emeriti'
veterans performed their deadly duty.

I confess that at eight o'clock on the morning of
September 17, 1891, when I came out of my hut
after an early breakfast, I was in a bad temper and
low spirits.   In spite of the excellence of my Lapp
hunter, Elias, a man of great experience and
thoroughly familiar with the country, and of his
dog Pasop, the most perfect leash-hound I have
ever met with †—superior, I am bound to say, even
to my own Huy; in spite of the considerable
number of elk seen up to date—in all, twenty-five,
including cows, calves, and two-year-olds—at these
I would not draw trigger ; and in spite of hard work
day by day from early morn until dusk, I had killed
but one bull, and, to my sorrow, wounded another,
which escaped in a dense fog on the high ground,

* This hunting-ground, comprising the districts round Mo
and Oplo, on the Indre Folden fjord, was a huge freehold
estate belonging to that perfect gentleman, prince of timber
merchants, and kindest of landlords, the late Herr Albert
Collett, of Christiania.   His successor is his eldest son, Herr
Johan Collett, who now conducts the business on another
immense family estate at Bangsund, not far from Namsos.
Mo and Oplo have been for some years deserted by the
lumbermen, as no more timber will, I believe, be felled in
those forests for at least another generation.

† It must be understood that this was not the dog mentioned
in the previous chapter, 'An Apprentice to Elk-hunting.'   The
name, which means 'take care,' is a common canine appellation
in Scandinavia.

and could never be found again. All things, as in
the case of Sisera, had conspired to fight against us.
A whole valuable week had been consumed in the
search for and vain pursuit of an enormous beast,
magnificently horned, who, in the company of an
extremely wary cow with a calf, and a younger bull,
frequented a wide expanse of open fjeld, and de-
feated during that time all our efforts to get within
shot. At length, with supernatural cunning, he
separated himself from his companions, and took up
his abode in the large tract whereon I had already
slain one of his kindred, and there, by operation of
the law which forbids the killing of more than one
elk on each registered division of the land, was in
perfect safety. Two attempts to dislodge him from
this sanctuary being unsuccessful, we had to leave
him in peace and move on.

Therefore, I say, when I came out of my hut on
the 17th, I was discontented and dispirited. It had,
as usual, been raining all night, as it had poured, after
two months of splendid summer, ever since the elk
season began, and there was not a sign of improve-
ment in the wretched weather. Beneath the canopy
of dark cloud which rested on the fjeld the lower
pine-clad slopes showed as black as the ' invisible
green ' of the rifleman ; a chilly breeze, laden with
drizzle, ruffled the leaden waters of the lake, whose
extremity was veiled by the curtain of another
approaching rainstorm. My outer clothing and boots
were still suggestive of their last soaking—on these
occasions one's wardrobe is perforce limited—and the
boat in which I was about to embark looked abomin-
ably damp.

Even my four cheery followers, Peter, Johannes,

Eric, and the ever-hopeful Nils, accustomed as
they were to hard work and hard weather, were
somewhat dejected. We were to shift quarters
that day, and they had before them a long wet
tramp over the hills, under their heavy burdens.
And had the elements been only fairly kind, how
delightful would everything have been! The log-
hut stood close to the margin of a narrow channel,
which connected with a swift current the two
divisions of the lake, and commanded from its
spacious ' altan,' or verandah-porch, a glorious view
of the upper sheet of water, girt by the terraced
hills. The last built, it had been constructed with
all the improvements suggested by experience. The
lake in front was full of trout and char ; game, big
and small, abounded in the adjacent forests. Nothing
was wanting but a little blue sky and sunshine to
render it an ideal residence for a sportsman. And
yet here was I leaving it with a kind of sullen thank-
fulness that my next quarters would be in a small
farmhouse. All the attractions of its position and
the wild beauty of its surroundings were neutralized
by the vileness of the weather.

But, be it fair or foul, the hunter whose legal
opportunities will be exhausted in forty days * must
not shirk the obligations of the chase. Artemis is
a hard mistress : her votaries, especially those who
pursue the elk, must offer, day after day, their
resolute homage of action and toil. There must be
no slackness in her cult, lest the irate goddess turn
from them the light of her countenance, and cause
them to miss the best chances of the season.

---

* It was so at that time. The season is now limited to
twenty-one days.

Leaving to the men the task of packing up, and the use of a large watertight boat adapted for the transport of baggage, Elias and I, with the dog Pasop, the only member of the party whose spirits seemed unaffected by the weather, entered a small and leaky one, and crossed the lake. My dear Huy, whose vivacity is now tempered by mature age, regarded our departure with melancholy resignation.

During the passage the fresh rainstorm overtook us, and increased the dismal tone of my reflections. There is an old song that has been a favourite of mine from my youth up. I believe that in former years I used to sing it ; on occasion I still hum or whistle the air. It begins in this fashion :

> ' Some love to roam on the dark sea foam,
>   Where the wild winds whistle free,
>   But a mountain-land and a chosen band,
>   And a life in the woods for me !'

I thought of it that morning. I reflected with some bitterness that the author, whilst noticing the fact that the sea may be dark and foamy, and the winds thereon wild and free, ignores altogether the possibility of the woods being sodden with rain, the mountain-land shrouded in mist, and the chosen bánd down upon their luck.

> ' When morning beams on the mountain streams,
>   Oh, merrily forth we go !'

But how if there are no beams of morning ? What if the streams are all muddy torrents ? How about your merriment then ? Under these conditions, my good sir, I think you would be inclined to modify your cheery refrain of 'Yoho ! yoho-oo !' with its prolonged high G.

We landed at the mouth of a very narrow glen, scarcely more than a ravine, and found ourselves forthwith in a copse of birch and alder, with dense undergrowth of tall ferns, sow-thistle, sorrel, and other highland herbage. Before we had penetrated thirty yards I was conscious of being moist all over; but this unpleasant consciousness was speedily ousted by the varied signs of wild animal life which revealed themselves in the thicket. There was the spoor of elk to begin with, certainly not more than a few hours old. The markings were those of a cow and calf only, but where a cow is a bull may be not far off, and hope is happily eternal. Then appeared the signs of a bear that had been feeding on the rank mountain sorrel, very much the reverse of fresh, and difficult to interpret by reason of the incessant rain. Then again, all within the same small area, came the traces of a marten-cat, a fox, and an old cock caper-cailzie. But, for the moment, the tracks of the big game only had any real interest for us.

Quitting the thicket, which extended but a short distance from the beach, and was succeeded by thin birch-wood, we began to slowly ascend the steep, narrow ravine by the side of its central watercourse, now filled with a foaming torrent. Above the tree-tops we could see the inland boundary of the gorge, a smooth wall of black precipitous rock, shining with wet and crested on its skyline by a bank of motionless gray fog. As we climbed, the fresh elk and old bear tracks always preceded us. About halfway up they separated, the latter crossing the stream and the former still following its course.

We imitated the bear, and, after gaining the opposite bank, not without trouble, by risky leaps from
boulder to boulder, emerged from the wood on to a
little open platform, where the inequalities of the
rock beneath were overlaid with a carpet of thickest
moss, unbroken by bush or stone, and equal in
moisture power to several million sponges.

Behind a mound of this matted primeval growth
we subsided—my previous sense of universal dampness recurred at that moment—and took out our
field-glasses. We were nearly in the centre of the
glen. To the right of our platform ledges of rock,
crested with brushwood, closed the view abruptly ;
to the left its edge overhung the bed of the torrent,
which, curving round to our front, separated us by
a secondary ravine from the final barriers of black
cliff and the screes immediately beneath it. The
latter, only a few hundred yards distant, were bare
of all trees, and covered with sheets of gray boulder
débris alternating with patches of low vegetation, on
which the taller foliage of the angelica was conspicuous even to the naked eye. Intent upon finding elk amongst the birch-scrub on the hill directly
opposite, we did not trouble to carefully examine
these slopes, where so large an animal could, even
if lying down, scarcely fail to be at once visible.

After a long and fruitless search we were shutting
up our glasses, when it occurred to me to ask Elias
how long he supposed it might be since the bear
made the signs we had seen below. The narrow,
gloomy gorge seemed to me a haunt so suitable to
the beast that I felt he ought, as a matter of duty,
to be there.

' Fourteen days or more,' replied the Lapp, as

he rose from the moss; 'but after such rain who can say? Nevertheless,' he added in a few seconds, and with his usual low, quiet tone, 'there *is* the bear now!'

And there he was, sure enough. High on the slope under the black cliff, and, as far as I could guess, between four and five hundred yards away, the carnivorous vegetarian was grubbing about amongst the herbage, looking, as I thought, very small and insignificant. Down dropped the Lapp, out came the glasses again, and we lay flat on our faces to inspect him.

Just then an eddying, wanton gust, the frequent bane of the hunter in a mountain-land, swept past us round the hollow of the glen and upwards to the black cliff, bearing with it a whiff of humanity, as instantaneously caught as is the image by the plate of the camera. We saw the bear raise his head, sniff the air, and then start to run along the slope. 'He is aware of us,' whispered Elias; 'you must shoot at once.' 'He is a mile off,' I murmured, with some excusable exaggeration. 'Shoot, nevertheless,' urged the Lapp; 'shoot! it is the only chance.' I felt that it was, and a very poor chance, too. The bear had a considerable distance to run before he could reach any covert, and I did not hurry my shot. Resting the rifle, as I lay, on the mound of moss, and putting up the sight for four hundred yards, its longest range, which had more than once done good service, I took the bead full, and, with a most careful aim, pressed the trigger.

For all my care, I had the least possible expectation of influencing the bear's movements, beyond making him run faster; but, to my surprise, directly after the shot he abandoned his horizontal course, and begun to bustle straight downhill in such a head-long, reckless fashion that I dared to indulge a faint belief in his being hit. As this change of direction brought him considerably nearer, I took the sight fine for the second barrel, which was discharged just as he made a momentary halt on a narrow ledge of rock. I believe the bullet to have struck the stone in front of his nose ; anyhow, I was intuitively aware at the instant that I had held too far forward.

The smoke hung heavily round the muzzle of the rifle on its rest of wet moss, as the bear plunged off the ledge into the bushes below, and, thereby losing sight of him altogether as I lay, I rose to my feet to put in fresh cartridges. ' Be ready,' said Elias ; ' he is still coming down '; and even as I was closing the breech the Lapp dropped his habitual whisper, and ex-claimed almost loudly, ' Here he is !'

In and out of the ravine, and through the inter-vening wood, that bear, wounded as he was to the death, must have galloped like a racehorse ; and now, as Elias spoke, he broke at the same pace from the covert on to our little platform, apparently charging straight at us. But the sight of two men and a dog—Pasop, so steady and mute to elk, but unac-customed to bear, was barking furiously—caused him to swerve slightly to the left ; and he was passing at the distance of fifteen feet, his head and chest slued round towards me, when I threw up the rifle and fired at him, as one often fires at a rabbit, with a timed snap-shot, and, for all the world like the little rabbit when hit well forward, the big beast turned clean head over heels and lay motionless, stone-dead on the instant.

It proved to be a she bear ; but this fact not being
ascertainable until after death, I have hitherto used
the masculine pronoun, for which I apologize. That,
having found her way into the little glen along the
beach some time before, she should have elected to
remain there was fortunate ; that I should have hit
her with the first shot at such a distance whilst
running along the slope was more so ; but that
she should then have hurried down right into our
teeth was an extraordinary piece of luck not easy to
explain. She had had our wind, we were posted
conspicuously in the open, the dog was barking.
We found that the first bullet had gone clean through
her, inflicting injuries that probably incapacitated
her from travelling uphill ; but had she taken any
other direction, had she even kept on down the
little ravine when once in it, she must have escaped
for the time, and given us a great deal of extra
trouble. The last shot had entered in front of the
shoulder, and the ragged lead rested against the
skin of the opposite side.

I acquit her of the faintest original idea of charging. Possibly, as Elias suggested, had she, on
reaching the platform, found a single hunter, she
might have gone for him ; but this is pure conjecture, and I feel that it is not for me, now that she is
dead, to unduly criticise her judgment, actions, or
intentions. And I also apologize for my contemptuous estimate of her proportions when far up on
the hillside ; at closer quarters I considered them
ample. From the tip of her black nose to the point
where a tail ought to have been she measured
five feet eight inches, and, if minded to stand on her
hind-legs, would have attained a stature of well over

six feet. No one, observing the powerful springy
gallop with which she covered the deep moss, could
doubt that, had her life been spared, and had it
pleased her to show fight, she might have proved a
formidable antagonist. Her skin was in splendid
condition, and her body, weighing, as near as could
be estimated, three hundred and fifty pounds, was
loaded with what Elias assured me was most valuable
grease. I will answer for it that a small portion
thereof, melted to oil, mingled with whisky, and
applied externally — its co-ingredient being at the
same time used internally—cured me, some days
later, of an incipient attack of rheumatism. In
conclusion, she furnished the party with a great deal
of doubtless excellent meat, which the majority
seemed to enjoy. I have to regret that three of us
—Elias, Huy, and myself—with no desire to be
intentionally rude, found ourselves unable to appreciate it.

There is strong reason for believing that during
the rest of the day the elements behaved as badly
as ever ; but our success with the bear having dis-
persed my depression, and caused the psychical
barometer to run up instantaneously to ' set fair,'
I ceased to trouble myself about the state of the
weather. For aught I knew or cared, it might have
been brilliantly fine, or very much the reverse, as,
stretched on a luxurious—if dampish—couch of moss,
I smoked my pipe and watched Elias artistically per-
forming his most needful but somewhat sanguinary
task.

And has there ever been smoked in the world a pipe
more sweet than that which is consumed by a hunter
on an occasion like this ? Through the blue fragrant

wreaths I gazed upon a picture perfect in its way.
The narrow, gloomy gorge, with its deep birch-clad
sides, and glimpses of white foaming water; the
treeless upper slopes, with their gray torrents of
stone, and, based on them, the colossal wall of
black rock, with its roof of cloud; in the centre, on
the one clear space of foreground, a hound couched
by a rifle, and a Lapp bending over a dead bear.
That day we did no more hunting, but, returning
down the glen to the boat, rowed to the beach where
the men had landed, and reached our next quarters,
the little farmhouse of Skrovstad, early in the afternoon. There was a 'kinder boom' in the quiet
homestead that evening.

Since I recorded* the experiences of a novice in
elk-hunting, it had generally been my lot in the same
pursuit, when under the guidance of a native hunter,
to trudge for many a weary mile through the depths
of the pine-forest and the interminable morasses of
the comparative lowlands, and to submit to the use
of the loose dog. Now, in this mode of hunting
everything depends, to begin with, on the courage
and stanchness of the hound, who, having found
the elk, must stick to him until he either slackens
his pace or is brought to bay; after which any novice
who can run and shoot fairly, and has coolness and
common-sense enough to avoid gross blunders, but
neither experience nor knowledge of woodcraft, may
achieve success. That it is a noble sport, at times
testing to the utmost the quality of both man and
hound, cannot be denied; but it affords little scope
for any study of the object of the chase, for the
niceties of woodcraft, or the art of the stalker.

* *Fortnightly Review*, January, 1888.

Moreover, in order to avoid disappointing the dog, and perhaps losing him for half the day, it becomes necessary to kill any animal that he has succeeded in stopping. That the hound, to insure his stanchness, *must* have blood, is a rigid maxim amongst the sportsmen of Sweden, where this style of hunting is chiefly practised, and the result in that country is the indiscriminate slaughter of both cows and calves, as well as of young bulls with no honours to speak of. Fortunately, the older bulls are most easily brought to bay—in such a case it is not even necessary to run—but a really good dog will stop anything. Arbitrary custom, based on a sense of dependence on the hound, refuses to the shooter the right of selecting or sparing. This is undoubtedly a great blot on the system, and could only be tolerated in a land where men think far more of the meat than of the sport or trophy.

It had, therefore, given me the greatest satisfaction to find that, under the guidance of Elias, who is a master in woodcraft, elk-hunting was in a great degree assimilated to deer-stalking. He was all for pursuing the chase on the highest possible ground. ' There are, of course, always elk in the low pine-forest,' he would say, ' and in winter it is full of them ; but at this season of the year the place to find and *kill* them is the high fjeld, or thereabouts.' That this dictum was in the main correct is proved by the fact that during thirty-two days' hunting in the season of 1891, about which I am writing, we sighted—including both sexes and all ages—no fewer than forty-one distinct elk, over two-thirds of which were found on the high terraces and slopes just under the crest of the mountains, or in the quiet dells and hollows of the fjeld itself, where the birch-copse often grew barely high enough to conceal them. They were occasionally seen lying out in the open, like red-deer. The term 'high' as applied to the fjeld is, of course, relative to the general elevation of the country. In my district the hills are grouped in masses of imposing bulk, often divided by deep, precipitous gorges, but in actual height they seldom exceed 1,500 or 2,000 feet. When, here and there, the summits reach 3,000, the rolling plateau of the fjeld between them becomes a mere wilderness of gray stone, avoided, or only traversed, by the hunter.

It is true that our habitual climb to the high ground made the work harder, and that often whilst crossing the bare summits we were exposed—the weather being such as it was—to the full fury of the elements ; but the sense of freedom, of escape from the monotonous tramp beneath a sombre canopy of dripping woods, the occasional rock-climbing and general variety of the march, the ever-changing glimpses of grand, wild scenery, amply compensated for increased exertion and exposure. To me the fiercest rain that ever fell is less pitiless and disheartening than the vicarious deluge of a thoroughly soaked forest.

Pasop, the dog, was never by any chance loosed, indeed, he never had been in his life while 'paa jagt,' but his wonderful nose utilized to the utmost. The perfect understanding between him and his master, and the panther-like progress of the pair whilst stealing on the elk, was a treat to witness. We both carried field-glasses, and habitually used them with much success. This was in itself a pleasant and to me almost novel feature in the sport, for although never without glasses, I had hitherto found them all but useless. I was now frequently able to study the appearance and movements of the deer for some hours. On the open expanse of a delightful fjeld called Grönlien (Greenlea), where there was abundance of pasturage, I remember having the pleasure of watching four separate lots of elk, all in view at the same moment. They were chiefly cows and calves, and there was no bull of any size amongst them, but I fancy that it falls to the lot of few hunters in the North of Scandinavia to enjoy such a sight.

The bear had yet to be skinned, and the pelt and meat brought home. On the following morning, therefore, we trudged back again with Nils and Johannes to the spot where the carcass lay, and, leaving them to do their work, picked up again the spoor of the cow and calf, which we followed past the end of the cliff to the higher terraces of the mountain. These we searched without success until the early afternoon, when we arrived at the mouth of a pass leading through a gap in the crags to the upper fjeld.

Here, as Elias had anticipated, the tolerably fresh tracks of several elk, including those of the cow and calf, converged, all making for the open ground above; and here, feeling extremely hungry, and there being a partial lull in the tempestuous weather —the hills were powdered that morning with the first snow—I proposed that we should halt and lunch. But Elias explained that another hour's walk across the fjeld would bring us to the head of what he described as ' a little quiet dale, very for-

tunate for elk,' for so I may translate his words, and
his proposal was that we should defer our meal until
we had reached it. To this, my personal barometer
still standing at ' set fair,' I consented.

Once clear of the pass, it was no longer possible,
however serene in mind, to treat the outward atmo-
spheric phenomena as altogether unworthy of notice.
A bitterly cold half gale was blowing in our teeth, and
about every ten minutes there burst upon us fierce
squalls laden with heavy sleet, so that in front we
were plastered all over with a kind of imperfect
freezing mixture. Now and then, when it was
difficult to see ten yards ahead, we lay down behind
ridges of rock until the fury of the blast was abated.

At last, during a lull, we sighted the head of the
little dale, a deep, dark notch in the fjeld, buttressed
with rock and filled with birch-scrub. At the bottom
a circular patch of gray light, the waters of a tarn,
showed like a hole right through the earth or a
window in the dusk.

Elias, like all true hunters and children of the
wilderness, never forgets to be observant and cautious, and is consequently seldom taken by surprise.
He is never guilty of careless approach or of throwing
away a chance. As a rule, his keen black eyes see
all round him ; I believe that on entering a room
they would not fail to note instinctively what was
immediately behind the door as well as in the opposite corner. On the very rare occasions when I
caught a glimpse of an elk before he did, I used to
feel uncommonly proud. And now, although Pasop,
as far as I know, had given no signs of game being
ahead, he slipped over the edge of the fjeld into a
groove between two of the rock buttresses, and

peered round the corner of an enormous block into
the valley below. I was a few yards behind him,
and, I confess, for the moment, not so keen about
the chase as I ought to have been, reflecting that
now, before searching the valley, we should assuredly
get our lunch ; that my fingers, despite the woollen
gloves I had put on, were decidedly cold ; that, as
for the sample of weather we were having—my
stoical unconcern of twenty-four hours' duration
was rapidly dying out—it was without exception
the most—— Here, just in time to save the credit
of my equanimity, I saw Elias drop suddenly into
the runlet which trickled down the cleft, and begin
to open the breech and remove the stopper of the
rifle. I had taken out the damp cartridges, and
given it to him to carry. Having learnt to instantaneously imitate these abrupt movements of the
Lapp, I did so now, and, quite unnecessarily, being
all the time concealed by the high rock, crawled
through the water to his side. Then without speech
he pointed stealthily over the low brushwood, and
about a hundred yards down the slope, which at this
point was excessively steep, I saw the broad back of
a bull elk, quietly feeding.

It was clear that the Lapp meant me to shoot, and
there was no time to lose. A fresh squall was
driving up the valley; the opposite hill and the tarn
below were already blotted out, and, although the
snow had not yet reached us, the flakes were beginning to cut the dark hide of the elk with white
lines. In half a minute he would be invisible. He
looked very big and black in the gray light, but as
I squatted and took aim with my elbows resting on
my knees, I had strong misgivings about the size of

his horns. They were, however, partly concealed by the brushwood and his position in feeding. Directly after the crack of the rifle Elias laid his hand gently but firmly on my shoulder, and I knew at once that I had held straight, for thus does he always express his silent congratulations on a good shot. Before the driving snow quite obscured all view I saw that the black mass was no longer erect, but plunging on the ground among the brushwood. At the same moment Elias detected the shadowy form of a second bull disappearing behind a lower ridge. When we had scrambled down we found the elk unable to rise, and the Lapp, gliding in like a cat, seized the horn, and pressed down the huge head with hand and knee; then, knowing the exact spot to the fraction of an inch, he passed in his keen blade without an effort at the junction of spine and neck, and in ten seconds life was extinct.

We were now enveloped in a hurricane of whirling snow, and were lucky to find shelter close at hand beneath the projecting slab of an immense mass of rock fallen from the upper cliff. From the edge of this huge eave, the result of cleavage and fully three feet wide, moisture continually dripped; but right under it the rock and moss were absolutely and incredibly dry, and there for a while we made ourselves fairly comfortable and ate our lunch. When everything is soaking, even the touch of dryness is a positive luxury, be it only the inside of a pocket. Thoroughly grateful was I for such shelter, for the thick woollen jersey—knitted by crofter hands in 'The Rosses,' in far-off Donegal—the dry cap, and the warm neck-wrapper, all produced from the rücksack. From the same receptacle came an axe guarded as to its edge by a bit of grooved horn, a scrap of whetstone, some twine, a white flag made of half an old handkerchief, and a small bag of snowy linen.

' Smoke now a little pipe,' says Elias, when, after his meal of rye-bread and reindeer cheese, and a drink of cold water—he touches neither spirits nor tobacco—he has piously clasped his hands and moved his lips in a silent grace : ' I will to the elk ; you can presently come and help me.'   When I do so I find him making the first artistic incisions round the hoofs of a very large five-year-old bull, and am, as I expected, disappointed with the horns, which are stunted and misshapen, and of ten points only.   Depending from the lower jaw is a fine specimen of the ' baton,' or long black beard, exactly like a big fox's brush in shape.   This curious and characteristic appendage disappears in older elk, and is replaced by a heavy bunch of coarse hair.   On account of it I resolve to preserve the head.

To get a full-grown elk into a nice position for the ' gralloch ' is a job for two men, although it may be accomplished single-handed.   But Elias is always very particular about doing his butcher's work in an artistic manner, and requires the huge carcass to be firmly propped by birchen shores at the right slope, to insure there being no slip or roll during the operation, and a free run from stem to stern.   A young birch-tree has also to be transformed by lopping with the axe into a temporary larder, and the breast and other selected portions spiked thereon, to be left till called for.   Within the linen bag are deposited the fillet and one or two tit-bits, which the hunter—quite superstitious on the point—always insists on carrying home himself.   Whenever, on our approach, that small bundle, white, with ruddy stains, is seen dangling from his hand, there is joy in the camp, notwithstanding the concomitant prospect of severe toil on the morrow.

Then, when all is ready for the start, Elias fastens the little white flag to the most conspicuous bough he can find, and produces a couple of sheets of the *Daily Telegraph*, with which I periodically supply him. For even when hunting in the wilds it is pleasant to be in touch with the outer world, and one or other of the men has to travel weekly to the sea in search of the post. All down the slopes and through the lower ravines and woodlands we leave behind us a conspicuous trail, like that of a paper-chase, until, at a spot where the main feeder of the tarn is joined by two tributary rivulets, Elias stops and impales the rest of the paper on a ragged tree-stump. ' It is enough,' he says ; ' they can find the elk without me this time '; and then rehearses the directions he will give this evening to the bearers of the slain : ' From the farm to Kværn Vand, thence upstream until the three becks meet, then follow the paper to the deer.'

These precautions are due to the trouble that arose in the finding of the last dead bull. He lay a very long way from camp in so secluded a position that the three bearers, who knew every yard of the country, and had been duly instructed by means of my big map—on the scale of an inch to the English mile—as to the whereabouts of the slain, were wandering about for some hours in the forest before Peter stumbled on the carcass. Nils, who accompanied them, and did not know the country, put his faith in Huy, who, he declared, would lead him straight

up to the quarry. But the little dog was not to be
balked of his fun for dead meat ; he dragged the
weaponless Nils a couple of miles astray, and eventually brought him face to face with a living bull,
who for some minutes stood and regarded the pair
with calm defiance.

Of the 19th, a blank day of inexpressibly bad
weather, during which the unfortunate bearers had
to bring home the elk meat, I must omit farther
mention, having to brace myself for a dismal narrative of greater interest. On the 20th, being Sunday,
it was allowable to lie late abed, in calm enjoyment
of coffee and farm-made cakes, of newspaper and
pipe, followed by a deliberate toilet, with bath and
razor complete. To my surprise and joy, when Nils
appeared at eight o'clock with the first-named
luxuries, the sun was shining brightly in at the windows, unprovided as they were, according to the
custom of pastoral Norway, with either shutter,
curtain, or blind. By throwing one open I was able
to survey from my pillow an extraordinary range of
shattered cliffs, which formed one side of the valley,
and nearly overhung the farm.

The fallen masses of rock were grouped in most
fantastic shapes. With an immense isolated mono-
lith, a hundred feet high, there was connected, as Nils
informed me, some local legend having to do with
giants and witches. I am inclined to believe that
they still exist in that valley, for I made, as I lay
in bed, a pencil sketch of a terrible crouching
monster, with human face and pendent ears, who
kept watching me between the stems of the pine-
trees. More pleasing, and scarcely less remarkable
—for in the forest valleys of Norway bird life is

scarce—was the sight of a feathered assembly feeding on a strip of fallow ground close to the house. There must have been a dozen magpies, as many common jays, twice as many ring-ouzels, and a large mixed flock of starlings, fieldfares, redwings, mountain finches, and wagtails.

After breakfast, as I was admiring, on the other side of the house, a waterfall which tumbles into the vale just opposite the front-door, and is grand enough to make the fortune of any district less remote, Elias approached. 'That river,' said he, 'comes out of Skrovdal.' Now, Skrovdal was a place that I had set my heart on seeing. On my map it is broadly indicated by a tint three times as black as that of any other gorge, and suggestive of the gloom and profundity which its name also implies. Elias went on to explain that it was easily accessible by a path close to the brink of the waterfall, and continued thence along the bank of the river. We agreed to start at once and explore it. 'You cannot shoot an elk there,' said the hunter, 'for the last was killed on Skrovstad ground. But you had better take the rifle: it is a likely place to meet a bear.' When I heard these words I felt sure that a bear we should not see, but in all probability the finest elk in the North of Europe.

The path on the brink of the waterfall consisted in a great measure of single logs supported on stakes driven into the crevices of the slippery shelving rock, with a tumble-down rail fence between it and the abyss, altogether, as Elias remarked, an awkward place on a dark night. The approach was promising, but Skrovdal itself was not as I had seen it in my dreams. To begin with, from its lie it was flooded with the noonday sun, and no place could in reason look gloomy under such conditions. Then, although narrow, with high, steep sides, half-bushy slope and half precipice, it was bottomed with natural meadows of rich grass, through which the river ran broad and clear, so gentle in current that it seemed incapable of producing the violent cataract we had just passed. The trout were rising merrily, and I began to wish that I had brought a rod instead of a rifle. For about three miles we followed what I must still by courtesy call the path up the glen, and a very delightful stroll it was. At intervals we sat down to examine the slopes with our glasses. Then, in a pleasant spot, we lunched and chatted, and I smoked a pipe or two before we rose to retrace our steps.

At this point I begin to hesitate. I feel that I have not the heart to describe in detail the melancholy conclusion of that Sunday stroll. Let the abridgment of the sad tale, as extracted from my diary, suffice. The painfully graphic jottings run as follows: 'After lunch turned back, the wind then in our faces. About halfway to the fos Pasop told us that there was game directly ahead—made sure we should see the biggest elk in the world. Elias went suddenly down on all fours; I followed suit. Had spotted bear feeding like a cow in meadow across river, about a hundred yards off. Owing to hollow meadow and high bank, could only see three inches of his back. With idiotic impatience, left Elias, who grabbed at my coat-tail and missed it, and tried to gain place for clearer shot. Pasop whined, bear put up his head, saw me, turned tail and bolted. Jumped to my feet and let off both barrels at his stern; waded river, and found no blood on spoor; followed it

some way uphill.   When it came to hands and knees,
Elias said we had better go home, for we should not
catch that bear.   Home accordingly.   Savage with
self.   Had I waited must have got clear, easy shot.
Gloomy place, Skrovdal.   Rain began again before
reaching farm—wretched evening.'

Yes ; the lead that then whistled from the grooved
steel is not in my handful.   It found a bloodless
grave in the sward of the glen, and added in a trifling
degree to the mineral wealth of the country.   That
evening there was the reverse of 'a boom' at
Skrovstad.

The bad weather which my diary, quoted above,
records as having recommenced, after a brief lucid
interval, on Sunday afternoon, is in full swing again
when I rise early on Monday.   To-day there is to
be another change of quarters, but the men will, I
am glad to say, have a fairly easy time of it.   They
can embark with the luggage close to the farm, drop
down the river into the lake, and row all the way
to Strömmen, the next halting-place.

We who do the hunting start long before them, and
are landed a mile away on the bank of the lake, whence,
by a circuitous route, we shall make the same point.
We begin by a stiff climb up the face of the mountain.
Elias, slim and light, generally goes, after the manner
of his people, pretty straight at an ascent; but,
fortunately for one who is—well, just a trifle less
active than he was a great many years ago, the hills
in this part of Norway are of 'trap' formation;
that is to say, they generally rise in a series of giant
steps ('trapper,' Norsk) or terraces, whereby the
climber gains at intervals a brief spell of fairly level
walking.   When, despite one's age and infirmities,

one is in tolerable condition, it is astonishing what complete and almost instantaneous relief to wind and muscle is obtained by a very few yards on the flat. One begins the next ascent with renewed vigour, and with the inspiriting knowledge that such moments of ease will shortly repeat themselves. Our long pull against the collar lands us in a region abounding in wooded dells and rocky basins, which always contain water in one form or another, either as tarn, stream, or swamp.

The wood consists chiefly of birch and mountain ash, but dotted over the landscape are a fair number of Scotch firs, and these picturesque trees occasionally mass themselves into small groves. The rocks are for the most part sheep-backed, and significant of their treatment by the ice in very remote ages. Here and there, however, a low range of crags, which seems to have overtopped the universal glacier, and escaped the general grinding down and polishing, stands up boldly, weather-worn, cloven, and splintered, but still defiant of the merciless centuries. Bounded by these crags are fairly level tracts, partly clothed with long heather, and partly with the spongiest moss through which the shooting-boot of unfortunate man ever laboured. I am positively ashamed to be always querulous about the state of the weather, but when a month of thirty days grants only four which may fairly be considered fine, how is it possible to avoid complaint ?

To-day we halt for the usual hour, and eat our lunch under much the same conditions as those described a few pages back, except that the rock beneath which we crouch affords less shelter, and that we have not killed an elk. We have, however,

seen five : a cow and calf lying down under cover of
a group of Scotch firs, and three cows feeding together
in a covert on the side of the hill.   One of these was
a remarkable animal—we watched them for a long
time with the glass—very light in colour, almost a
yellow dun, with a black head and, strange to say,
a long ' baton ' beard.   Query : Was she in a tran-
sition state, and assuming with age the characteristics of the male ?   I had half a mind to shoot her
—she was about the ugliest beast I ever saw—and
keep her skin as a curiosity, but am right glad before
the end of the day that I did not.

The afternoon is drawing towards evening when
Pasop again encourages us by his evident but
repressed excitement, and at last leads us up to
very fresh and magnificent spoor.   There is no
doubt about it this time ; we are upon the track
of a really big bull.   The length and spread of
the slot is unmistakable evidence.   From his
devious course it becomes evident that he is
restlessly wandering about, probably in search of
the cow, but of her we see no signs.   After awhile,
however, his trail is joined and crossed more
than once by that of a second animal, which Elias
pronounces to be a younger bull.   There is also
proof of some kind of skirmish : one has chased
the other for a short distance, and further relieved
his feelings by tearing up the ground and knocking
a young fir-tree all to bits.   The desire for blood
and the hope of success are now strong in Elias.   His
eyes glitter, he radiates an aura of keenness and
stealthiness.   I am sympathetically filled with a
sense of perfect reliance on his craft and patience,
and the unerring instinct of his hound.

The difference is often very striking, irrespective of the mere change of pace, between the movements of elk when ignorant that the hunter is after them and when they know for certain that he is. In the latter case they will resort to every kind of artifice to hide their trail and baffle their pursuer. This same season I was following for two successive days the tracks of a family—bull, cow, and calf—which we had disturbed. I am inclined to regard the mother as the inventor of the stratagems by which, for the time being, they all profited.

Amongst the most remarkable of them were these : The family, to begin with, entered one end of a long, shallow lake on the open moor, and waded or swam to the opposite end. A mile or two farther on they made as though they would enter another lake, but on the very margin turned along the stony beach, and thereby gained a causeway, also stony, where their footings were invisible. This causeway they did not follow out, but near the middle of it scrambled down over the boulders to a lower level, whence they described a huge S, the first curve thereof being to leeward of their previous line. They walked very slowly, in three long zigzags, up the face of a hill covered with brushwood, and overlooking a great morass behind them, across which we were bound to pursue. Here they probably sighted us, for at the top they hurried on at a great pace. They descended a range of pine-clad hills in a long slant to a considerable stream, which they pretended to cross. In reality they turned straight back up the bed of it for two hundred yards, and issued therefrom at an acute angle to their former course. Eventually they reached a big river, half

18—2

canal, half rapid, running out of a rushy lake; and
there their footings, clear on the soft bottom near
the edge, led into a deep, broad pool, and there, as
far as my personal knowledge goes, may the elk be
to this day. Carefully all round the lake, and for a
considerable distance down both sides of the river,
did we search, but neither the nose of Pasop nor the
eyes of Elias could recover the lost trail. The Lapp,
however, was sufficiently familiar with the trick,
and never doubted that, time permitting, we could
have found their place of exit a long way downstream. But it was late on the second day; we were
far from home, and were forced to abandon the chase.

The bull we are now after has no suspicions, and
is above all such low cunning. His bold trail is
easy to follow. The chief danger is that, in his
erratic course, he may execute an involuntary flank
movement, and surprise himself by detecting us.
Therefore, as we advance, the Lapp's intense
scrutiny, backed by my own efforts, makes every
yard of ground safe on either side.

As we are descending the steep bank of a ravine,
with the usual stream of considerable size at the
bottom, certain unmistakable signs, of the very
freshest, warn us that the elk must be close at hand.
We tread like cats, for at the very moment he may
be standing to listen. It appears that he has crossed
the river; but Pasop, whilst acknowledging the spoor
to the water's edge, keeps facing the breeze, which
is quite favourable and blowing strongly down the
ravine, thus showing that he gets the wind direct
from the elk himself. Hence Elias argues that
the bull, after the manner of his kind, when restless
and roving, must have recrossed higher up; and

examination proves that he is right. The tracks regain our bank close to a densely thick little wood which lines one side of the ravine from top to bottom for two hundred yards. He is probably in that wood, and to approach him through it without noise is all but impossible.

The genius of Elias is equal to the occasion. 'Now,' says he, 'it is our turn to cross.' And, sneaking into the river, we wade over, gently and without splashing, on the very tracks of the bull, which are visible through the clear water. At this moment there passes high overhead, in a long curving line, a flock of several hundred wild geese, whose cackling, not unlike the distant cry of a pack of hounds, had for some time been audible. They doubtless notice what is going on below, and are making remarks on it; but, fortunately for us, the elk do not understand their language.

Up the bank we crawl like serpents, and coil up in a depression at the top, preparatory to searching the wood with our glasses. But there is no need for them. The first glance shows us both bulls, standing some distance apart on the flat open ground above the upper edge of the thicket; and also assures us that, whilst the one is a good beast with a fair head, the other, who even as we look stalks majestically along the flat, and halts directly opposite, is a bull of the first class, immense in bulk and blue-black in hide, with spreading antlers of a peculiarly bright red.

'He is a long way off,' I whisper to Elias; 'we must try to get nearer.' But the Lapp shakes his head. 'I dare not try,' he answers; 'the elk are uneasy, and may be off at any moment. Perhaps,

if we had time, it might be well to wait, but the
light is now failing. Will you not put up that long
sight which helped us to the bear, and shoot from
here ?' The 400-yard sight again ! To think that
my chance of that grand head over the way must
depend on such a shot ! ' I am certain you will hit
him,' whispers the Lapp encouragingly; ' but lose no
time. See, he moves !' And, indeed, at that moment
the elk advances a few steps, and stands again with
his full broadside towards us. Now or never it must
be. There is a single dead tree in our hollow ambush,
which I can reach without rising. Against the side
of the trunk I firmly press the tips of my fingers and
thumb, and steady the rifle on the rest thus obtained.

As the crack rings through the ravine, and the
smoke flies down wind, I see the bull drop forward
like a stumbling horse, but recover himself on the
instant and stand erect. Whilst his companion at
once swings round, goes off at best pace across the
flat, and disappears, the grand beast opposite never
stirs until the second bullet strikes, when he gives a
slight lurch and begins to move on, but with such a
dragging limp in his off fore-leg that I feel pretty sure
the shoulder is broken. Elias is not so certain
about this. ' It may be low down, perhaps in the
foot,' he says. ' He can yet reach the forest and
give us much trouble, possibly escape for the night.'
Accordingly, under pressure, I fire two more shots at
long and uncertain range, and without visible result,
for the elk has now gained a thin grove of Scotch
firs, and is slowly retiring among the stems. Then we
hurry down, wade the river, regardless of depth, and
struggle through the thickets up the opposite bank.

This kind of thing is not conducive to good shooting, and the light is getting worse every moment, but of the three cartridges I expend at the form of the retreating monster, who contrives to shuffle along at a somewhat better pace, I hear at least one tell loudly. Seven shots, and he is not down yet! As I tell Elias, I have but two more in my pouch. ' We must head him,' says the Lapp shortly. And off we go, swinging round in a considerable circuit, to find that the bull has suddenly disappeared. He must have dropped at last; and, sure enough, by careful search we detect one great red horn standing out from the broken ground. We approach with some boldness, believing caution to be now unnecessary, but all is not yet over. The prostrate bull hears us and raises his head.

This time I am determined to end his sufferings —which, with all the ardour of the chase upon me, cut me, I declare, to the heart—and when within fifty yards I aim as well as the light will permit me at a mortal spot in the neck. But just as I press the trigger he regains his feet with a convulsive plunge, and my penultimate bullet misses him altogether. Then, as he scrambles off again, I run in and give him the last shot at close quarters, right behind the shoulder. He halts at once, but, to my consternation, still keeps his legs. How are we to finish the tragedy? How is this monstrous vitality to be overcome? I cast myself and rifle despairingly on the heather, and appeal to Elias, who remains expressively mute. But the end is at length near. The gallant bull tries to ascend a low bank by which he is standing, fails in the attempt, staggers back, topples slowly over with a heavy crash, and lies before us in the majesty of death.

He is a beast of enormous bulk, probably about twelve years old, and in the prime of condition; for he has not yet entered upon that long period of complete fasting when the tender passion is tyrannically and exclusively dominant in the soul of a bull elk. The horns are heavy and yet graceful, symmetrical in their wide sweep, and without too much palmation; one has twelve and the other has eleven points — twenty-three in all. It appears that the first shot struck the very centre of the off shoulder, breaking the bone, and the hide reveals four other holes and a graze. I endeavour to illuminate the finishing touches of the ' gralloch ' by the aid of a few vesta fusees, and I shall not in a hurry forget our long tramp that evening over the roughest ground and in nearly total darkness, nor my relief when the ruddy stars of light in the homestead, visible far up the side of the mountain, broaden into distinct windows, and we hear—

> ' The honest watch-dog's bark
> Bay deep-mouthed welcome as we draw near home.'

At the next mountain farm to which we moved I was laid up for twenty-four hours by the attack of rheumatism which, as I have mentioned, was cured by the application of bear's oil and whisky. Whilst confined to the house I heard that the river close by was full of enormous mussels, some of the shells being as much as nine inches long. I therefore directed the men to bring me a couple of large buckets of the finest, from which Nils and I extracted twenty-three small pearls. The majority were discoloured and misshapen, but half a dozen of the little gems were quite round and of almost Oriental lustre. I have

no doubt that by devoting a fortnight to that river
at low water, when the mussels appear packed by
thousands in its bed, one might make a nice collection of pearls, but I have never since found time for
that kind of hunting. The natives did not seem to
trouble their heads about the matter. Many years
ago a friend of mine instructed several merchants
in the north of Norway to procure for him from
various rivers enough of the mussel-pearls to form
a double-row necklace. After eight years he received the ornament. The pearls were of large size
and good colour, well matched and graduated, and
the cost was £170.

Having got the better of my rheumatism, I killed
at Langotuva a bull who was for half the day lying
down, in sight, but unapproachable. We had to
wait patiently until it pleased him to rise and move.
Luckily, the weather was dry, or the rheumatism
might have returned.

And then, when I was hunting from the next hut,
within ten miles of my headquarters at Mo, occurred
the first act of the most lamentable drama in my
career as a pursuer of elk. For I had a chance at
' the big bull of Mo,' and only wounded him!

It must be noted that the season of 1891 was my
first in the great Mo Forest. For several years
previously, according to report, the said gigantic
deer had frequented the same wood and its vicinity;
a wood of great extent, and in one part, the elk's
favourite haunt, so thickly set with the stems of
small pine-trees that one could seldom advance
three yards in a straight line.

Whilst, having marked the mighty spoor and
got the wind, we were creeping stealthily through

this sylvan maze, which the daylight itself could hardly penetrate, the enormous gray bulk of the bull suddenly reared itself up from behind a hillock, and stood facing us. I was for some moments completely baffled by the stems, but while all the vital parts of his body were protected, the upper part of his head with the huge horns showed clearly between two of them, and I believe that I ought to have tried for a bull's-eye in the forehead. But the shot seemed too risky at the time, and I moved slowly round, searching for a chance at the body. When, however, I fired at what I took in the uncertain light to be the centre of his chest, the first bullet cut a groove along his shoulder, and the second cracked into a tree. And then the monstrous gray phantom melted silently away among the gray columns, after the fashion peculiar to elk, affecting, I know not how, a noiseless passage amid innumerable obstacles.

Strangely enough, the giant had also been wounded by my predecessor, Colonel Walker, who was the first English tenant of the forest, and had it for four years, up to 1890. And I may as well state at once that, still more strangely, in the following year, 1892, the second act of my crowning calamity, which I never shall forget, took place. I had another chance at the big bull, and again touched him, but so slightly that ten days later, when the season was over, he was seen by a travelling peasant calmly nibbling the birch-trees on the margin of the lake which bounded one side of his labyrinthine domain.

But on that occasion, although I had shot hurriedly and badly with the first barrel, his life was undoubtedly saved by the old-fashioned safety-bolt

of the left barrel having been shut by the awkward
fashion in which the Lapp carried the rifle on his
shoulder.   We were going up a steep hillside after
a rather sumptuous lunch in the hut with a fishing
friend, William Sargent, commonly called ' Bill,'
brother of John, and I was smoking the end of an
excellent cigar.   We came on the bull unexpectedly
and in the most unlikely place, there being neither
wind nor spoor to help us ; and when Elias quickly
handed me the rifle, I thought that I had cocked both
barrels, but the hammer of the left was held fast by
the treacherous bolt; before I could rectify the
mistake the bull had vanished.   Otherwise I think
he would have died, for he offered a broadside shot
at less than sixty yards, and as I vainly pressed the
trigger I knew that the sight was steady an inch
behind his broad shoulder.   It is possible that I was
rightly served for overeating myself at lunch and for
lazily smoking while the Lapp carried the rifle; but
we had not left the hut ten minutes.   I had been
hunting all the morning on the other side of the lake
without success, and did not often get a friend to
share my meal, which was on that particular day,
by favour of the good Johannes, rather out of the
common, and consequently prolonged.   It was just
the luck of ' the big bull of Mo.'   No wonder he was
regarded as a trold-elk, and practically invulnerable.

But by the next season he had disappeared, and,
as far as I know, was never seen or heard of again.
I fear that the travelling peasant reported him to
some of the poaching fraternity, to whose machina-
tions he fell a victim during close time.   Beyond
his haunt was a vast tract of uninhabited forest-land,
stretching to a desolate branch of the fjord—it is

known to us by the name of 'the Silent Land'—and
by that route the meat, horns, and hide might have
been smuggled away without anyone being the wiser.
At all events, my diligent inquiries about him were
in vain ; my men would not allow that such an elk
could have been killed without their hearing of it.
For he was quite unmistakable ; I much doubt if
there was another bull like him in Norway. He
always shed his horns in the same tract of forest,
and several of them were picked up. They were
always of the one type, with very broad palmation
and a row of short points set like daggers along the
edge of it.

The biggest horn of his which I possess—a
left antler, without a fellow—measures 35 inches
along the inner curve to the frontal tine, which is
only 4½ inches in length. The palmation has a
fairly uniform breadth, being 13 inches at its widest
and 11¾ inches at its narrowest ; the points are
sixteen, the longest of which is 7¼ inches. The base
of the horn to the curve of the first frontal tine is
very short—2½ inches—and the circumference below
the burr 7½ inches. It was picked up in 1886,
freshly shed, and now weighs 13 pounds. The bull
was therefore six years older in 1892, and, as far
as I could judge during our brief interview, his
honours had not deteriorated. The spread must be
a matter of conjecture and comparison with other
horn measurements, but if I set him down as a 34
or 36 pointer with 54 or 56 inches spread, I think
I shall be about the mark, and for a Scandinavian
elk these dimensions are enormous.

It will be readily understood that during the last
three days of the 1891 season we did not cease

to search for the big bull. After being shot at, he travelled at a great pace, as elk frequently do under similar circumstances, in an immense circuit among the hills, and, aided by his conspicuous spoor and Pasop's nose, we laboriously followed every yard of his course, in the hope that he might halt and lie up somewhere. The blood-marks from the cut in his shoulder which at first stained the foliage through which he passed soon ceased, for there was, of course, no internal injury. We found that he had returned to within a few hundred yards of the spot whence he started, and crossed a deep, narrow channel between two lakes. We therefore took boat the next day at the hut and followed him ; but in the end he evaded us, and we never saw him again until the following year. In all probability he recrossed the water some miles further up, and regained his favourite fastness. Such is the cunning of elk, and the distances which they can accomplish over hill and dale in two or three hours occupy the poor biped man for a whole day, even if he be not stopped by lake or river. But whilst we hunted, Peter had instructions to patrol the waterways, keeping a sharp look-out for swimming deer.

But man also can exhibit cunning, and thereby sometimes outwit the elk. A rather remarkable instance of this occurred on the very last day, when, distracted for the time being from the rather wearisome, stern chase of the big elk, we were following on low ground up wind the spoor of a bull and cow which had caught a glimpse of us, but were not much scared. After trotting for some distance they subsided, as we saw by the tracks, into a walk. But on reaching a spur of rock which jutted into the forest, the extremity of a ridge which ran up to a considerable height, they rounded it and at once turned down wind, thereby placing us in their rear to windward had we continued to pursue them. Without hesitation the Lapp faced about, and, after following the back trail for some way under the ridge, began to ascend the slope of the latter in a slanting direction at such a pace that I needed all my forty days' training to keep up with him. As, however, I guessed what he was after, there was no need to waste breath in asking questions. In about five-and-twenty minutes we reached the top of the ridge, which was quite open and mattressed with thick moss, on which we lay down. We are not given to talking much during the chase, and for ten minutes did not say a word. My business was to recover my wind for shooting, and I was content to leave the rest to Elias and Pasop. I found that we were on the brink of a little cliff, perhaps eighty feet high, immediately under which was a fairly level terrace about a hundred yards broad, and covered with birch-trees and brushwood, with a few Scotch firs at intervals; beyond this the ground dropped rather suddenly to the distant landscape.

I had forgotten all about my rapid climb, when the Lapp gently pressed my elbow and pointed to the left, and in a few seconds I saw the horns and broad back of a bull elk surge up amongst the brushwood. He was walking behind a very small cow, who preceded him by five yards or so; we had got well ahead of them, and they were now approaching us down wind and without the slightest suspicion. The cow gave the line to the bull just along the edge of the bank where the terrace ended, and where the

The End of the Season.

trees were thickest ; by watching her, I could tell
where he would appear a few seconds later. Fortunately, just in front of us there was a clear space
amongst the branches about as long as an elk's body,
and when the cow filled this gap I got the rifle up,
in a sitting posture with my elbows on my knees,
and as soon as the point of the bull's shoulder
crossed the sight pressed the trigger. He fell over
at once, and disappeared, all but one motionless horn,
whilst the little cow danced in towards the cliff until
she was close under us, and then made off. We
found that the bullet had struck the centre of the
base of the neck, and the elk had died so instantaneously that his hind-quarters were still hoisted
up by the stem of a young birch against which he
had fallen under the edge of the bank.

Of course, in this case, being fired from above,
the bullet penetrated downwards ; but in my experience, confirmed by that of others, the neck-shot is
with elk always very deadly.   Even when hit behind
the shoulder, they will sometimes travel a considerable distance, but when the lead strikes fairly in the
centre of the broad neck they usually drop within a
few yards at the outside.   In stalking, owing to the
utilization of knolls and other eminences, a large proportion of shots are fired from above.

And so ended my first season in the great Mo
Forest.   The next day we quitted the hut in our
biggest boat and in fine weather, and formed, I
think, amid the grand scenery, a picture not altogether unworthy of the brush of Landseer.   The
men, who worked four pair of sculls, the fourth man
facing stroke and steering the boat, had lashed to
the tall beak in the prow the head of the last bull

just as it was cut off, for I intended to have it stuffed ;
in the centre was packed the baggage, surmounted
by the meat and hide; and on the top of the pile
squatted the quaint figure of the Lapp in charge of
the rifle.   Seated luxuriously in the stern, I attended
to the rod on which I was trailing a spoon, with the
shot-gun handy in case of ducks ; and beside me sat
Pasop, conscious, I believe, that his work for the
season was over, but still with quivering nostrils
testing the breeze that swept down to us from the
wooded shores.   Huy had been sent back to Mo
some time before.

And whilst I sat, there arose in me a great longing
and hope that, when once more the cold, white
mantle had vanished from the hills of Norway ;
when the bear had crept out from his winter lair, and
the elk had renewed his horns ; when the crow of
the ryper should be heard on the fjeld, and the wail
of the loons on the lonely tarn ; when the trout
should be rising in lake and stream, and the salmon
plunging in the pool, I might again find myself in
that grand region of the North, with health, strength,
and spirits to enjoy hard work, in defiance of bad
weather and occasional disappointment.

BILLING AND SONS, LTD., PRINTERS, GUILDFORD.